This welcome contribution to the marketing literature builds on three decades of social scientific research to provide an invaluable demonstration of the way producing a meal lies at the heart of an intricate and overlapping set of practices that are embedded in the food provisioning cycle that runs, time after time, from shop, to kitchen, to plate, to waste bin.

Anne Murcott, *Honorary Professorial Research Associate, SOAS University of London, UK*

This volume is a veritable smorgasbord of texts catering to those craving the intellectually savory, without neglecting those lusting after something sweet. Scholars with a gluttonous inclination might want to feast on the book in one setting, but I would probably recommend enjoying the chapters as tidbits from time to time, allowing plenty of time for digestion.

Jacob Östberg, *Professor, University of Stockholm, Sweden*

This is by far the most creative and innovative group of papers on food I have read in many years. The authors mount a cohesive expedition into the terra incognita of the everyday meal, discovering and exploring important rich veins of consumer culture which have been hitherto neglected. Using advanced theoretical tools, they take us far beyond the comfortable fiction of the happy family dinner.

Richard Wilk, *Provost's Professor of Anthropology, Indiana University, USA*

T0270829

The Practice of the Meal

Reflecting a growing interest in consumption practices, and particularly relating to food, this cross-disciplinary volume brings together diverse perspectives on our often taken-for-granted domestic mealtimes.

By unpacking the meal as a set of practices – acquisition, appropriation, appreciation and disposal – it shows the role of the market in such processes by looking at how consumers make sense of marketplace discourses, whether this is how brand discourses influence shopping habits, or how consumers interact with the various spaces of the market. Revealing food consumption through both material and symbolic aspects, and the role that marketplace institutions, discourses and places play in shaping, perpetuating or transforming them, this holistic approach reveals how consumer practices of 'the meal', and the attendant meaning-making processes which surround them, are shaped.

It will be of great interest to a wide range of scholars interested in marketing, consumer behaviour and food studies, as well as the sociology of both families and food.

Benedetta Cappellini is a senior lecturer in Marketing at Royal Holloway, University of London, UK.

David Marshall is Professor of Marketing and Consumer Behaviour at the University of Edinburgh, UK.

Elizabeth Parsons is a Professor of Marketing at the University of Liverpool, UK.

Routledge Interpretive Marketing Research

Edited by Stephen Brown and Barbara B. Stern
University of Ulster, Northern Ireland and *Rutgers, the State University of New Jersey, USA*

Recent years have witnessed an 'interpretive turn' in marketing and consumer research. Methodologists from the humanities are taking their place alongside those drawn from the traditional social sciences.

Qualitative and literary modes of marketing discourse are growing in popularity. Art and aesthetics are increasingly firing the marketing imagination.

This series brings together the most innovative work in the burgeoning interpretive marketing research tradition. It ranges across the methodological spectrum from grounded theory to personal introspection, covers all aspects of the postmodern marketing 'mix', from advertising to product development, and embraces marketing's principal sub-disciplines.

The Practice of the Meal

Food, families and the market place

**Edited by Benedetta Cappellini,
David Marshall and Elizabeth Parsons**

LONDON AND NEW YORK

First published 2016 by Routledge

2 Park Square, Milton Park, Abingdon, Oxfordshire OX14 4RN

52 Vanderbilt Avenue, New York, NY 10017

Routledge is an imprint of the Taylor & Francis Group, an informa business

First issued in paperback 2019

British Library Cataloguing in Publication Data
A catalogue record for this book is available from the British Library

Library of Congress Cataloging in Publication Data
Names: Cappellini, Benedetta, editor. | Marshall, David, editor. | Parsons, Elizabeth, editor.
Title: The practice of the meal : food, families and the market place / edited by Benedetta Cappellini, David Marshall and Elizabeth Parsons.
Description: 1 Edition. | New York, NY : Routledge, 2016. | Series: Routledge interpretive marketing research | Includes bibliographical references and index.
Identifiers: LCCN 2015040444 (print) | LCCN 2016009486 (ebook) | ISBN 9781138817685 (hardback) | ISBN 9781315745558 (Master ebook)
Subjects: LCSH: Food consumption. | Food–Social aspects. | Food waste.
Classification: LCC HD9000.5 .P665 2016 (print) | LCC HD9000.5 (ebook) | DDC 394.1/2–dc23
LC record available at http://lccn.loc.gov/2015040444

ISBN: 978-1-138-81768-5 (hbk)
ISBN: 978-0-367-87098-0 (pbk)

Typeset in Bembo
by Wearset Ltd, Boldon, Tyne and Wear

Contents

Illustrations

Figures

Tables

Contributors

Søren Askegaard is a Professor of Marketing at the University of Southern Denmark. He has a postgraduate degree from the University of Paris 1 Panthéon-Sorbonne and a PhD in business studies from Odense University. His research interests are oriented towards consumer culture theory. Current research projects include globalism and localisms in consumer culture and branding and ideologies of food and health. From 2008–2014 he was an associate editor at the *Journal of Consumer Research*. He is one of the founders of the university–business collaboration project *Brand Base* and the creator and director of the study programme in *Market & Management Anthropology*.

Alex Barnard is a doctoral student in the Department of Sociology at the University of California, Berkeley. He conducted two years of ethnographic research on freegan anti-waste activists in New York City from 2007 to 2009; his first book, *Freegans: Diving into the Wealth of Food Waste in the United States*, is forthcoming in 2016 from the University of Minnesota Press. His doctoral dissertation compares mental health care systems in the United States and France, focusing on how states and public policies influence the classificatory practices that construct persons with mental illness as deviant, dangerous, deserving or disabled.

Alan Bradshaw teaches and learns at Royal Holloway, University of London and at the University of Stockholm.

Dorthe Brogård Kristensen is a trained Anthropologist with an MSc in Medical Anthropology from the University College London and a PhD in Anthropology from the University of Copenhagen. She is currently an Associate Professor of Consumption Studies at the University of Southern Denmark. Her research interests include consumer culture, medical sociology, food sociology, medical pluralism, body and identity. She has recently published in the *Journal of Consumer Culture*, *Journal of Marketing Management*, *Appetite* and *Journal of Consumer Behaviour*.

Robin Canniford wears socks with sandals. Accordingly he works at the University of Melbourne where he is a Director of the Cluster for Organisation, Society and Markets.

Benedetta Cappellini is a Senior Lecturer in Marketing at Royal Holloway, University of London. Her research interests are in food consumption, material culture and family consumption. She has published in referred journals including *Sociology*, *The Sociological Review*, *Journal of Business Research*, *Consumption, Markets and Culture*, *Journal of Consumer Behaviour* and *Advances in Consumer Research*.

Teresa Davis is an Associate Professor in the Marketing group within the University of Sydney Business School. Her research examines consumption and marketing from a sociological perspective. Her focus lies in examining 'cultures of transition' such as consumption of/in childhood and migrant groups. Related areas of research include the socio-historical analyses of culture and consumption. Her papers have been published in *Sociology* and *Consumption, Markets and Culture*, among others. She is the Co-Convenor of the Australian Food, Culture and Society. She also co-leads the University of Sydney Business School's Health and Business Research Network.

Janice Denegri-Knott is an Associate Editor of *Marketing Theory* and Co-editor of the *Journal of Promotional Communications*. She is Principal Lecturer in the Faculty of Media and Communication at Bournemouth University where she teaches Consumer Culture and Insights. Her research interests span conceptualising and documenting digital virtual consumption and its practices, the emergence of media technology, and more generally the subject of power in consumer and marketing research. Her work has been published in journals including the *Journal of Macromarketing*, *Journal of Marketing Management*, *Journal of Consumer Culture*, *Consumption, Markets & Culture* and the *European Journal of Marketing*. She has done consultancy work for a range of media companies like *The Daily Telegraph*, ITV, Channel 4 and Hearst.

Karin Ekström is a Professor in Marketing at University of Borås, Sweden. Her research interests are the meaning(s) of consumption, sustainable consumption, consumers' relations with artefacts, collecting, consumer socialisation and family consumption. Current research projects involve culinary tourism and market orientation of art museums. Recent publications include *Waste Management and Sustainable Consumption: Reflections on Consumer Waste* (ed., 2015), 'Conformity and Distinction in Scandinavia's Largest Department Store' in *Being Human in Consumer Society* (ed. A. Néstor García Martínez) and 'Reuse and Recycling of Clothing and Textiles: A Network Approach' (with N. Salomonson) in the *Journal of Macromarketing* (2014).

Malene Gram PhD, is an Associate Professor and Head of the School of Culture and Global Studies at Aalborg University, Denmark. Her main research interests are within consumer culture with a special focus on family, parent and child consumption, motherhood, and intergenerational relations. She has a special interest in cross-cultural studies and in gaps between ideals and practice in everyday culture. She has published in *Childhood, Journal of Consumer Culture, Advertising and Society Review, International Journal of Consumer Studies, Young Consumers, Journal of Marketing Communications, Higher Education* and *Journal of Youth Studies.*

Paul Hewer is a Reader in the Department of Marketing at Strathclyde University, Glasgow. His research focuses on theorising contemporary consumer culture, from unpacking cookbooks and celebrity chefs, 'lifestyle' gardening texts, to car cultures and exploring consumer's practices of 'debadging'. His work can be found in a range of journals from the *Journal of Marketing Management, Journal of Consumer Culture, Consumption, Markets and Culture,* to the *Scandinavian Journal of Management* and *Advances in Consumer Research.* He has co-edited the *Journal of Marketing Management* with Professor Mark Tadajewski since 2010 and co-edited books on *Expanding Disciplinary Space: On the Potential of Critical Marketing* (Routledge, 2014) with Professor Douglas Brownlie and Professor Mark Tadajewski and *New Directions in Consumer Research* (Sage, 2015) with Dr Ali Jafari and Dr Kathy Hamilton. He is often to be found cooking, enjoying family life, reading and (now and again) writing at speed in kitchens.

Margaret Hogg holds the Fulgoni Chair of Consumer Behaviour and Marketing in the Department of Marketing at Lancaster University Management School. Her work has appeared in refereed journals including the *Journal of Advertising, Journal of Business Research, Consumption, Markets and Culture, Journal of Marketing Management, Journal of Services Marketing, European Journal of Marketing* and the *International Journal of Advertising.* She edited six volumes of papers on consumer behaviour in the Sage Major Works series (2005 and 2006), and, along with Michael Solomon, Gary Bamossy and Søren Askegaard, she is one of the co-authors of the *6th European Edition of Consumer Behaviour* (2016).

Annilotta Hukkanen received her Master's degree in Marketing in 2013 from the School of Management, University of Tampere, Finland. Her research interests include food consumption, consumption practices and online consumer behaviour. She has published her research in *Advances in Consumer Research.* Currently she works closely with customer experience and business development in the insurance industry.

Rebecca Jenkins is a Senior Lecturer in Advertising, specialising in Consumer Culture and Behaviour in the Faculty of Media and Communication at Bournemouth University. She has published research in the areas of consumption in the imagination, the role of consumption in interpersonal relationships, non-market-mediated consumption and in relation to Higher Education. Her co-authored paper "Just Normal and Homely": The Presence, Absence and Othering of Consumer Culture in the Everyday Imagination' was awarded Editor's Choice in the *Journal of Consumer Culture,* highlighted as one of the journal's most noteworthy manuscripts since its launch in 2005. Currently involved in research projects about the role of digital devices in a variety of consumer practices, access-based consumption, and health veganism and sustainability, she is particularly interested in the contextualisation of consumption in everyday life and consumption in transitional periods/life stages.

Alice Julier is an Associate Professor and Director of the Graduate Program in Food Studies at Chatham University. She writes about material life, social movements, domestic life, labour, consumption and inequality in food systems. Her work includes: 'Mapping Men onto the Menu' in *Food and Foodways*, 'Family and Domesticity' in *A Cultural History of Food: The Modern Age*; 'The Political Economy of Obesity: The Fat Pay All' in *Food and Culture: A Reader*; 'Julia at Smith' in *Gastronomica*; and 'Hiding Race and Class in the Discourse of Commercial Food' in *From Betty Crocker to Feminist Food Studies*. Her book is entitled *Eating Together: Food, Friendship, and Inequality*. She is the past president of the Association for the Study of Food and Society and is on the board of the Agriculture, Food, and Human Values Society. She is the co-editor of *Food and Culture: A Reader*.

Alessandra Marilli is a Post-Doctoral Researcher at the Department of Sociology and Political Studies, University of Florence, Italy. Her research interests are media consumption, media representation of gender and ethnicity and family consumption. She held various research and teaching positions at the University of Florence. She has just concluded a European Union funded research project on the Italian media representations of immigrants.

David Marshall is a Professor of Marketing and Consumer Behaviour at the University of Edinburgh Business School. His primary research interests include research on food access and availability; consumer food choice and eating rituals; and children's discretionary consumption in relation to food advertising and marketing. He edited *Understanding Children as Consumers* (2010) and *Food Choice and the Consumer* (1995) and has published in a number of academic journals including *The Sociological Review, Journal of Marketing Management, Consumption, Markets and Culture, Journal of Consumer Behaviour, International Journal of Advertising and Marketing to Children (Young Consumers), Appetite, Food Quality and Preference, International Journal of Epidemiology* and *Journal of Human Nutrition*.

Nina Mesiranta received her PhD in Marketing from the University of Tampere, Finland in 2009. Her research focuses on understanding consumers in the online environment utilising interpretive methods such as netnography. Specifically, her research interests relate to online shopping, such as consumer online impulsive buying, and social media, such as fashion and food blogging. She has published her research for instance in the *Journal of Fashion Marketing and Management, Journal of Retailing and Consumer Services* and *Advances in Consumer Research*. She has worked in various research and teaching positions mainly at the School of Management, University of Tampere since 2001.

Susanna Molander is a Post-Doctoral Researcher at the Stockholm Business School, Stockholm University. Her research focuses on consumer culture with a particular interest in theories of practice and issues related to food, motherhood, fatherhood and consumption. She also studies fashion branding from a cultural perspective. With the Nordic context as her primary empirical base, she explores how political projects shape the way consumption is enacted.

Marie Mourad is a doctoral student at the Center for the Sociology of Organizations and Sciences Po, Paris. Her research focuses on public policies, corporate initiatives and social movements to address 'food waste' in France and the United States, analysing how different actors value and manage excess food throughout production, distribution and consumption. She also carried out ethnographic work with freegans and dumpster-divers in both countries. In addition to her academic work, she has collaborated on food waste studies with the French Waste Prevention Agency (ADEME), the French Ministry of Agriculture and the National Resources Defense Council in the United States.

Elina Närvänen is a Lecturer of Marketing at the School of Management, University of Tampere, Finland. She defended her PhD thesis on the collective consumption of brands in 2013. Her research interests include consumption practices, consumption communities, food consumption and interpretive research methodologies. She has published her research for instance in the *International Journal of Consumer Studies*, *Advances in Consumer Research*, *Managing Service Quality*, *Journal of Consumer Behavior* and *Journal of Marketing Management*.

Elizabeth Parsons is a Professor in Marketing and Consumer Research at University of Liverpool Management School. Her research interests include consumer culture, critical marketing, and gender, identity and subjectivity at work. Recent co-edited texts include *Branded Lives: The Production and Consumption of Meaning at Work* (Edward Elgar) and *Key Concepts in Critical Management Studies* (Sage). She is also co-editor of the journal *Marketing Theory*.

Alan Petersen is a Professor of Sociology, School of Social Sciences, Monash University in Melbourne. His research spans the fields of the sociology of health and medicine, science and technology studies, and gender studies. He has published books and articles on health and risk, the body and society, the new public health, the sociology of bioscience and bio-technologies, constructions of sex/gender, and gender and emotion. His most recent book is *Men, Masculinities and Modern Medicine* (Routledge, 2013) (edited with Antje Kampf and Barbara Marshall).

Tanja Schneider is a Research Fellow in Science and Technology Studies at the Saïd Business School and the Institute for Science, Innovation and Society, University of Oxford. Her areas of expertise include social studies of markets and marketing, media and consumer culture as well as the politics and practices of food governance with a particular interest in food marketing. Tanja is also a fellow at the Unit for Biocultural Variation and Obesity and member of the Oxford Martin Programme on the Future of Food at the University of Oxford.

Monica Truninger (PhD) is a Senior Research Fellow at the Institute of Social Sciences, University of Lisbon, Portugal. Her research interests include school meals and children's food practices, domestic technologies and cooking practices, sustainable consumption and food provisioning systems, and food security. She has published widely in national and international journals, e.g. *Journal of Consumer Culture*, *International Journal of Sociology of Agriculture and Food* and *Young Consumers*. She is currently preparing a couple of monographs contracted with established international and national publishers. She has recently completed two nationally funded projects on school meals and food insecurity among families with children. She is a board member of the Research Network of Sociology of Consumption in the European Sociological Association and she co-chairs the Sociology of Consumption section of the Portuguese Sociological Association.

Sofia Ulver is an Associate Professor at Lund University, Sweden. Her research interests reach from general critical marketing studies to empirical investigations into social trends in consumer culture (such as consumer activists, foodies, runners, urban farmers etc.) and their relationships with, and consequences for, social structures at large.

Ann Veeck is a Professor of Marketing at Haworth College of Business, Western Michigan University, USA. She has studied food marketing systems in China and other emerging markets for over 20 years. Her most recent projects include studies of the development of food consumption patterns in Chinese teenagers and a life course analysis of food-related practices of elderly Chinese. She has a Masters of Marketing Research from the University of Georgia and a PhD in Marketing from Louisiana State University.

Carl Yngfalk holds a PhD from Stockholm University and is currently Post-Doctoral Research Fellow at the Stockholm Centre for Organizational Research (Score) and Stockholm Business School, Stockholm University. He teaches in marketing and his research interests include critical marketing, consumer culture, consumerism, identity politics, the body, sustainability and market development.

Hongyan Yu is a Professor of Marketing at the School of Business, Sun Yat-Sen University, China. His main research interests are market orientation, customer engagement and food consumption behaviour in China. His recent projects include customer experience, Chinese teenage food consumption and the food practices of the elderly. He has a PhD in Business Statistics from the Tianjin University of Finance and Economics.

Fang (Grace) Yu is a PhD student of Marketing at David Eccles School of Business, University of Utah, USA. Her most recent projects include studies of the food consumption behaviour of Chinese teenagers and competitors' response strategies to negative spillover effects. She has two master's degrees, from Brock University and City University of Hong Kong.

Foreword

There has perhaps never been so much popular, public and collective discussion of food as at present. The question of what to eat has become much more open for even the poorest sections of affluent societies. Industrialisation of agriculture, intensification of world trade, and concentration of retailing dramatically altered the supply of food in the later twentieth century. Accompanied by increased global flows of people and ideas, many more diverse ways of eating have become possible. This much we know.

How ordinary people in their everyday lives adapt to these new possibilities is less clear. Many scholars in the cultural and interpretive social sciences have mused over the condition that Claude Fischler described as 'gastro-anomie', the incipient dissolution of authoritative reassurance about how best to eat. With uncertainty comes anxiety. How, he asked, can people, faced with an unprecedented range of options – ones which potentially present themselves several times a day – determine what they should eat?

At the time he raised this question, still less than 40 years ago, we knew how much households spent on which foods and about the volume of outputs of industry; but we knew relatively little about what ordinary people ate and what arrangements they made to obtain their daily sustenance. In the last couple of decades the social sciences have made considerable progress in understanding the process of food consumption as the cultural and symbolic aspects of eating have come to be investigated more intensively. Nevertheless the topic is vast and the picture remains complicated.

A central topic in the sociology of food, the meal is recognised as an occasion where highly significant social relationships are formed, affirmed and expressed. It is considered precious in most societies for its religious, social and personal significance. Meals have considerable analytic potential because they pull together social aspects of household organisation, temporal rhythms, practical priorities, social (and actor) networks, social conventions and rituals. As this book demonstrates, meals can also be used as a focal point for understanding connections between the production, distribution and consumption of food. The meal as an institution orchestrates several ineradicably intertwined practices up and down the food chain. The linkages between procurement, preparation, presentation, enjoyment and disposal by households permit a thorough analysis of the phases of the food chain which are consummated in the eating of meals.

If meals matter, so too do markets. The furnishing of meals in modern industrial and post-industrial societies is ever more intricately bound up with market processes. Markets operate as a bridge between commercial organisations and social modes of consumption. To examine the mutual interdependence of consumption and markets highlights qualities like convenience, freshness and cheapness which are invoked to structure understanding and steer purchases.

The Practice of the Meal provides a raft of valuable empirical studies of the later phases of the food chain. It is a perennial task for social science to capture in detail the many variants of everyday practice, describing and explaining what different sorts of people do, and why. There can never be enough case studies of the varied and alternative ways in which groups of people engage with their specific environments. Adaptation to changing circumstances is often ingenious. It is both instructive and intriguing to be able to comprehend the arts of dumpster-diving, the substitution of digital communications technologies for cookbooks in the process of food preparation, the ways that children negotiate with their parents in the supermarket and at the table, and the social costs for middle-class Italian women providing food for their families in straitened times. Such case studies are the pieces in the jigsaw which answer the question of how the myriad of diverse experiences and variable conditions fit together to form a picture of both mainstream and minority activity.

Such cases also give us perspective on change. Another recurrent social scientific endeavour, often even more intriguing, is to determine to what extent practices have changed over time, and where they are likely to go next. Is 2015 really very different from 1975? How will we be eating in 2050? The interpretive social sciences require repeated inquiries to deal with the task of documenting change, and to challenging myths about change. Recurrent angst about the collapse of the family meal is just one striking instance; its crisis has been repeatedly announced since at least Edwardian times in the UK. Only iterated empirical investigations demonstrating the contrary – or rather, in this case, showing modes of adaptation of an ideal to changing circumstances – allows a myth to be dispelled.

Empirical investigations take on additional value when they contribute to theoretical development. In recent years, in a parallel move across many disciplines, theories of practice have been employed to explain consumption. This volume explores how the concepts of practice theory might explain processes attendant upon meals. It thus helps to establish the value of a theoretical conjecture whose fate remains in the balance. Certainly it seems that social processes occurring in supermarkets, kitchens and bin cupboards can be effectively framed by strings of concepts like habit – routine – sequence – convention – ritual, and, acquisition – appropriation – appreciation – disposal.

The Practice of the Meal provides a stimulating and varied set of investigations which give a thorough analysis of the the interrelated stages whereby foodstuffs move from the point of procurement by consumers, through preparation, to consumption and waste. This set of case studies helps to elucidate the contribution of theories of practice to social scientific explanation and shows that the meal can be used as a lens for investigating the social relations surrounding the many dimensions of food consumption.

Alan Warde, Manchester, 6 July 2015

Acknowledgements

We would like to thank the following people for their support and input throughout the development of this project: Alan Warde for his encouragement and his insightful foreword, Sinead Waldron, Editorial Assistant at Routledge, for guiding us through the production process and three anonymous reviewers for their useful and encouraging comments on the book proposal. A special thanks is for colleagues who refereed the contributions collected here: Pia Albinsson, Antony Beckett, Shona Bettany, Helene Brembeck, Marylyn Carrigan, Norah Campbell, Aaron Darmody, David Evans, Joan Gross, Vicki Harman, Heli Maria Holttinen, Ben Kerrane, Dannie Kjeldggard, Stephanie O'Donohoe, Klara Scheurenbrand, René ten Bos and Luca Visconti. Finally, we are very grateful to the contributors for their inspiring and thought-provoking chapters and for being so accommodating in helping us to realise this project.

Benedetta Cappellini
David Marshall
Elizabeth Parsons

.

1 Introduction

The practice of the meal

David Marshall, Benedetta Cappellini and Elizabeth Parsons

Among the many cookery programmes that currently crowd our television screens is *Jamie's 15 Minute Meals*. Here the ubiquitous celebrity chef Jamie Oliver conjures up tasty treats speedily, effortlessly and with plenty of style. The viewer is treated to a whirlwind of high energy cooking resulting in a meal which is a feast for the eyes and (we are led to believe) the taste buds. We highlight this particular show because it is a good example of a much wider popular media obsession with cookery skill, style and aesthetics. Often hidden is the highly necessary work of planning, shopping, preparing, disposing of unwanted food and cleaning up afterwards. Also rendered invisible are the systems of provision that make an array of (arguably exotic) ingredients available to the average consumer. In fact, watching *Jamie's 15 Minute Meals* we felt utterly cheated, aside from the cost of the ingredients and small size of the portions (certainly not big enough to feed a family of four) where did he get the ingredients? How long did the shopping take? And what about the time spent in preparation and washing up? Not to mention, who is looking after the children? While there are a whole host of texts which individually explore each of these aspects of the meal we found little recent work that takes a holistic view of consumer practices across the meal provisioning cycle (Warde, 2010; Marshall, 1995; Goody, 1982). Exploring consumer practice across the different stages of acquisition, appropriation, appreciation and disposal allows us to look beyond the acts of cooking and eating and to reflect on how consumers engage in what are a whole host of other mundane often taken-for-granted activities. Our aim however is not merely to reveal the everyday work of the meal (indeed this has been done excellently elsewhere – see for example DeVault, 1994) our additional focus is to examine the intersection of these practices with the marketplace. We explore how consumer engagement in, and understanding of, these practices is shaped by marketplace discourses and institutions.

Food consumption and the market

The Practice of the Meal is a celebration of thinking around the bundle of consumption practices centred on, what for many Western consumers is an everyday activity, creating and eating meals. US households spend around 7 per cent of total household income on food or $43 per person per week (*The Economist*, 2013), UK households spend 11.4 per cent of household spend or an average of £42.18 per week on food and drink, of which around one-third goes on eating out (DEFRA, 2014). Expenditure across European households averages 14.5 per cent but is up to 30 per cent in parts of Eastern Europe. But eating and drinking goes far beyond household expenditure and in order to understand this consumption practice we need to look at the time and effort engaged in food- related activities from acquiring, preparing, cooking and eating through to the disposal of food across the food provisioning cycle (Warde, 2010; Marshall, 1995; Goody, 1982). All of the stages have to be 'performed' but in contemporary societies we begin to see a new focus on the earlier stages of the process with concerns about how food is sourced and procured, how it is processed and the various activities surrounding its production pre- and post-farm gate as well as concerns over the sustainability and environmental impact (Barber, 2014). These issues have become an integral part of food policy in an increasingly 'ecological public health approach' to food (Lang, Barling, & Caraher, 2009) that influences both what is made available to consumers and what they choose to eat. We can add to this the debates about local food supply, community farms, and alternative food networks that are shaping how we think about food supply, or consider changing household structures and the continued dependence on women in full time work that place different challenges on each of the food provisioning stages, through to the concerns about growing demand for food and food waste and pollution that are reshaping how we consume. We see these concerns reflected in consumer practice, for example around initiatives to reduce food waste, source from sustainable suppliers, or pay for plastic shopping bags. Some of these practices are driven by legislation, others by individual choices in response to changing beliefs or austerity (see for example, Cappellini, Marilli, & Parsons, 2014). On another level we see evidence of new technologies in the home and food industry changing how people prepare and cook food, from greater use of ready prepared foods and meals through to sous vide products that promise new taste experiences. The demand for diversity, the need for convenience or better quality has not gone away – government and the food industry constantly face new challenges. Where there are choices, and not every household has a choice, consumers can elect to act more sustainably, or economise, or indulge themselves. But these choices are not always clear and are often contradictory; as Alan Warde (1997) notes there are a series of antinomies of taste that include novelty and tradition, health and indulgence, economy and extravagance, convenience and care that contribute to our understanding of the complexity around food consumption and expressions of taste that represent dilemmas of contemporary practice. In this text we consider how these practices are played out across the food provisioning process by focusing on the meal and considering key discourses that relate to and illuminate each of these different stages.

Our interest is in how these practices are influenced by, and in turn influence, the commercial market. As food provisioning is increasingly 'marketised' how is consumer practice driven by producers, manufacturers, processors and distributors? How are consumers reacting and responding to what is, in essence, a highly industrialised food system (Moss, 2013; Ochs & Beck, 2013; Blythman, 2006; Schlosser, 2002; Klein, 2000)? While some yearn for a romantic notion of returning to the land and producing our own food, for most urban and rural dwellers this is simply not practical. There are some great alternative food outlets, fantastic community food scheme initiatives and farmers markets but few households can exist solely on these sources for sustenance. What is clear is the extent to which industrial food supply is omnipresent; there is no getting away from it. The first thing is to acknowledge our reliance on the food industry and work to improve the quality and healthfulness of the food we eat, the second is to ensure that affordable good quality healthful food is available to all, and the third, to ensure that in producing good food resources and people are not exploited. This is what books like Moss's do, they generate a discussion about how our food is produced, processed and marketed (see also Blythman, 2006). What this all adds up to is convenience and the 'heat and serve' foods of the middle of the last century were seen as a great advancement saving the 'housewife' from endless chores (Carrigan, Szmigin, & Leek, 2006).

This book is not necessarily intended as a critique of our food system or a comment of food policy – although these issues will emerge in the course of the book – rather a reflection on contemporary food systems and an examination of how consumers are contributing through their practices to the commercial (re)construction of the food system and (re)interpretation of mealtimes. Meals, and mealtimes, involve a wide range of eating activities from the festive through to the everyday family dinner. They involve debates around food and nutrients, food availability and access, preparation and cooking skills, family structures and female employment, as well as existing and new technologies that contribute to the manufacture, storage and cooking of foods that go into the meal. This is a complex multi-faceted system and one that requires us to consider meals and food choice more broadly, from a range of disciplinary perspectives.

Mealtimes

'The term "meal" refers both to foods that are ingested and to the encompassing social arrangements of an event involving locations, times and companions, reflecting the empirically observed interconnection between occasions and the foods served' (Yates & Warde, 2015). As these authors note, the practice of meals is about selecting foods, combining them into an acceptable sequence appropriate for the occasion. While the structural approach adopted by researchers like Douglas (1975, also Douglas & Nicod, 1974) may be seen as too rigid to capture the complexity of the meal and its various nuances, it does provide the basis on which to construct a hierarchy of meals that reflects the nature of the occasion (Cappellini & Parsons, 2012; Marshall, 2005). Yet, changing work patterns and market forces have converged to alter the social organisation, content and practice of eating (Yates & Warde, 2015; Warde et al., 2007). Despite these changes the orthodox pattern of three meals per day remains prevalent in Britain although differences can be seen over the previous 50 years in the nature of the domestic meal. Meals are becoming restructured, simpler, and more likely to be eaten alone, reflecting changes in domestic food practices (Gatley, Caraher, & Lang, 2014).

The family dinner

Despite the aforementioned changes in domestic food practices, one of the most enduring modes of eating meals is undoubtedly the family dinner. Why is family dinner, that quintessential meal, a challenge for contemporary families? In addition to work demands, children's extracurricular activities and scheduling conflicts it seems that even when families are together the abundance of convenience foods, individualised meals and snacks contrive to usurp the family meal. Despite this, over three-quarters of (American) families manage to eat dinner together at least one evening a week and while only one-fifth ate all dinners together[1] the majority of these involved one or more family members. In contrast almost a quarter of the families never ate together and a high proportion of dinners eaten at different times or in different rooms involved convenience or takeaway foods, like chicken nuggets, or ready dishes with processed convenience accompaniments. This reliance on commercially prepared convenience foods is exemplified by the now ubiquitous 'home-cooked' dinner (Atlantic, 2013). All meals, it seems are not made equally. Could convenience be the latest threat to the family meal?

The Atlantic article, based on Ochs and Beck's (2013) anthropological account of family dinners in American and Italian families, suggests that this demise of the family meal begins in the supermarket with large-scale purchases of packaged convenience foods and reflects differences in the domestic environment. Italian families have smaller refrigerators and purchase food more infrequently using neighbourhood stores (we assume stocking similar items to the supermarkets!). In contrast American families stockpile food leading to an abundance of convenience foods that facilitates snacking and encourages family members to eat at different times and in different places. Moreover, the focus on health over taste is apparent in the discourse around the table, reflecting broader cultural differences between the US and Europe (Ochs & Beck, 2013; Blythman, 2006; Rozin, Fischler, Imada, Sarubin, & Wrzesniewski, 1999). Educating families about the health benefits of eating meals together can be seen in a series of British government initiatives[2] aimed at getting families to buy, cook and eat healthier food (McArdle, 2015). Ochs and Beck question the extent to which convenience foods and ready meals may actually help us to recreate the formal mealtime (without the time and effort – see Hallsworth, 2013). Underpinning this is an ongoing debate around the alleged demise of the family meal as part of a broader moral debate (Jackson, 2009; Meiselman, 2009; Murcott, 1982, 2012). However, the debate has been somewhat focused on meals at home with much less work on meals eaten outside the home (Warde & Martens, 2000).

Mealtimes as consumption practice

Theories of practice have recently become popular in consumer research (Boulaire & Cova, 2013; Echeverri & Skålén, 2011; Halkier, Katz-Gerro, & Martens, 2011; Watson & Shove, 2008; Warde, 2005). They have been used as a way to shift emphasis away from the consuming subject to embrace more fully the ways in which collective/shared understandings of consumption, as well as the material stuff of consumption, shape the way in which that consumption proceeds (Southerton, 2006; Shove & Pantzar, 2005). In this respect consumption may be best seen as embedded in particular practices (Warde, 2005). Moreover, practices have also been used as a way to explore the more macro shaping of consumption through the operation of marketplace discourses (Halkier, Katz-Gerro, & Martens, 2011; Warde, 2005). As 'routinised types of behavior' that are closely interconnected, practices represent background knowledge in terms of know-how, understanding, emotional and motivational states of knowledge (Reckwitz, 2002: 249). These practices represent 'conventional' ways of doing things that stress the routine and collective, as opposed to individualistic, aspects of consumption, with wants and preferences emanating from practices (Holm, 2013; Gronow & Warde, 2001). In the case of food consumption these practices include acquisition, preparation, eating and disposal – part of the food provisioning process. Therefore, while we explore the series of micro activities surrounding the meal we also examine the more macro influence of marketplace spaces, institutions and discourses on everyday mealtime practices. As such we think of the contemporary food marketplace as made up of a range of retail spaces (supermarkets, farmers' markets, etc.), discourses (the ethical shopper, brands) and institutions (retailers, the media). This holistic marketplace focus explores the shaping of consumer practices of 'the meal' and the attendant meaning-making processes surrounding these practices that include both material and symbolic aspects of consumption and the role(s) that marketplace institutions, discourses and places play in reshaping, perpetuating or transforming such practices. This brings together the micro and macro, allowing us to more comprehensively examine the meal through the lens of *consumption practices*. Meals, like all practices, are dynamic and change over time and through history in response to food production, manufacturing, processing and retailing which all impact across the food provisioning process.

To this extent we are interested in the role(s) of the market in such processes and how consumers make sense of marketplace discourses through their practices (i.e. how brand-based environmental discourses influence consumers' shopping habits), how consumers interact with institutions (i.e. what consumers do and 'make' with the advice of celebrity chefs when they serve their meals), and how consumers interact with the various spaces of the market (i.e. how supermarkets influence food shopping practices). The book brings together work from a range of disciplinary perspectives to systematically examine *mealtime practices*.

The practice of the meal

Some texts treat the meal as an eating event but look at it from a multidisciplinary perspective that includes a scientific (psychology, physiology, nutrition, sensory, food service, product development, economics), as well as a social science perspective (sociology, anthropology, cultural studies, history and business marketing) (Meiselman, 2000, 2009).

Our focus is on the social sciences drawing on the social and cultural aspects of eating and the locus of practice theory. Meals are complex and we hope that in focusing on meals we can offer some insight into that complexity by offering a range of social science perspectives and new thinking about these practices in relation to the food provisioning practice that consumers experience in an everyday context. This is not the subject of laboratories and food halls but located in the mundane and everyday life of consumers faced with the diurnal task of provisioning for themselves, their families and their friends.

Taking inspiration from the food provisioning process by Goody (1982) and its more recent application to consumption (Marshall, 1995), the book unpacks the meal in a set of practices to include: acquisition, appropriation, appreciation and disposal. In this deviation from earlier models we combine planning and cooking into appropriation that reflects a range of emerging influences on this stage in the process, and open up the disposal stages to reflect some of the broader environmental concerns. Each of these practices forms a key section of the book. While we start by looking at practices of acquisition and end with practices of disposal it is important to note that we do not consider the everyday meal a linear process involving discrete practices, but rather a circular process of interrelated practices that embody a certain theoretical 'messiness' (Hill, Canniford, & Joeri, 2014) that we hope to unpack.

Part I on *acquisition* deals with the processes through which consumers interact with the market for their food provision. It investigates the current changes in food provision, including the way grocery stores orient themselves towards an increasingly multi-cultural food market and how consumers distinguish between branded authenticity and authentic branding. It also looks at individual, relational and collective family identities at play during mundane food shopping practices. This part reflects the way in which the market responds to broader social change at both the micro and macro level, as the increasingly diverse demands offer new opportunities for retailers and consumers alike, and notes the corresponding shift in consumer practice. Some of these emerging tensions are elaborated upon in Chapter 2 by Askegaard, Kristensen and Ulver, who consider the role of authenticity in the quest for 'real food' and 'healthiness' in the branded ubiquity of the marketplace. Chapter 3 (Gram) develops the idea of good versus bad food and suggests that the practice of food shopping, in this case with children, may involve less conflict than previously suggested, thus dispelling some of the myth around this everyday consumption activity. Chapter 4 (Cappellini, Marilli and Parsons) reveals how Italian women deal with their reduced household incomes by changing their shopping habits and intensifying their social and cultural capital to maintain a pre-austerity lifestyle. Chapter 5 (Ekström) examines how Swedish grocery retailers target foreign-born consumers.

Part II on *appropriation* unpacks the main issues surrounding the process that takes place at home once acquisition is accomplished. This part will look at how practices such as planning and cooking a meal are entangled with technology media devices, and interlaced with brands and celebrities. It explores the impact of marketplace discourses and materials on what people do and make in the kitchen, examining the influence of brands, cookbooks and kitchen gadgets and technologies. Chapter 6 (Julier) looks at how, through this process of appropriation, there is a continual adaptation, of both products and consumers, to accommodate social and technological change as convenience products become incorporated into even the most iconic of festive meals. In turn this changes how we think about meals at home and when eating out. One is left in little doubt as to the impact of the commercial marketplace on the kitchen. Chapter 7 (Truninger) considers a technological revolution in the kitchen and the way in which material culture impacts on the meal providing links with existing practice while transforming that practice. This debate is opened up in Chapter 8 (Denegri-Knott and Jenkins) which considers the impact of digital virtual devices in the kitchen as smartphones, tablets and laptops are increasingly used to guide meal preparation, opening up new spaces and opportunities for the cook. They show how this digital technology reconfigures food-preparation practice as devices augment the cook's creative capacity. This links neatly to the final chapter (Hewer, Chapter 9), which explores the influence of the media and the role of the celebrity chef in shaping our culinary practice, saving time while simultaneously investing in the celebrity 'brandscape'. This re-stylising of the everyday meal involves new practices that are closely tied to the market and offer inspiration and new forms of 'believing'.

Part III on *appreciation* looks at discourses and practices of mealtimes while food is shared in the household. Through a socio-historical analysis of women's magazines, changes to market discourses of the family meal over time are analysed. It also explores how sharing the everyday meal is connected to individual family identities with a specific focus on middle-class single mothers. Finally this part looks at children's snacking as a practice related to the organisation of the family meal and children's role and influence on family food consumption. The opening chapter (Davis, Marshall,

Hogg, Schneider, & Petersen, Chapter 10) shows how the family meal acts as a discursive device in two popular women's magazines centred on the image of the 'happy' family and notes the recent shift in how mothers are depicted in food advertising. This discussion around mothers is developed in Chapter 11 (Molander) which looks at a range of the mealtime practices of single mothers and the ways in which bodily disruptions and 'deviant' practices challenge existing conventions. These pressures on the family dinner are examined in Chapter 12 (Veeck, Yu, & Yu) which focuses on competing practices as family life and school life vie for time, leading to reshaping practices around the family meal. Finally, Chapter 13 (Marshall) shifts attention towards children's snacking and considers the range of practices associated with these less formal eating occasions and the ways in which commercial practice actually reaffirms the importance of the meal. Across these chapters we see the changing nature of meals as new schedules and demands are accommodated within existing practice.

Part IV focuses on *disposal* of the meal. Here we explore market discourses of food labelling as a powerful means of reshaping household food disposal. It also explores consumers' practices and associated discourses of re-using and transforming food leftovers. Finally the often neglected aspects of bodily waste and their cultural and social consequences in consumer society are examined. The part opens with Chapter 14 (Yngfalk) on the growing problem of food waste and an examination of the way in which its disposal centres on date labels as part of an institutionalised practice and bio-political struggle. This consumer responsibility can be seen in Chapter 15 (Närvänen, Mesiranta, & Hukkanen) which shows how social media (specifically food blogging) can be used to discourage food waste and illustrates the complex ways in which this disposal impacts across the range of practices associated with food provisioning. This examination of food blogging is another example of how technology can be used to shape consumer food practices. Questions about food provisioning practice are addressed next in Chapter 16 (Mourad & Barnard) which looks at how issues around waste are changing practices among 'dumpster-diners' living off the waste as a reaction against the food industry on both sides of the Atlantic. There are clear links here with the first chapter in this part on how we evaluate food as acceptable but the chapter shows how the meal is driven by what is available rather than what we want and have in the fridge, while retaining the culinary rules and meal aesthetics. We end with a discussion of the 'outcome of the meal' (Canniford & Bradshaw, Chapter 17), beyond waste and digestion, the final stage of (bodily) disposal as food is transformed into excrement. This chapter highlights our unease in talking about meals in this way and the extent to which we have become 'civilised' to ignore this aspect of eating.

We hope that this edited collection will provoke and inspire more research in this area of consumer food practice by illustrating some of the complexity that surrounds everyday eating and the increased marketisation of our meals. Despite concerns over the disappearance of the meal it seems as if these eating events continue to dominate our ideas about eating and we are increasingly reliant on others to produce, process, assemble and even dispose of what we eat. In the end the interpretation and practice of the meal remains with us as consumers.

Notes

1 This was over the research period (three days).
2 The article covers an initiative by the Scottish Government – Eat Better Feel Better www.eatbetterfeelbetter.co.uk/ – a response to the challenge of getting families to buy, cook and eat healthier food (McArdle, 2015). This community initiative aimed at C2DE mothers, centres on providing healthier home-cooked family meals in response to the growth in ready meals and takeaway foods. The associated website offers a series of recipes and hints that include shopping and preparing dishes that young families will eat. Research by the Scottish Government reports that up to one-third of the mothers surveyed report eating ready meals at least three times a week. What underpins all of this is a focus on meals and the practices that surround these events. It will be interesting to see if this initiative is successful in changing practices that have become increasingly reliant on outsourcing food preparation and meals to the food industry.

References

Atlantic. (2013). *Serving Convenience Foods for Dinner Doesn't Save Time*, (11 March 2013). Available at: www.theatlantic.com/health/archive/2013/03/serving-convenience-foods-for-dinner-doesnt-save-time/273729/ [Accessed 22 May 2015].

Barber, D. (2014). *The Third Plate: Field Notes on the Future of Food*. London: Penguin Press.

Blythman, J. (2006). *Bad Food Britain: How A Nation Ruined Its Appetite*. London: Fourth Estate.

Boulaire, C., & Cova, B. (2013). The dynamics and trajectory of creative consumption practices as revealed by the postmodern game of geocaching. *Consumption, Markets and Culture, 16*(1), 1–24.

Cappellini, B., & Parsons, E. (2012). Sharing the meal: Food consumption and family identity. *Research in Consumer Behaviour, 14*(1), 109–128.

Cappellini, B., Marilli A., & Parsons, E. (2014). The hidden work of coping: Gender and the micro-politics of household consumption in times of austerity. *Journal of Marketing Management, 30*(15–16), 1597–1624.

Carrigan, M., Szmigin, I., & Leek, S. (2006). Managing routine food choices in UK families: The role of convenience consumption. *Appetite, 47*(3), 372–383.

DEFRA. (2014). *Food Statistics Pocketbook*. Available at: www.gov.uk/government/statistics/food-statistics-pocketbook-2014 [Accessed 27 June 2014].

DeVault, M. L. (1994). *Feeding the Family: The Social Organization of Caring as Gendered Work*. Chicago: University of Chicago Press.

Douglas, M. (1975). Deciphering a meal. *Daedalus, 101*(1), 61–81.

Douglas, M., & Nicod M. (1974). Taking the biscuit: The structure of British meals. *New Society, 19*(December), 744–747.

Echeverri, P., & Skålén, P. (2011). Co-creation and co-destruction: A practice-theory based study of interactive value formation. *Marketing Theory, 11*(3), 351–373.

Gatley, A., Caraher, M., & Lang, T. (2014). A qualitative, cross cultural examination of attitudes and behaviour in relation to cooking habits in France and Britain. *Appetite, 75*(1), 71–81.

Goody, J. (1982). *Cooking, Cuisine and Class: A Study in Comparative Sociology*. Cambridge: Cambridge University Press.

Gronow, J., & Warde, A. (2001). *Ordinary Consumption. Studies in Consumption and Markets Series*. London: Routledge.

Halkier, B., Katz-Gerro, T., & Martens, L. (2011). Applying practice theory to the study of consumption: Theoretical and methodological considerations. *Journal of Consumer Culture, 11*(1), 3–13.

Hallsworth, A. G. (2013). Food retailing. In A. Murcott, W. Belasco, & P. Jackson (Eds.), *The Handbook of Food Research* (pp. 275–292). London: Bloomsbury Publishing.

Hill, T., Canniford, R., & Joeri, M. (2014). Non-representational marketing theory. *Marketing Theory, 14*(4), 377–394.

Holm, L. (2013). Sociology of food consumption. In A. Murcott, W. Belasco, & P. Jackson (Eds.), *The Handbook of Food Research* (pp. 324–337). London: Bloomsbury Publishing.

Jackson, P. (ed.) (2009). *Changing Families, Changing Food*. London: Palgrave Macmillan.

Klein, N. (2000). *No Logo*. London: Flamingo.

Lang, T., Barling, D., & Caraher, M. (2009). *Food Policy: Integrating Health Environment and Society*. Oxford: Oxford University Press.

Marshall, D. (ed.) (1995). *Food Choice and the Consumer*. London: Chapman and Hall.

Marshall, D. (2005). Food as ritual, routine or convention? *Culture, Markets and Consumption, 8*(1), 69–85.

McArdle, H. (2015). Scottish families shunning home cooking for 'cheaper' ready meals. *The Herald*, (9 January 2015). Available at: www.heraldscotland.com/news/health/scottish-families-shunning-home-cooking-for-cheaper-ready-meals.115807500 [Accessed 27 March 2015].

Meiselman, H. (2000). *Dimensions of the Meal: The Science, Culture, Business and Art of Eating*. Maryland: Aspen Publishers.

Meiselman, H. (2009). *Meals in Science and Practice: Interdisciplinary Research and Business Applications*. Oxford: Woodhead Publishing.

Moss, M. (2013). *Salt, Sugar, Fat: How the Food Giants Hooked Us*. London: WH Allen.

Murcott, A. (1982). On the Social Significance of the 'Cooked Dinner' in South Wales. *Social Science Information, 21*(4/5), 677–695.

Murcott A. (2012). Lamenting the 'decline of the family meal' as a moral panic? Methodological reflections. *Recherches sociologiques et anthropologiques, 43*(1), 97–118.

Ochs, E., & Beck, M. (2013). Dinner. In E. Ochs, & T. Kremer-Salik (Eds.), *The Fast Forward Family* (pp. 48–66). Berkeley: University of California Press.

Reckwitz, A. (2002). Toward a theory of social practices: A development in culturalist theorizing. *European Journal of Social Theory, 5*(2), 243–263.

Rozin, P., Fischler, C., Imada, S., Sarubin, A., & Wrzesniewski, A. (1999). Attitudes to food and the role of food in life: Comparisons of Flemish Belgium, France, Japan and the United States. *Appetite, 33*, 163–180.

Schlosser, E. (2002). *Fast Food Nation: What the All American Meal is Doing to the World*. London: Penguin Books.

Shove, E., & Panzar M. (2005). Consumers, producers and practices: Understanding the invention and reinvention of Nordic walking. *Journal of Consumer Culture, 5*(1), 43–64.

Southerton, D. (2006). Analysing the temporal organization of daily life: Social constraints, practices and their allocation. *Sociology, 40*(3), 435–454.

The Economist. (2013). *Thought for Food,* (12 March 2013). Available at: www.economist.com/blogs/graphicdetail/2013/03/daily-chart-5 [Accessed 23 January 2015].

Warde, A. (1997). *Food, Taste, and Consumption.* London: Sage.

Warde, A. (2005). Consumption and theories of practice. *Journal of Consumer Culture, 5*(2), 131–153.

Warde, A. (2010). *Consumption. Benchmarks in Culture and Society.* London: Sage.

Warde, A., & Martens, L. (2000). *Eating Out: Social Differentiation, Consumption and Pleasure.* Cambridge: Cambridge University Press.

Warde, A., Cheng, S.-L., Olsen, W., & Southerton, D. (2007). Changes in the practice of eating: A comparative analysis of time-use. *Acta Sociologica, 50*(4), 363–385.

Watson, M., & Shove, E. (2008). Product, competence, project and practice: DIY and the dynamics of craft consumption. *Journal of Consumer Culture, 8*(1), 69–89.

Yates, N., & Warde, A. (2015). The foods we eat now: Meal content in UK eating patterns, 1955–2012. *Appetite, 84*(1), 299–308.

Part I
Acquisition

2 'Authentic food' and the double nature of branding

Søren Askegaard, Dorthe Brogård Kristensen and Sofia Ulver

Introduction

There was a time, not too long ago, when the food of the future was imagined as a highly processed and industrialised product, basically imitating the fascinating creations of NASA and other space agencies for the booming space age. The first author of this chapter, just like Boyle (2004), remembers avid discussions among peers around the age of ten of the futuristic possibilities of producing and consuming pork roast or meat balls from tubes 'just like the Apollo astronauts'. While pork roast in a tube is still not to be found on the supermarket shelves, it is definitely a matter of fact that food engineering has conquered new territory and created types of food that only few grandmothers would recognise as such, to paraphrase Michael Pollan (2008).

However, industrialised foods are increasingly under pressure from a variety of movements, promoting 'slow food', local produce offered in public markets, customer-supported agriculture and similar initiatives (see e.g. Visconti, Minowa, & Maclaran, 2014; Press & Arnould, 2011; Petrini, 2001). These (and numerous other similar) works investigate the morality and ethics behind an emerging – oftentimes simultaneously utopian, nostalgic and very real – variety of alternative systems of production and consumption (see Julier, Chapter 6), that promote better food quality and a more direct and traceable link between the consumer and the spheres of food production.

Much of the contemporary policing of food is discursively constructed around the notion of authenticity. This chapter investigates consumer navigation between what they qualify as 'authentic' or 'real' and, conversely, 'unreal' food. The purpose of the chapter is to propose a semiotics of food authenticity and reflect on the impact on meal practices. We build our arguments based on the results of a Danish health branding project, notably drawing on results reported in prior publications (Chrysochou & Grunert, 2014; Ulver, Askegaard, & Kristensen; 2011; Chrysochou, Askegaard, Grunert, & Kristensen, 2010). These studies all contained dimensions that directly or indirectly inform consumer reflections on food authenticity. The following chapter builds on these insights but we will also be adding data collected in the context of the health branding project but not previously used.

This chapter is thus both a reflection upon and an extension of these prior studies.

The health branding project was carried out in a cross-disciplinary and cross-institutional cooperation between Danish researchers between 2008 and 2012. The general purpose was to investigate the possibility of using branding techniques as a supplement to standard informational campaigns in a public policy-oriented pursuit of nutritionally improved food consumption among Danish consumers.[1] The project included ethnographic, survey and experimental data collection methods.

Food as a politicised domain

The health branding project thus inscribes itself in a contemporary policing of food. The ubiquitous addressing of food consumption by national health institutions as well as the abovementioned movements address what is considered 'carelessness' in consumption and production processes; although 'careless' production in neoliberal market contexts seems more difficult to address once we get beyond what is outright dangerous to the consumer. Even if the motivations and practices behind a quest for better health and for food products of higher quality are far from homogeneous and concordant, the search for better quality food products in contemporary society becomes deeply intertwined with the increased focus on health, in personal terms, for the family, and (for some) also for the planet (see Yngfalk, Chapter 14).

The emergence of 'caring consumers' and 'caring producers' (Kneafsey, Cox, Holloway, Dowler, Venn, & Tuomainen, 2008) is thus a paradoxical and contradictory mix of nutritional and culinary discourses and practices (Chrysochou et al., 2010), which leads to a situation where not only for the 'caring consumers' investigated by Kneafsey and her colleagues, but for consumers in general, healthy lifestyle and food consumption is intimately tied, as witnessed by the omnipresent food-and-health-advice, contemporary public-mediated and private discourse. Thus, while tendencies towards more agentic participation in the food market may still pertain to relatively narrow segments of the population, one of the most important – if not the most significant – drivers of this as well as other processes of contemporary food choice, namely a contemporary public focus on food and health, has a much broader base among various segments of food consumers (Chrysochou et al., 2010).

The policing of food thus points to an increased consumer agency in pursuit of health and of better culinary life quality, sometimes but not necessarily in combination. The perceived ethics and sustainability of the public market relations (Visconti et al., 2014), the growing interest in customer-supported agriculture (CSA) (Press & Arnould, 2011; Thompson & Coskuner-Balli, 2007) and other such collaborative schemes also point to a more agentic encounter between producers and consumers. All such agentic encounters between producers and consumers and decoding of quality produce constitute a central dimension of contemporary politics of food and food culture. But the highly politicised food culture and food market is by consequence also a field of tension, where different value schemes for what constitutes 'good' and 'proper' eating compete, and which products and brands may or may not be included in acceptable foodways.

These tensions also find their ways into ordinary family lives and lie at the root of the current cultural reflexivity around the significance of many individuals' and families' attempts at maintaining control over their daily food intake, including a quest for relative transparency of the nutritional and gastronomic qualities of the products available in the marketplace. Furthermore, this contributes to explaining steady confirmations about 'how enduringly powerful and yet seemingly elusive the ideal of the "family meal" proves to be' (Cappellini & Parsons, 2012: 126). Cappellini and Parsons point to the tensions and contradictions in daily foodways between the ideal governing the imaginary of family mealtimes and the rough realities of daily temporal stress and temptation of convenience-based meal solutions. Their reflections also draw on the distinction between homemade and market-made (Moisio, Arnould, & Price, 2004) and its role in family identity formation. Given that the market for food products in modern, globalised market economies tend to be a juxtaposition of local and global players, hypermarkets, specialised stores, farmers' markets, direct selling from farms, food cooperatives and other types of consumer supported agriculture, how do people navigate and make sense of all the qualifiers that are supposed to separate 'real food' from its opposite? We think here of qualifiers such as 'organic', 'natural' and 'local', but also 'home made' 'traditional' and the like. Some of these labels are subject to strict regulations, in particular the qualifier 'organic', but they are understood and used by consumers in highly differentiated ways. So the problem remains, how do consumers find out what is 'real food'?

Authenticity and branding

Consequently, it may not be so surprising that contemporary markets have witnessed an upsurge in the quest for authenticity (e.g. Holt, 2002). This is not least the case for food and drink markets, where concepts of 'origin' and 'terroir' become particularly salient locally and globally (e.g. Beverland, 2005; Groves, 2001; Wilk, 1999). However, as Peterson (2005) notices, with reference to cultural critic Lionel Trilling, authenticity is an inherently polemic concept and consumers in search of authenticity for their daily food consumption are treading dangerous grounds, with room for much dispute of what constitutes an authentic product.

Grayson and Martinec (2004), using a Peirceian conceptual framework, argue for a double relationship between authenticity and commercial produce and distinguish between indexical and iconic representations of authenticity in a museum context, thus suggesting a distinction between a more positive type of authenticity and a more experiential type. The more positive, indexical authenticity, for example, refers to a consumer perception of an authentic native American tool, something that was actually made and used by a historical tribesman, whereas iconic authenticity would be a representation of said tribesman as realistically as possible given historical sources about tribal customs in terms of personal look, clothing, and accessories. However, as argued by Peterson (2005), even those types of authenticity that could be qualified as indexical, and thus more positive, are inscribed in a social constructed idea of authenticity since they are connected to, and obtain their authenticity through, some process of performativity or, as Peterson qualifies it, 'authenticity work' (2005: 1086). Consequently, authenticity is not just something that *is* but also something that is also *done*.

With this opening up of authenticity to performativity and social construction, the path is also paved for introducing the uneasy relationship between brands and authenticity – a relationship that divides consumers in terms of trustworthiness and which kind of brands are able to 'perform' authenticity through the trustworthiness of disclosed information. The brand format's origin as an indexical authenticity sign, in principle guaranteeing and thus clarifying a certain biography of a commodity, is mixed with the brand as a performative narrative that generates opacity in terms of the background and origins of the commodity. This double nature of the brand plays a pivotal role in the quest for authentic foods, as we shall see.

This problematic aspect of the brand has been analysed by Holt (2002), who argues for a 'flight forward' kind of relationship between brands and consumer markets. In this process, brand managers are on a perpetual quest for authenticity in the form of cultural resources that are 'untouched' by commoditisation or even 'modernity' in general; a process that leads to increased brand inflation and brand fatigue and an authenticity extinction through a breakdown of the distinction between culture and commerce. Brands, therefore, much like tourists searching for unspoiled and pristine environments, cause trouble through a simultaneous construction and mediation of authenticity while also undermining it through the very staging and commoditisation processes (Holt, 2002; cf. also Jones, 2010).

How do brands perform authenticity? It is suggested that authenticity in a market context can be considered as something that is 'projected via a sincere story that involves the avowal of commitments to traditions, passion for craft and production excellence, *and* the public disavowal of the role of modern industrial attributes and commercial motivation' (Beverland, 2005: 1025). From this follows that the coupling of market offers and authenticity first and foremost is based on narrative and that it therefore becomes possible to analyse conditions for authentic brand narratives (Visconti, 2010). Visconti furthermore underlines that from such a perspective, the authenticity of the brand narrative is constructed through the interaction between companies and markets/consumers. In a recent study, Napoli, Dickinson, Beverland and Farrelly (2014: 1091) identified seven cues of brand authenticity: heritage, nostalgia, cultural symbolism, sincerity, craftsmanship, quality commitment and design consistency. These cues were reduced through a confirmatory factor analysis to three explanatory factors of brand authenticity: quality commitment, heritage and sincerity.

Authenticity is thus both depleted and requested. Consequently, in the words of Jones, 'we need to ask why people find ideas of authenticity so compelling and what social practices and relationships these ideas sustain' (Jones, 2010: 183). Even if we accept that the basic dimensions in perceived authenticity are quality commitment, heritage and sincerity, as suggested by Napoli and her colleagues, we are still not able to say much about the dilemmas that consumers are confronted with when judging offerings in the marketplace. Thus, we need to situate the idea of authenticity in relation to the daily practices of shopping and cooking and the impact on the meals.

The mundane brand resistance

One attempt at analysing such a linkage is provided in one of the ethnographic accounts from the health branding project mentioned in the introduction. Based on ethnographic studies, various elicitation techniques, and interviews of a total of 40 contemporary Danish and Swedish consumers, Ulver, Askegaard and Kristensen (2011) analysed consumer navigation of industrialised versus homemade or generic produce, as well as the expression of this dichotomy in an evaluation of branded food products as they represent either clarification or opacity. They concluded that Scandinavian food consumers, and in particular the more 'caring' ones, seemed to sport a particular kind of negotiated relationship to brands that is both indicative of brand scepticism, and of the salience of the brand as an inescapable cultural form.

The analysis focused on how ordinary middle-class consumers who do not see themselves in any particular consumer activist role, nevertheless engage in a mundane type of brand resistance. This type of resistance is covered by Izberk-Bilgin's (2010) notion of agency and empowerment discourse against 'the dominant order' of industrial food in the contemporary market, 'emphasizing "everyday" micro-tactics; how consumers in subtle but skillful ways use consumption to oppose the dominant order [...] in line with de Certeau's view on the power of mundane tactics' (Ulver et al., 2011: 220). This resistance emerges through a number of bridging processes that consumers use to navigate the co-presence of good and bad food products and good and bad brands in the marketplace. More particularly, a problematic relation to the presence of brands in the alternative food sector was revealed, thereby pointing to consumers' difficulties in reconciling a branding logic from the food industry – with which they indicate that they are only all too familiar – with the alternative food sector. At various points, for example, consumers qualified brands from the caring food production as 'brands, OK, but not *real* brands' as known from the food industry and the supermarket (Ulver et al., 2011).

They argue that, seen from these middle-class consumers' perspective, the decisive principles for evaluation of food quality are inscribed in a kind of contemporary work ethic. Consumption as well as production represents kinds of work, and when you engage in such work processes, the moral duty is to engage well. Only then, is there basis for taking pride in the resulting product whether it is an agricultural product, a craft-based production of, for example, jam or a home-cooked meal combining a variety of ingredients that may not all live up to normative standards of organic, local, or other such production processes (Ulver et al., 2011).

Consequently, and still according to Ulver and her co-authors (2011), the issue of craftsmanship, both as a virtue of producers but also of consumers (Campbell, 2005) is fundamentally structuring consumer relations to the food produce, they encounter. This way, such food encounters reflect the significance of the cultural biography of food as something that comes with an origin, a history, and a trajectory (Kopytoff, 1986), and also a reaction of relative decommodification against the overwhelming dominance of industrial food in the contemporary food market. As we conclude 'the middle-classification of the crafting citizen–artist makes necessary the proliferation of the crafting industrialist' (Kopytoff, 1986: 233).

How to choose 'the right thing'

The usefulness of considering health and food quality, in terms of the origin of produce as interconnected features, was underlined in a different study from the health branding project. In an experimental study of health-related advertisement information, Chrysochou and Grunert (2014) distinguished between three types of communication elements that potentially can convey health-related meanings to the consumer and test their impact on consumers' perception on product healthfulness and purchase intentions. The first and most classical of these communication elements is what they term functional claims. Functional claims are advertising elements about nutritional properties that are deemed as beneficial to consumer health, as for example 'contains omega-3 fatty acid' or 'low fat content'. The claims included (Calcium, vitamin B-12 and Omega-3) were tested with and without explanatory remarks such as 'contains Omega-3 that helps to enhance memory functions' or 'contains vitamin B-12 that promotes cardiovascular health'. The second type of communicative element tested is what is termed 'process claims'. Process claims include claims about 'organic production', 'natural product', and 'locally produced' since, as we have discussed, consumers perceive such food production processes as linked to health benefits. The third type of communicative element included in the study is 'health imagery'. Health imagery refers to the visual elements, in this case the visual background that is used in the advertisement. Such visual imagery, from a cognitive psychological perspective, communicates healthiness through inference. Visual health imagery included in this study was 'exercise' (a man on a running machine), 'diet' (an apple and a bowl of salad) and 'well-being' (a woman superposed on the background of green meadows). The mock ads produced presented a

Figure 2.1 Two illustrations of mock advertisements displaying health branding claims.

combination of presence and absence of these health claims for two product types: cheese and yogurt.

Interestingly, the conclusions of the study run counter to a number of assumptions concerning how consumers evaluate the benefits of products. For example, it was concluded that while functional claims did increase the likelihood that consumers would perceive the product as healthy, they had no effect on the purchase intention. In other words, functional claims did not seem to enhance the likelihood of consumers buying the product. Second, the process claims were found to have an impact both on the evaluation of the healthiness of the products and on the purchase intention, that is, consumers perceive organic, locally produced or natural products to be both healthier and more attractive for purchase. However, by far the strongest impact on perceived healthiness and purchase intention was produced by the health imagery. In other words, the inclusion of a health oriented visual background was more effective in communicating healthiness of the product and enhancing the chances of consumers buying the product.

Also interestingly in this context is their finding that consumers with enhanced health motivations rely more on process claims for perceived healthiness and purchase intentions. This primacy of the process arguments found among health motivated consumers resonate well with the indication of the importance of work ethic and craftsmanship pointed out by Ulver et al., (2011).

The brand's double nature

So what to conclude about health branding on this basis? One central finding is that the visual imagery is a significant part of the communication of 'health'. To the extent that health is communicated through visual cues (for which there is little regulation and none in terms of health) and not through more factual claims, this finding represents a challenge to public policy makers and social marketing communicators interested in promoting healthier eating behaviour (Chrysochou & Grunert, 2014). More generally speaking, it is an indication that product qualities (in terms of health or other) need to be *shown*, not *told*, in advertising, packaging etc. Second, the results of Chrysochou and Grunert indicate the increased salience of process arguments – arguments about the product being 'natural', organically produced or of local origin, or any combination thereof – for the more health motivated segment of the population.

Once again, we are brought back to the double nature of the brand as informer and trickster. The brand, in the modern market, is the dominant vehicle for linking the producer and the consumer and it thus becomes a *discloser* of the origins of something. It is not alien to think of the farm shop in branding terms. The narrative of authenticity is still a narrative, and narratives of commodities in contemporary society are understood as 'branding'. However, as is well known, these days the brand is far more than a reference to the origin. Quite the opposite, it is the general scheme of valorisation of commodities (Arvidsson, 2006), it is just as performative as the notion of authenticity, and it refers to the concordant and conflicting set of producer-generated strategic and market and consumer generated narratives that is circulating about a product or a producer. In other words, the brand is also indicative of the narrative elements that *conceal* the origin of something, not necessarily due to ill will but because the aim is to tell a different story (or many different stories). Branding therefore causes trouble (Holt, 2002) and represents a dilemma to consumers who are trying to figure out, how to choose good, healthy, high-quality, authentic products for their, and their families' and friends' food consumption.

Sorting good from bad

Now the time has come to introduce fresh data in this chapter, which so far has been mainly a cook-up of leftovers from previous studies. In the context of the ethnographic study included in the health branding project, informants were asked to perform a sorting exercise. For this part of the data collection, we asked informants to sort a pre-selected set of branded products promoting some dimension of 'authentic' quality, classifying these products in the most and least trustworthy in terms of the authenticity of their claims. It may be important to note, that the informants sorted the actual products so they had access to all printed information on the packaging, concerning details about origin, source, size and type of the producer, etc.

The branded products included such items as organic whole milk from a cooperative (that is competing with Danish–Swedish dairy giant Arla), ProBio, a health-positioned yogurt brand from Arla, an organic lime drink from a small-scale producer, a ketchup from a local brand (as opposed to global market leader Heinz), an organic salami from a medium-scale producer, a micro-brewed beer, bread made from white wheat from a major industrial bakery, a honey-crunch muesli from an established Danish health food producer, a store brand of chips made from various roots and Asian ('Macau') spring rolls from a major Danish producer of frozen foods of predominantly Asian type. Other products were included as well, but this list gives an indication of the span of products and claims that were included.

This sorting exercise seemed to indicate both a high degree of variation in the relation to the specific brand, for example made explicit in varying degrees of confidence in the store brand mentioned above or in some of the fat-reduced products. There was however, a clear tendency to a higher ranking in terms of trust for products that came from what the consumers perceived as small-scale producers, such as the organic lime drink or the organic salami. On the other end of the scale were health product offerings from large-scale producers, such as fat-reduced brand extensions and other such health-profiled industrial produce. It is also interesting to note that the ranking is relative in the sense that organic *Beauvais*, the ketchup brand that received relatively good rankings, presumably not because it is from a small-scale producer or that it is perceived as crafted in any sense – but for what it is *not*, namely global market leader Heinz. In that market context, the local brand (formerly a family-owned business, now overtaken by a Norwegian holding company) stands out as a good choice.

The general impression from the sorting exercise is one of varying criteria, from relative market positioning to the general poor imagery of the producer (Arla, Kellogg's) and to a relative acceptance, sometimes based on prior product knowledge but often on the production process cues given by the packaging. But the informants of this sorting study also expressed widespread brand scepticism, in particular vis-à-vis the major corporations included in the sample:

and it is a nice piece of work, impressive advertising, super intimidating ... but also a piece of shit, I mean really, really bullshit, clever branding, good marketing, but by God there is nothing in it.

(Per, 32)

'There's nothing in it' is an idiomatic expression indicating shallowness and false promises and as such a quite strong statement. The scepticism makes consumers turn towards smaller-scale producers and their brands for a more reliable relation between product and claim:

Grønnegården and Hanegal and such brands, it is somebody who [want to] work there, they said yes to that job – it's not the same, [...] but it generates trustworthiness that these are someone who just really would like to make a nice product [...] and when it gets too big one just loses the ability to look through all that.

(Nina, 25 and Camilla, 24, double interview)

Behind these reflections, we find the same kind of longing that was also found by Ulver and her colleagues (Ulver et al., 2011), that a fundamental mythology which prevails with representatives of this consumer group is the myth of the generic and unspoiled food product which is conceived as completely natural.

The thing is that I would never consider buying any of these products. If I want something healthy, I will rather go directly to the source instead of buying something that has been through so many processes and then mixed into a sort of product.

(Nina, 25)

As indicated in the quote, this involves a maximum of 'care' in the production process (Kneafsey et al., 2008), and a minimum of processing since 'we eat food, not brands' as one informant quipped.

Towards a semiotics of food authenticity

We can now slowly see an 'order of things' emerge from the navigation between various types of food products, branded or not, in the contemporary marketplace. In order to summarise the insights presented in the preceding sections of the chapter, we would like to suggest a semiotic square of the relationship between branding and authenticity in the food market. The choice of a semiotic square, which is excellent for highlighting key tensions and paradoxes in meaning systems, reflects the complexities pertaining to brand perceptions in the food market and food consumption. As we have seen, the brand in contemporary food culture operates in a paradoxical mode where the brand is simultaneously embraced and despised, depending on the actual context. This is particularly the case for the more food- and health-savvy consumers of the North European middle classes, such as the populations investigated in the key studies from the health branding project.

An obvious basic juxtaposition that emerges from our previous discussion is the contrariety between the generic food produce (by which we mean gathered, grown in the garden or even bought in bulk format at the farmers' market) perceived as coming directly from its natural source with its absolute counterpart, the artifice of the industrial product. However, with reference to the informant who underlined the fact that we as consumers eat food, not brands, we would like to draw attention to an even more profound distinction, namely that between the manifest and material food object which plays a biological and gastronomical role as a physical and cultural building block – a tactile, olfactory and gustatory experience and, conversely, the symbolic and communicative realm of the brand. Even if the brand oftentimes is presented to us in a highly material context (Moor, 2007), our critical informants first and foremost think of the brand in its standard versions in the food market-place as an immaterial epiphenomenon that is linked to some kind of edible object, often with the purpose of disguising its (lack of) fundamental qualities. We would thus like to follow Arvidsson's (2006: 7ff.) qualification of the brand as informational capital and, consequently 'as a means of production, informational capital is immaterial capital'. The contrariety that juxtaposes the generic food product with its brand is thus a contrariety of materiality.

The contradiction of the generic (natural, unprocessed, unpackaged) produce is the non-generic produce. What does it mean that something is

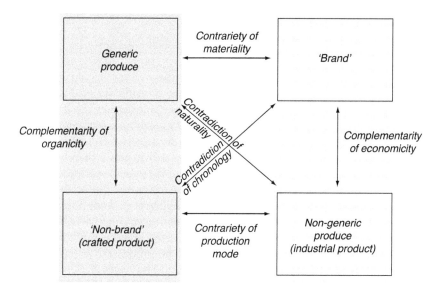

Figure 2.2 A semiotic square of meanings structuring perceptions of brands and authenticity.

non-generic? It means that it has been manufactured and removed from its natural state. In the purest form, it is a food product that fails to live up to Pollan's (2008) already cited advice never to eat anything that one's grandmother would not recognise as food. Although, obviously, not all food products from the food industry are this remote from any kind of natural state, our interpretation of this element in the semiotic square is the manufactured type of food that we find in standard products from the food industry, an interpretation that we find justified in the findings of Ulver et al., (2011). The contradiction between what is generic and what is industrial can consequently best be represented as one of naturality.

The other logical contradiction in our semiotic square is between the immaterial brand and the 'non-brand'. What is the meaning of a non-brand? According to informants in the studies quoted above, it is a brand that has all the material qualities of the generic produce, it just happens to come in the guise of a brand. For example, small-scale producers may still use branding techniques, for example a logo, a reference to the farm where the production takes place, etc. But it is perceived as a 'brand' that lacks the fraudulent qualities of the food industry's brands. As we have seen, it is a matter of whether the brand is at the service of the produce or the product at the service of the brand. By this we mean that for industrial (food) brands, the informants think of the food object as a mere vehicle for and carrier of the immateriality of the brand and its (hollow) promises, much in line with Arvidsson's (2006) arguments. The brand is the prime element of the constellation of the material and the immaterial. For non-brands it is the inverse. The prime element is the physical food object, the physical, gustatory, olfactory and tactile thing that can be eaten. The brand is an add-on that plays a secondary role in these food- and health-savvy consumers' perspective. The global ideoscape of branding, a notion that refers to branding as a globally dominant form of valorisation of products (Askegaard, 2006; cf. Arvidsson, 2006), necessitates some kind of brand-based representation and storytelling around the food product but the symbolic content is secondary to the culinary quality. There is first and foremost an object of quality and care (Kneafsey et al., 2008) that subsequently gets branded through the necessity of symbolic representation in the marketplace. For our critical consumers, it is a matter of differentiating between a brand that gets an object or the object that gets a brand. Crafted production is considered a production type where the care for the product and its qualities is primordial, and the brand is attached post hoc due to the necessity of branding in the markets of contemporary promotional culture (Wernick, 1991). Contrary to this, the idea circulating among our critical consumers concerning industrial food products is that the brand is cared for much more than the product because the purpose of the production is profitability rather than craftsmanlike pride in the final product. The contradiction is therefore one of chronology: brand before product or product before brand.

This makes for a secondary contrariety between the non-brand and the non-generic produce, or the crafted versus the industrial product. This contrariety is, obviously, one of mode of production, juxtaposing the craft-based production with an industrial production mode. It is a juxtaposition of *homo faber* against an *animal laborans*, the appendix to a capitalist mode of production. This also leaves us with two sides of complementary meanings. The generic produce and the crafted non-brand are complementary in terms of their working on the basis of what is perceived as 'natural transformation processes' (natural growth or the work of *homo faber* on nature's resources). They are, as such, both organic processes that belong to a 'natural' mode of being in the world, for living organisms, humans, plants and animals alike. The opposite complementarity of the brand and the industrial product is, on the contrary, a complementarity rooted in the particular socio-historical form known as capitalism. The complementarity is based on the fundamental commoditisation that lies at the roots of the capitalist form of production.

The contrarieties and contradictions in the meanings structure help us to better understand the consequences for consumers' meal practices. We see that consumers do not only rank the moral currency of food brands according to the meanings of the right chronology, naturality and organicity in the exercises, and perhaps more importantly, in our prior observations and interviews, the way social relations are valued corresponds with this ranking; the given importance to certain guests relative to others, child-caring versus self-caring, and the normative pressure surrounding traditions, to mention only a few. In contexts where guests have been involved, practices worth emphasising are, for example, hiding and even *masking* industrial products but showing off non-brands, making ironic remarks and thereby flashing one's consciousness at occasions when industrial products and brands are the only ones at hand, telling lengthy stories about the true marketing chronology when using non-brands and pointing out their organicity and crafted production. But also in more everyday situations with family members, the meanings of organicity, naturality and the absence of commercial immateriality are manifested through the temporal and emotional dedication and commitment that goes into every meal. When the meal is experienced to be of a predominantly non-generic and branded character, the event is quickly got over with, and not at all verbally elaborated. As if it never happened. On the other extreme, when the meal was seen as mostly organic, natural and dominated by non-brands, a lot of time and analytical engagement was spent elaborating upon various ingredients, textures and origins.

Conclusion: the *hau* of authenticity

Branding has always been caught up in a contradictory logic of clarification and opacity (see Hewer, Chapter 9). On the one hand, branding is fundamentally a signifier referring to a particular site of origin. Thereby it is indicative of an object's biography (Kopytoff, 1986), generating an often value-laden historical trajectory back to a product's 'birthplace'. On the other hand, exactly because it is based on a particular narrative of a history of values, branding is an exemplar of the human version of the sign; the sign which is a notion that, as Eco (1976) reminded us, refers to everything that can be used to tell a lie. Reading food brands is therefore a matter of constant negotiation of the trustworthiness of various indexical and iconic (and, retaining the Peirceian taxonomy, we should obviously add symbolic) 'signs of authenticity'. And it is a reminder how the 'perception of authenticity can depend on the simultaneous application of imagination and belief' (Grayson & Martinec, 2004: 310).

Let us conclude with a daring proposition, which is too complex to be pursued in the context of this chapter but which to us makes an obvious starting point for future research. This combined imagination and belief in the selection of 'real food' takes a form that, without being the same, is reminiscent of the anthropological concept of the *hau* so central to Marcel Mauss' study of the gift, 'a Maori term for the force of the identity of the owner of an object, which is attached to the object' (Wilk & Cliggett, 2007: 159). When an object is given away, some of that spirit will follow it, and it requires something in return. When we look at the attachment of some of our informants to their food providers, and we reflect upon what exactly it is that differentiates the left side of the semiotic square from the right, the branded authenticity from authentic branding, it is difficult not to get the idea that the permeating force of craftsmanship – of quality commitment, heritage and sincerity (Napoli et al., 2014) reflects some kind of *hau*. In the Maori belief system, the *hau* that leaves the owner wants to come back, which provides the foundation for an intricate system of reciprocal exchanges. The standard capitalist mode of production and market exchange, according to Mauss, has lead to a loss of the *hau* and de-personified and alienated the social ties of the exchange process (Wilk & Cliggett, 2007). In the alternative food market, however, an at least somewhat similar reciprocity exists – the *hau* must be returned to the crafting producer through some form of loyalty, endorsement, help (in consumer supported agriculture programmes for example) or other kinds of reciprocal engagement that links consumer and producer beyond the mere market transaction. If the produce is generic, we likewise owe the *hau* to nature as a giver and provider, in the form of natural protection, environmental and climate consciousness and the duty not to over-exploit, over-fish, over-harvest.... What we are asking ourselves, what we ultimately use as a basis for judgement of whether a food product is 'real' or not is: Is it an object that contains the *hau* of the producer?

This has consequences for the practice of the meal insofar as the perspective of the *hau* provides increased depth to the idiom 'you are what you eat'. Usually applied rather physiologically in order to provide a sense of responsibility (or guilt) in terms of choice of healthy (or unhealthy) food products, it becomes meaningful in an existential sense. Buying and consuming the *hau* of the food producer supposedly provides your existence with the same qualities that were put into the object in the first place, not in a biological but also a sociological sense. The practice of the meal thereby becomes not only the consumption of certain qualities but also the reproduction of these same qualities and an element in their circulation. The *hau*, as we have discussed, is present both in terms of the practices attached to the preparation and consumption of the meal but also discursively constructed and circulated through the verbalisation of the qualities of the food eaten.

Note

1 The project was supported by the Danish National Strategic Research Council.

References

Arvidsson, A. (2006). *Brands. Meaning and Value in Media Culture*. London: Routledge.

Askegaard, S. (2006). Brands as a global ideoscape. In J. Schroeder, & M. Salzer-Mörling (Eds.), *Brand Culture* (pp. 91–102). London: Routledge.

Beverland, M. (2005). Crafting brand authenticity: The case of luxury wines. *Journal of Management Studies, 42*(5), 1003–1029.

Beverland, M. B., & Farrelly, F. J. (2014). The quest for authenticity in consumption: Consumers' purposive choice of authentic cues to shape experienced outcomes. *Journal of Consumer Research, 36*(5), 838–856.

Boyle, D. (2004). *Authenticity. Brands, Fakes, Spin and the Lust for Real Life*. London: Harper Perennial.

Campbell, C. (2005). The craft consumer: Culture, craft and consumption in a postmodern society. *Journal of Consumer Culture, 5*(1), 23–42.

Cappellini, B., & Parsons, L. (2012). Sharing the meal: Food consumption and family identity, In R. W., Belk, S. Askegaard, & L. Scott (Eds.), *Research in Consumer Behavior, 14*(1), 109–128. Bingley: Emerald.

Chrysochou, P., & Grunert, K. G. (2014). Health-related ad information and health motivation effects on product evaluations. *Journal of Business Research, 67*(6), 1209–1217.

Chrysochou, P., Askegaard, S., Grunert, K. G., & Kristensen, D. B. (2010). Social discourses of healthy eating: A market segmentation approach. *Appetite, 55*(2), 288–297.

Eco, U. (1976). *A Theory of Semiotics*. Bloomington: Indiana University Press.

Grayson, K., & Martinec, R. (2004). Consumer perceptions of iconicity and indexicality and their influence on assessments of authentic market offerings. *Journal of Consumer Research, 31*(2), 296–312.

Groves, A. M. (2001). Authentic British food products: A review of consumer perceptions. *International Journal of Consumer Studies, 25*(3), 246–254.

Holt, D. B. (2002). Why do brands cause trouble? A dialectical theory of consumer culture and branding. *Journal of Consumer Research, 29*(1), 70–90.

Izberk-Bilgin, E. (2010). An interdisciplinary review of resistance to consumption, some marketing interpretations, and future research suggestions. *Consumption Markets and Culture, 13*(3), 299–323.

Jones, S. (2010). Negotiating authentic objects and authentic selves. *Journal of Material Culture, 15*(2), 181–203.

Kneafsey, M., Cox, R., Holloway, L., Dowler, E., Venn, L., & Tuomainen, H. (2008). *Reconnecting Consumers and Producers of Food*. Oxford: Berg.

Kopytoff, I. (1986). The cultural biography of things: Commoditization as process. In A. Appadurai (Ed.), *The Social Life of Things* (pp. 64–91). Cambridge: Cambridge University Press.

Moisio, R., Arnould, E., & Price, L. (2004). Between mothers and markets. Constructing family identity through homemade food. *Journal of Consumer Culture, 4*(3), 361–384.

Moor, L. (2007). *The Rise of Brands*. Oxford: Berg.

Napoli, J., Dickinson, S. J., Beverland, M. B., & Farrelly, F. (2014). Measuring consumer-based brand authenticity. *Journal of Business Research, 67*(6), 1090–1098.

Peterson, R. A. (2005). In search of authenticity. *Journal of Management Studies, 42*(5), 1083–1098.

Petrini, C. (2001). *Slow Food: The Case for Taste*. New York: Columbia University Press.

Pollan, M. (2008). *In Defense of Food: An Eater's Manifesto*. London: Allen Lane.

Press, M., & Arnould, E. J. (2011). Legitimating community supported agriculture through American pastoralist ideology. *Journal of Consumer Culture, 11*(2), 168–194.

Thompson, C. J., & Coskuner-Balli, G. (2007). Countervailing market responses to corporate co-optation and the ideological recruitment of consumption communities. *Journal of Consumer Research, 34*(2), 135–152.

Ulver, S., Askegaard, S., & Kristensen, D. B. (2011). The new work ethic of consumption and the paradox of mundane brand resistance. *Journal of Consumer Culture, 11*(2), 215–238.

Visconti, L. M. (2010). Authentic brand narratives: Co-constructed Mediterraneaness for L'Occitane brand. *Research in Consumer Behavior, 12*(1), 231–260.

Visconti, L. M., Minowa, Y., & Maclaran, P. (2014). Public markets: An ecological perspective on sustainability as a megatrend. *Journal of Macromarketing, 34*(3), 349–368.

Wernick, A. (1991). *Promotional Culture*. London: Sage Publications.

Wilk, R. R. (1999). 'Real Belizean food': Building local identity in the transnational Caribbean. *American Anthropologist, 101*(2), 244–255.

Wilk, R. R., & Cliggett, L. C. (2007). *Economies and Cultures. Foundations of Economic Anthropology*, 2nd ed. Boulder: Westview Press.

3   The supermarket revisited

Families and food shopping

Malene Gram

Introduction

Bringing children to the supermarket is stereotyped as being a 'nightmare'. As Holden notes, the supermarket visit with a child means dealing with marketing stimuli in a public place while at the same time having to buy necessities for one's everyday life (Holden, 1983). Pettersson, Olsson, and Fjellstrom (2004) found that some parents avoid shopping for food with their children as they experience this as stressful and exhausting. However, when actually looking at studies on parent/child supermarket shopping, very few signs of coercive and pestering behaviour are found, and other types of relational interaction seem to be much more important in family supermarket practice (Gram, 2014; Marshall, 2014; Commuri & Gentry, 2000). This chapter shows that shopping with children can also be a pleasant experience and is an opportunity for both doing and displaying family (Finch, 2007; DeVault, 1991) in an everyday life that is relatively segregated between work, school, spare time activities and electronic devices. As noted by Phoenix (2005: 88) declining birthrates have meant that children have taken the central role in parents' lives and 'are seen to reflect on their parents' identities and affluence', and family food consumption is not just about product choice but also about social interaction and identity (Jackson, 2009).

This chapter is about families shopping for food together. Going to the supermarket has become, if not an everyday routine, then at least a very frequent part of our food practices in the Western world. The arenas of food (Halkier, 2010), childhood and motherhood (Eyer, 1996; Zelizer, 1985) are loaded with values, norms and ideology, which parents and children need to navigate (see Marshall, Chapter 13). In the following account family supermarket visits are seen as collective processes with high levels of routinised behaviour intertwined with ideals and social norms about which food ought to be eaten, how parent/child interaction should take place, parents' and children's positions when interacting in the supermarkets, while at the same time being tempted by the food products on offer, and parents and children possibly having different ideas about what the family should eat. Practices of buying food involve at the same time pleasant intergenerational togetherness and anxiety and tension. The study is based on 50 observations of adults and children shopping for food together in the northern part of Denmark.

Background

From 'pester power' to a more nuanced understanding of the child consumer

The word 'pester power', meaning that children nag their parents to get what they want, appears in the literature on family consumption. The notion of 'pester power' was, according to Oxford English Dictionary, used for the first time in 1979 in the *Washington Post*, but has since been applied persistently, especially in the 1990s and early 2000s (Lindstrom, 2003; McNeal, 1999), and is in current publications often used to set the scene of children and consumption (Tyler, 2009; Coakley, 2003). However, 'pester power' does not seem helpful in understanding the more complex processes at stake when parents and children buy food together and has been problematised by several authors (Gram, 2011; Marshall, O'Donohoe, & Kline, 2007). While 'pester power' indicates that children are selfish and cannot take the perspective of others, children must be seen as 'not only self-centered in their seeking of resources from their parents' (Phoenix, 2005: 91), which for example is evident in studies of children in poor families, where children sometimes avoid asking for products because they know that parents' cannot afford them (Hamilton & Catterall, 2006). In opposition to what is implied in the 'pester power' concept, children can also take the position of the empathic helper, which is very far from the image of the pestering child, and the win–lose perspective of the pester power concept. 'Pester power' is therefore not an adequate means for understanding family consumption (Marshall et al., 2007; Commuri & Gentry, 2000). Being a family is a 'vitally important collective enterprise central to many consumption experiences' (Epp & Price, 2008: 50), and both parents and children are part of this enterprise.

In many previous studies an emphasis has been on the child's developmental stages, to a large extent inspired by Piaget's work, classifying the young child as incompetent and the older child and adolescent as more competent. This approach has, however, been problematised by a number of researchers (de la Ville & Tartas, 2010), drawing on Vygotsky's work and arguing that the level of competence of the child is much more related to the context in which the child lives, and the experiences the child has had, than the perceived universal level of cognitive development. Children are exposed to and participate in consumption at a much younger age than ever before. Because of a general interest in most Western countries in child participation in family processes this means that children acquire consumption and negotiation skills earlier than previously assumed, as will be exemplified later in this chapter. Children start taking part early on in family food purchasing in some ways – even from the moment they start talking and pointing, simply because they are part of these practices from the beginning of their lives. The argument is therefore that children are not just incompetent and consumers-to-be but – just like adults (Miller, 1998) – jumping in and out of competent versus incompetent roles (Ekström, 2010).

From rationalised individual processes to collective, habitual and embodied practices

In previous studies on families buying food, significant emphasis has been placed on the rational and individualised decision-making process, for example, by focusing on distinct decision-making phases, such as assessing how much each family member influenced each phase. In newer writings a much stronger focus has been on consumption as collective and relational processes (Cook, 2009), to a high extent embedded in habitual behaviour (Warde, 1997), in which emotions play a much more significant role than earlier assumed (Illouz, 2009). Emotions are part of consumption practices, and affectionate relationships between family members must be considered when seeking to understand family consumption (Hamilton & Catterall, 2006; Park, Tansuhaj, & Kolbe, 1991). Particularly in relation to parenthood and motherhood, feelings of guilt, fear, pride and love are at play (Miller, 1998; Eyer, 1996; see Veeck, Yu, & Yu, Chapter 12).

Consumption of food is best understood as intersecting practices which encompass a number of elements at the same time: routinised embodied behaviour including doing and saying, understandings and objectives (Halkier, 2010). The supermarket visit is characterised by habitual mechanic behaviour such as walking the same route in the supermarket, taking down the usual goods from the shelves, sometimes without thinking, but is at the same time related to ideals for healthy eating, for good parenthood, and a pragmatic trade-off between what was planned, what can be found in the supermarket and what urges of desire and temptation the consumer might feel. Multiple practices can be at play at the same time (Halkier, 2010) for example while shopping or cooking, but as argued by Molander (2011) motherhood can be seen as a meta-practice, dominating other practices (see also Molander, Chapter 11). Children become part of, internalise and co-create these routines, too, and also play into social norms by seeking to take the position of 'the good child' at least some of the time (Gram, 2014).

Many parents and children are found to be well informed about what healthy eating is perceived to be by authorities, but do not always act accordingly (Fagt, Christensen, Groth, Biltoft-Jensen, Matthiesen, & Trolle, 2007; Warde, 1997). Some characterise parents as being 'inconsistent' (Hoy & Childers, 2012), in their juggling with health-indulgence dilemmas (Hughner & Maher, 2006; Warde, 1997). This is quite in contrast to the way parents have often implicitly been presented in family decision-making studies – as 'good' parents in contrast to 'bad' children. Several studies have found that children are very active in shopping trips and that they often influence what the parent accepts to buy (Ebster, Wagner, & Neumueller, 2009; Buijzen & Valkenburg, 2008) and shopping trips are characterised by ongoing interaction (Pettersson et al., 2004).

Summing up, acquiring food has come to be seen as less of a conscious and rational process than earlier assumed and more anchored in habit and routines, social relations and emotions. It seems fruitful to consider family food shopping as joint practices where skills of shopping, knowledge of nutrition, desire for certain food items, wishes to be 'good' parents and 'good' children come together in a messy jumble of acts and aspirations, interpretations and justifications. Buying food is no finished practice but is to some extent (re) invented as both adult, child and market offer develop.

Method

In this chapter parents' and children's food shopping practices are explored in an interpretive perspective, not assuming that parents and children are or should be rational, but rather that they are engaged in complex micro-processes including intentionality, desire, habit and normativity as part of several intersecting practices (parenthood, healthy eating, being interesting partners, cool kids, etc.). Considering families buying food as practice emphasises that focus should not only be on mindful processes but also on embodied, emotional and habitual behaviour (Reckwitz, 2002). Human beings move between different positions (Schatzki, 1996) and do not necessarily take on the same position all the time.

The theoretical approach to the child is guided by the view from childhood sociology (James, Jenks, & Prout, 1998). This challenges the view that the child in society is seen as an unfinished individual who needs protection and is unable to act on what is best for him or her. It is argued that children should also be understood as active and competent actors in their own lives (James et al., 1998) as part of a network and involved in collective action (Kerrane, Hogg, & Bettany, 2012; Miller, 1998). However, children are at the same time also sometimes vulnerable, just as adults (Sparrman, Sandin, & Sjöberg, 2012).

This chapter is based on 50 situations of brief unobtrusive observations among Danish middle- and upper-middle-class families. Supermarket practice was observed among parents shopping with children between 0 and 16 years of age. The supermarkets chosen for observation were situated in middle- and upper-middle-class areas in the northern part of Denmark. The observations were carried out in 2009 and 2010 over 36 different days, where one-third of the observations took place on weekends. On weekdays, observations were mainly carried out between 4:00 and 6:00 p.m., on weekends mainly in the mornings. The aim was to observe what happens when parents and children make food decisions and to understand the positions and unwritten rules at play. The strength of this approach is that it allows insight into routinised behaviour. Since consumption is seen as, to a large extent, habitual behaviour, self-reporting approaches to studying family consumption pose difficulties, as informants cannot fully explain processes of which they are hardly conscious (Gram, 2010). Unobtrusive observation, however, also has some limitations. The observer only sees a tiny bit of the family members' interaction and shopping routines, which might not be enough to understand all aspects of what is going on. In the following, 'healthy' and 'unhealthy' foods are in quotation marks, as these concepts are contested.

The fact that Denmark is the context for the observations no doubt plays a role for the findings. In Danish society there is a long tradition of including children, and strong ideals exist for anti-authoritarian upbringing with an emphasis on independence and autonomy. This means that child-rearing practices probably stimulate the involvement of children and inclusion of their voices in family life more than in non-Scandinavian countries.

Findings

Little shopping trolleys, colourful packaging appealing to children and certain goods placed at children's eyelevel show that supermarket managers and food manufacturers consider children as part of their customer group. As the super-market study presented here was carried out in Denmark, where most mothers and fathers work outside the home, children are in daycare, kinder-garten or at school during the day. Therefore when parents and children buy food together, this takes place in the late afternoons or on weekends. When in the supermarket, the parents and children who were observed moved quickly among the shelves, often chatting as they went along. The children typically suggested numerous food items (cf. Ebster et al., 2009; Buijzen & Valkenburg, 2008), and parents accepted or rejected and discussed with their children as they moved along. Below, some central findings will be presented to illustrate the collective and social aspects of family food shopping, the embodied and routinised aspects, the importance of 'healthy'/'unhealthy' food and finally parents' and children's navigation in norms and expectations of being the 'good parent' and the 'good child'.

Collective and social processes in acquiring food

Several practices intersect when parents and children buy food: motherhood practices, cooking practices, etc. (Halkier, 2010). The following example shows the complexity of parents' and children's positions in the supermarket:

> A Friday afternoon in May a mother and a boy, around 12 years of age, looked for dinner. The boy pointed several times at a display freezer with frozen instant chilli-con-carne, and tried to direct his mother to that freezer. 'Look' he said. But the mother did not appear interested. They browsed on. The boy went back to the display freezer, picked up a product and read out loud so that his mother could hear it: 'It only takes

5–7 minutes in the microwave oven…' he read on. His mother was not uninterested now and joined him and looked with him at the other goods in the display freezer. Another customer came by who apparently knew the mother. 'O hi, so this is where you shop', he said. The mother started talking: 'Yes, we do because….' The boy appeared a little annoyed. He had almost succeeded in getting the instant dish. He started taking up three packets of the dish. The man was interested: 'And what is that?' The mother said: 'Well, [boy's name] can't resist things like that, and when it only costs 10 kroner [£1.25 pounds] each then….' The man said goodbye and left. The boy put the three packages into the shopping basket. They moved on.

As the example above shows both parent and child played a role in food selection practices, and the observation shows a complex interaction. The boy appealed to his mother through consistency and information campaigning and he convinced her to purchase the meal by emphasising for example that this dish was both quick and easy to prepare. Ready meals are not very well-accepted, not connoting love, care and quality as homemade food (Moisio et al., 2004), and the mother clearly needed to legitimise their purchase when an acquaintance came by and observed. The mother argued that she bought the ready meal because the child wanted it and it was cheap. She did not mention that possibly she liked this kind of product herself, too, and that the choice of convenience food was an easy solution for her as this would replace a meal that would have to be cooked, reasons which could jeopardise her status as a responsible and loving parent. Ideals about good taste and good parenthood seem to play an important role. The mother first rejected the product, possibly because of negative connotations regarding industrial food, but changed her mind as she was made aware by her son of the advantages of the product being quick and convenient to prepare. To put it crudely she took the position of the 'bad' parent in opposition to how parents are often implicitly presented in supermarket studies as consistent and sensible (Gram, 2015). She used significant energy on legitimising her choice, however, and one could argue that this is to make her act fit into the good parent position (listening to her child's wishes, getting a good bargain). The boy also acted according to ideals about good behaviour, and played the role of 'the good child', using argumentation rather than pestering. The example shows that parents and children take on varying positions, have and use significant knowledge about each other; the mother knew what the boy liked, the boy knew how to approach his mother; they listened to each other, and they had knowledge of each other's priorities and about how to behave in the space of the supermarket.

Embodied routinised behaviour

Following the shift in focus on intentionality, a larger focus comes to rest on the embodied habitual behaviour, how for example moving around in the supermarket is at least at times a routine which is barely conscious. An example of this stems from my own collection of data in the supermarkets, when I first set out to observe parents and children. Despite my plans to observe, when entering the supermarkets in the beginning, I slipped into routinised behaviour, putting goods into the shopping basket on autopilot, reacting to offers and new products, etc. and forgetting that I was supposed to observe, not shop. This serves to exemplify that habitual embodied behaviour plays an immense role when acquiring food. This is seen in various ways in the supermarket observations. Parents and children moved quickly through the supermarket often talking about other things than buying food. They seemed to follow more or less encoded routes in the supermarket moving from fruit to bread, from meat to dairy sections and finally through the contested area of confectionery.

Routinised behaviour such as collecting necessities in the supermarket is embodied, non-reflective behaviour, resting firmly on habits. Also the role division between parents and children appeared quite set, and was very rarely addressed. Whereas the child was typically very active in finding goods, showing and proposing goods to the parent, the parent was at all times the gatekeeper of what went into the shopping trolley (Marshall et al., 2007).

'Healthy'/'unhealthy' food

The concepts of 'healthy'/'unhealthy' food constituted an important part of the scaffolding of the interaction regarding what food to buy. As discussed in Gram (2015) 'healthy' and 'unhealthy' foods were a significant means of deciphering food in the supermarket and part of the interaction in food choice. Whether or not a product was labelled as 'healthy' was a valid argument in negotiations, mainly used by parents and mainly respected by children. Both parents and children were found to suggest 'unhealthy' food – but children did so more than adults. As a tool of minimising 'unhealthy' food items 'Friday sweets' is a common phenomenon in Denmark and is a concept often used in the observed negotiations. 'You can have that for Friday sweets' or 'Can I have this for Friday?' revealing firmly integrated rules for when 'unhealthy' food items can be indulged in without compromising responsible parenthood. 'Friday sweets' can be seen as a cultural practice of 'contained indulgence' as a way to balance the healthy versus indulgence antinomies (Warde, 1997). This concept is an important part of the cultural context in which the observations are situated, and perhaps 'Friday sweets' helps avoid conflicts between parents and children as a limited but acceptable way of consuming unhealthy food.

While there has been a focus on children's coercive behaviour, in these observations, this was by no means a dominant trait, even though tension and negotiation do take place as the first example illustrates. While children asked for a lot of 'unhealthy' goods, they appeared to be familiar with health dis-courses, too, and accepted parental refusal to buy items based on health claims. An example illustrating the complexity and various positions follows:

> A mother and her son of four or five entered the supermarket. The mother asked the boy if he wanted a small trolley or whether she should take a basket. He wanted a small trolley. They started shopping. The boy went directly to some cinnamon buns and said to his mother: 'Should I take two of these?' His mother said yes. They moved on. The mother wanted to look at meat. Her son said after a short while: 'Should we move on to the Kindermilchschnitte [sponge cake with cream filling kept by the dairy products] section?' His mother said: 'But you are not getting any Kindermilchschnitte today. You know you got the others [cinnamon buns].' The boy accepted. 'But can I have juice then?' 'Yes,' his mother said. 'When can I have it?' he asked. His mother wanted to take milk. The boy picked up full milk. His mother said: 'No, we are definitely not having that.' She opened the fridge with the skimmed milk. The boy said: 'I can take that. Do you want two or three or one?' The mother wanted to move away from the dairy section. The boy said: 'But I could have juice.' He pointed to some juice next to the milk. 'No, not that,' his mother said. She looked at frozen fish. The boy spotted another type of juice: 'Here is juice. Can I have this?' 'O no,' his mother said, 'That juice is disgusting.' The boy accepted. His mother said: 'We'll find those small ones.'

The mother took a dialogical approach to her son by letting him choose if he wanted the small trolley or not. She took the position of the indulgent parent, who gave in to the child's desire for cinnamon buns in one moment, but changed into the position of the health-conscious parent by minimising unhealthy food intake by rejecting the Kindermilchschnitte. She probably knew that he would suggest that they buy one, as he labelled the dairy section the 'Kindermilchschnitte-section' and probably because she knew he liked these. She referred to the fact that they had just chosen cinnamon buns and could not have both. Also in her 'health-mode' she rejected whole milk, but here she perhaps stepped a little out of her 'good parent' position, as she appeared somewhat impatient and irritated. As she rejected the juice, arguing that this was disgusting, she moved into an emotional realm, instead of explaining that this juice was perhaps made with artificial colour and taste additives, was not natural, or similar. She ended up in a constructive mode again, suggesting what kind of juice the boy could have. The mother thus moved between positions as the indulgent parent, the responsible health-conscious, patient and explaining parent, to an impatient and irritated parent and back to a constructive, consensus-seeking parent. The boy was active in suggesting products, but accepted rejections any way they were formulated in this observation. He offered to help by picking up the milk, and he insisted on having the juice that he was promised, but accepted the compromise of finding the small juices suggested by his mother.

The whole situation only lasted a couple of minutes, but illustrated how both the mother and her young son moved between different positions: the insisting and accepting attitudes from the child, and the mother between roles of the patient and reasonable parent, and the impatient and annoyed adult arguing through emotion rather than sense. The example of deal-making as a way of minimising ('if you get this, you cannot have that') was widely used and accepted, and helped to maintain a consensus-based shopping ambience.

Being the 'good' parent and the 'good' child

Both children and parents were found to navigate according to social norms of appropriate behaviour, and sought cooperation rather than warfare. When I first presented the findings from my observations in supermarkets in a research seminar, someone in the audience said towards the end: 'Does this mean that there were no screaming children in the supermarkets?' This view on children in supermarkets clearly represents a common myth, but has little to do with the majority of what is actually taking place in supermarkets – both according to my findings and the literature on children's coercive behaviour in supermarkets. Surely children are not little angels at all times, but in this study they are found to work hard on taking on the position of the 'good' child. More importantly the point to be made in this chapter is that an overlooked aspect in family food shopping studies is the changing positions of parents, who are not always behaving in the consistent position they are often assumed to take on (changing their minds on decisions to reject food items, being impatient or a little rude, suggesting unhealthy food items, etc.).

Children seemed to know the rules of appropriate supermarket behaviour. An example of this stems from a supermarket visit where two very young girls, approximately two and five years, were in the supermarket with their father. They were close to the check-out point, and while their father was engaged in looking at some other goods, the two girls examined the sweets displayed:

> The oldest girl said 'Look: sweets.' The 2-year-old said: 'We are not having any of that today.' The oldest girl said that she was just looking. The 2-year-old picked up a packet of Maoam sweets. The older girl said: 'That's not looking, that is touching.' She laughed. The young girl put it back.

Without any intervention from their father, who was not even looking, these two girls were enacting this little scene. Even though they were very young children, who according to the traditional way of perceiving children as incompetent should not be able to neither postpone needs nor navigate according to social norms, they indeed followed the norms of appropriate supermarket behaviour. They had clearly already internalised the family rules for sweets and did not even attempt to approach their father to ask for an exemption from these rules. 'We are not having any of that today' indicates a defined space of time for confectionery which was not the present, and they respected this rule in this situation. 'Touching' is tempting and underscores the embodied and tactile elements of buying food, but the two girls also accepted that this is not appropriate supermarket behaviour in opposition to 'looking'. The children helped in minimising 'unhealthy' food purchasing on their own, and the example shows that just as parents seek to be 'good parents', children seem to aim at being 'good children' (Gram, 2015).

Children were found to respect parents as gatekeepers. Some meta-communication regarding pestering took place but very little actual nagging. Children did a lot of helping out, suggesting and fetching goods, filling shopping bags and watching the goods when purchased. There was often an ongoing dialogue between parents and children throughout the shopping trips, about school, siblings, birthday parties, etc. Parents also in some instances sought inspiration from the children: 'What should we eat tonight?', and were concerned about children's desires: 'What do you feel like eating?'

Conclusion

Family food shopping is a continuous and repetitive act as food needs to be acquired in a constant flow into the home. The family shopping experiences have been presented as a war zone (with terminology such as winning and losing, mothers as tacticians, children's strategies, etc.) with a strong focus on conflict. While tension, anxieties, and negotiations using tactics and strategies on both parts certainly are part of shopping practices, family food shopping in this study comes across as marked by a high level of mutual understanding and respect. This is quite in contrast to previous stereotypical images of children behaving badly in supermarkets, but quite in line with the lack of evidence of children's pestering behaviour in the research literature. Just as parents seek to live up to images of 'good parents', children internalise rules for acting in public and are immersed in social norms, too, and are quite skilled in negotiating and persuading. The study finds that children navigated aptly in the meaning universe of the supermarket and the parental rules and desires.

Parents and children moved between different positions in relation to the various and intersecting practices at stake. The parent was at times patiently explaining about nutrients, and carefully listening to the child's wishes and argumentation. At other times the parent was being emotional and impatient, or took the lead in encouraging 'unhealthy' food items, which is actually how the child has implicitly been seen in earlier studies. The child suggested innumerable food items, using intensive persuasion and negotiation, but was also self-regulating and in many cases a genuine help in the practical work of acquiring food in teamwork with the parent.

Food purchase must be seen as relational and as a way of doing family, where all members compromise and most often respect prevailing rules and norms. The child and the parent go through routinised acts of taking food back home while dancing around the concepts of 'healthy' and 'unhealthy' and while enacting the conflicting positions of being 'good' and 'bad' parents and 'good' and 'bad' children.

References

Buijzen, M., & Valkenburg, P. M. (2008). Observing purchase/related parent/child communication in retail environments. *Human Communication Research, 34*(2), 50–64.

Coakley, A. (2003). Food or 'virtual' food? The construction of children's food in a global economy. *International Journal of Consumer Studies, 27*(4), 335–340.

Commuri, S., & Gentry, J. W. (2000). Opportunities for family research in marketing. *Academy of Marketing Science Review, 4*(5), 1–34.

Cook, D. T. (2009). Semantic provisioning of childen's food. *Childhood, 16*(3), 317–334.

de la Ville, V. I., & Tartas, V. 2010. Developing as consumers. In D. Marshall (Ed.), *Understanding Children as Consumers* (pp. 23–38). London: Sage.

DeVault, M. (1991). *Feeding the Family: The Social Organization of Caring as Gendered Work*. Chicago: Chicago University Press.

Ebster, C., Wagner, U., & Neumueller, D. (2009). Children's influence on in-store purchases. *Journal of Retailing and Consumer Services, 16*(2), 145–154.

Ekström, K. M. (2010). Consumer socialization in families. In D. Marshall (Ed.), *Understanding Children as Consumers* (pp. 41–60). London: Sage.

Epp, M. A., & Price, L. (2008). Family identity: A framework of identity interplay in consumption practices. *Journal of Consumer Research, 35*(June), 50–70.

Eyer, D. E. (1996). *Motherguilt: How Our Culture Blames Mothers For What's Wrong With Society*. New York: Times Books/Random House.

Fagt, S., Christensen, T., Groth, M. V., Biltoft-Jensen, A., Matthiesen, J., & Trolle, E. (2007). *Børn og Unges Maltidsvaner 2000–2004 (Children and Young People's Meal Habits 2000–2004)*. Søborg: DTU Fødevareinstituttet.

Finch, J. (2007). Displaying families. *Sociology, 41*(1), 65–81.

Gram, M. (2010). Self-reporting vs. observation: Some cautionary examples from parent/child food shopping behaviour. *International Journal of Consumer Studies, 34*(4), 394–399.

Gram, M. (2011). The death of 'pester power': Intergenerational food shopping. In A. Bradshaw, C. Hackley, & P. Maclaran (Eds.), EACR proceedings: European Advances of Consumer Research, 479–480.

Gram, M. (2015). Buying food for the family. Negotiations in parent/child supermarket shopping: An observational study from Denmark and USA. *Journal of Contemporary Ethnography, 44*(2), 169–195.

Halkier, B. (2010). *Consumption Challenged: Food in Medialised Everyday Lives*. Farnham: Ashgate.

Hamilton, K., & Catterall, M. (2006). Consuming love in poor families: Children's influence on consumption decisions. *Journal of Marketing Management, 22*(9–10), 1031–1052.

Holden, G. W. (1983). Avoiding conflict: Mothers as tacticians in the supermarket. *Child Development, 54*(2), 233–240.

Hoy, M. G., & Childers, C. C. (2012). Trends in food attitudes and behaviors among adults with 6–11-year-old children. *The Journal of Consumer Affairs, 46*(3), 556–572.

Hughner, R. S., & Maher, J. K. (2006). Factors that influence parental food purchases for children: Implications for dietary health. *Journal of Marketing Management, 22*(9/10), 929–954.

Illouz, E. (2009). Emotions, imagination and consumption. A new research agenda. *Journal of Consumer Culture, 9*(3), 377–413.

Jackson, P. (Ed.) (2009). *Changing Families, Changing Food*. London: Palgrave Macmillan.

James, A., Jenks, C., & Prout, A. (1998). *Theorizing Childhood*. Cambridge: Polity Press.

Kerrane, B., Hogg, M. K., & and Bettany, S. M. (2012). Children's influence strategies in practice: Exploring the co-constructed nature of the child influence process in family consumption. *Journal of Marketing Management, 28*(7/8), 809–835.

Lindstrom, M. (2003). *Brandchild*. London: Kogan Page.

Marshall, D. (2014). Co-operation in the supermarket aisle: Young children's accounts of family food shopping. *International Journal of Retail and Distribution Management, 42*(11/12), 990–1003.

Marshall, D., O'Donohoe, S., & Kline, S. (2007). Families, food, and pester power: Beyond the blame game? *Journal of Consumer Behaviour, 6*(4), 164–182.

McNeal, James U. (1999). *The Kids Market. Myths and Realities*. Ithaca, NY: Paramount Market Publishing.

Miller, D. (1998). *A Theory of Shopping*. Cambridge: Polity Press.

Moisio, R., Arnould, E. J., & Price, L. L. (2004). Between mothers and markets: Constructing family identity through homemade food. *Journal of Consumer Culture, 4*(3), 361–383.

Molander, S. (2011). Food, love and meta-practices: A study of everyday dinner consumption among single mothers. In R. W. Belk, K. Grayson, A. M. Muñiz, & H. J. Schau (Eds.), *Research in Consumer Behavior (Research in Consumer Behavior, 13*(1), 77–92. London: Emerald Group Publishing Limited.

Park, J.-H., Tansuhaj, P. S., & Kolbe, R. H. (1991). The role of love, affection, and intimacy in family decision research. *Advances in Consumer Research, 18*(1), 651–656.

Pettersson, A., Olsson, U., & Fjellstrom, C. (2004). Family life in grocery stores. *International Journal of Consumer Studies, 28*(4), 317–328.

Phoenix, A. (2005). Young people and consumption: Commonalities and differences in the construction of identities. In B. Tufte, J. Rasmussen, & L. B. Christensen (Eds.), *Frontrunners or Copycats?* (pp. 78–98). Copenhagen: Copenhagen Business School.

Reckwitz, A. (2002). Toward a theory of social practices: A development in culturalist theorizing. *European Journal of Social Theory, 5*(2), 243–263.

Schatzki, T. R. (1996). *Social Practices: A Wittgensteinian Approach to Human Activity and the Social*. Cambridge: Cambridge University Press.

Sparrman, A., Sandin, B., & Sjöberg, J. (Eds.) (2012). *Situating Child Consumption. Rethinking Values and Notions of Children, Childhood and Consumption*. Lund: Nordic Academic Press.

Tyler, M. (2009). Growing customers. Sales-service work in the children's culture industries. *Journal of Consumer Culture, 9*(1), 55–77.

Warde, A. (1997). *Consumption, Food and Taste*. London: Sage.

Zelizer, V. (1985). *Pricing the Priceless Child*. New York: Basic Books.

4 Working your way down

Rebalancing Bourdieu's capitals in times of need

Benedetta Cappellini, Alessandra Marilli and Elizabeth Parsons

Don't change your lifestyle, change your supermarket
(Lidl advertising campaign, Italy, Autumn 2013)

Introduction

More than just a catchy advertising slogan, the German discount supermarket Lidl seems to have captured the sea change in consumer behaviour in times of austerity. The recipe seems very simple: change your everyday shopping habits and you will be able to maintain your pre-recession lifestyle.[1] However, things are not as simple as switching supermarkets, especially when incomes are drastically reduced. In analysing the shopping practices of ten middle-class Italian women experiencing a reduction of family income, we found a series of other switching behaviours involving the development of marketplace and non-marketplace knowledges and competences. Importantly we find that these behaviours involve an intensification of social and cultural capital, and an overall rebalancing of capitals (social, cultural and economic) to maintain as far as possible a pre-austerity lifestyle and make up for drastically reduced household economic resources.

The purpose of this chapter then is to investigate Lidl's catchy slogan and understand how people have changed their food provisioning and how such changes may be linked to their lifestyles. We do so by providing a critical reading of the everyday practice of shopping and other food provisioning practices of ten middle-class Italian women living in Florence. Elsewhere we have unpacked the gender issues of the current austerity in Italy, claiming that recession has brought women back into their kitchens, exacerbating gender inequalities in the home (Cappellini, Marilli, & Parsons, 2014). We show how shopping is a practice linked to the domestic food provision circle and, as such, needs to be understood in relation to the cosmology of the meal rather than a distinct and disconnected practice (see also Marshall, 1995). These two claims are fundamental to contextualise and fully understand these women's food acquisitions. Here we draw from such claims, but we are interested in understanding the process of acquiring food as a set of practices enacting classed competences, knowledges and disposition. We apply a

Bourdieuian approach to practice, in order to understand how skills and competences related to different forms of economic, social and cultural capitals are at play during food acquisition. Inspired by Bourdieu's (1986) idea of conversions of capitals, we show how a reduced amount of financial resources to be spent in food acquisition, corresponds with an intensification of other practices derived from the other forms of capitals, including practices emerging from local social networks, and practices derived from individual culinary competences. Our study will offer theoretical insights into the relationships between the three forms of capitals, showing the compensatory nature of cultural and social capitals.

Social class and capitals

According to Bourdieu (1986), social class is the main determinant of people's lifestyle, which is understood here in its broader sense as the way people think of themselves, relate to others and perform their own identity through largely unreflected cultural practices, including consumption practices. Bourdieu's theory of social class is indeed a theory of taste, assuming that individual preferences reflect the person's class position in society. People sharing the same social class tend to share similar tastes, visible in similar patterns of consumption (i.e. sharing of likes and dislikes), which constitutes the symbolic dimension of class struggle, as taste is unequally and hierarchically distributed. Such a hierarchical distribution of taste results from the combination of three different capitals (economic, social and cultural), which contribute to the position of an individual in society. In his essay, *Forms of Capital*, Bourdieu (1986) provides an extended description of this notion of capitals explaining how they can be acquired, exchanged and converted.

For Bourdieu, cultural capital results from formal and informal education, mostly determined by family of origin and a non-reflective form of capital, also known as *habitus*. Habitus is a set of culturally structured individual dispositions, bodily skills and non-discursive knowledge. Sociological and consumer research studies have investigated the complexity of habitus in the way people like and dislike food (Johnston & Baumann, 2010; Warde, Martens, & Olsen, 1999; Wilk, 1997). Mindful that class is relational, these studies have shown how owning 'proper' middle-class cultural capital is a never-ending learning process, as displaying the 'right tastes' and 'possessing the logic in order to reproduce them' (Skeggs, 2004: 136) is fundamental for maintaining a privileged class position. Others have highlighted how middle-class cultural capital is also manifested in mundane domestic consumption in which, more than a matter of positioning in relation to others, such capital is a matter of being simply 'ordinary' and indeed conforming to the dominant normativity of the immediate and familiar class milieu (Kravets & Sandikci, 2014). Interpretive studies have confirmed both these theoretical positions of class, showing how food competences and skill operate at the horizontal (defining us) and vertical (distancing us from them) levels (Cappellini, Parsons, &

Harman, 2016 (forthcoming); Ulver & Ostberg, 2014). We take inspiration from this set of studies highlighting how cultural capital is not only relational and thus aimed at positioning in comparative terms, but it is also a matter of defining 'us' through performing skills, ideas, and verbalising sensibilities typical of 'us'. For example, studies on family food consumption show how women's performances of what they consider to be 'good mothering' are manifestations of their classed cultural capital. For middle-class women, being a good mother includes providing children with a diet considered healthy and varied (Willis, Backett-Milburn, Roberts, & Lawton, 2011; Bugge & Almås, 2006) 'socializing them [the children] into culinary competence' (Hollows, 2003: 186) and exercising control and discipline (Harman & Cappellini, 2015; Willis et al., 2011). For working-class mothers, good mothering is more a matter of providing filling food, giving instant gratification and teaching children to make autonomous choices (Willis et al., 2011).

If cultural capital has attracted attention in consumer research, social capital has been a less popular topic of investigation. According to Bourdieu, social capital is defined as 'the aggregate of the actual or potential resources which are linked to possession of a durable network of more or less institutionalized relationships of mutual acquaintance and recognition' (1986: 248). This definition highlights how social capital is a personal resource that can be accumulated, used for personal advantage and transformed into economic capital. Empirical studies looking at job markets have shown the advantages that social capital can provide. For example, Paul Du Gay's (1996) concept of the 'enterprising self' (see also Erickson, 1991) highlights how individuals become enterprising subjects, through developing social capital in order to secure stable employment, ultimately rendering the subject responsible for his/her own success in the marketplace. The few consumer studies showing the impact of strong or weak ties in shaping leisure consumption (Warde & Tampubolon, 2002) and food consumption (Cappellini & Yen, 2013) have not investigated the links between social capital with other forms of capitals.

In unpacking these links, we take inspiration from Bourdieu's understanding of the way social and cultural capitals are linked to economic capital. Following Bourdieu, social and cultural capitals cannot be simply reduced to economic capital but their acquisition and development derives from it. They can be converted into economic capital since the latter 'is at the root of all the other types of capital' and 'in the last analysis – at the root of their effects' (Bourdieu, 1986: 54). According to Bourdieu, in order to understand this conversion process, the analysis needs to combine an economic *and* cultural view of practices. As he said:

> The real logic of the functioning of capital, the conversions from one type to another, and the law of conservation which governs them cannot be understood unless two opposing but equally partial views are superseded: on the one hand, economism, which, on the grounds that every type of capital is reducible in the last analysis to economic capital, ignores

what makes the specific efficacy of the other types of capital, and on the other hand, semiologism (nowadays represented by structuralism, symbolic interactionism, or ethnomethodology), which reduces social exchanges to phenomena of communication and ignores the brutal fact of universal reducibility to economics.

(1986: 54)

Taking inspiration from Bourdieu's idea of exploring the three forms of capitals as a sort of conversion game between currencies (economic, cultural and social), we will look at how the three capitals are at play during food acquisition. Looking at food acquisition from a symbolic (called semiologism by Bourdieu), and material perspective (economism), we will investigate how cultural and social capital are at play when economic capital is drastically reduced. We will do so by looking at how participants use their social and cultural recourses to overcome their reduced household finances. In exploring participants' food acquisition involving the three forms of capitals, we examine if (and if so how) participants manage to maintain their pre-crisis consumption patterns. In other words, we are going to see if, as the Lidl slogan simply puts it, people manage to maintain a similar lifestyle despite their reduced household income.

Findings

This study emerged from a qualitative investigation exploring how ten Italian middle-class women – in their mid-thirties to early forties – cope with a reduced family income. We selected households in the city of Florence and surrounding areas, with pre-crisis incomes of more than 50,000 euros after tax, which had experienced a recent significant decline in income. Participants were recruited via the snowball sampling technique (Silverman, 2006). They are all in stable relationships and five have young children. Despite their different careers (some have professional jobs, others permanent clerical positions), levels of education, and family composition, they all self-identified as shouldering the main responsibility for family meals (see Table 4.1 for participants' profile).

In our semi-structured interviews we explored their coping strategies in the range of practices surrounding the provision of everyday meals. Discussions with our participants reminded us of Newman's comments on his fieldwork with American middle-class people falling from grace, who 'all are deeply sensitive to the lives they left behind. They spend hours reflecting upon what their old world meant and what the new one lacks' (Newman, 1988: 10). Our participants experienced a similar sense of disenchantment with their present situation combined with a sense of loss of their (middle-class) pre-crisis sense of entitlement and ability to consume. Ambitions of moving to a bigger house, travelling to exotic places, and buying new cars have largely been abandoned. In fact participants were very open in describing their reduced consumption patterns as visible indicators of their loss of middle-class status. However it seems that everyday meals are the last area to be cut and much effort is put into maintaining pre-austerity standards:

> We are not that bad! We are not the starving ones yet (laughing) we still manage to eat well, to have some treats and occasionally go for a take away. Things have changed and I would lie if I said that we have not reduced the money we spend on things, but we still manage. We are not one of those families living in poverty, eating with the support of a charity!
>
> (Amanda)

> I would lie to you if I said that I have stopped buying lots of things, but I am much more careful now. I do not buy branded products anymore; I buy only what I need for the week, and I constantly look at the special offers.
>
> (Costanza)

> I rely much more on what my parents are giving us. My mum often gives us vegetables from their allotment. They give us enough olive oil for the entire year, as they have their own olive trees and they make their own olive oil. They are little things here and there, but they do make a difference at the end of the month.
>
> (Caterina)

Despite their reduced incomes, participants continue to maintain where possible pre-austerity patterns of food consumption. For Amanda, maintaining pre-recession consumption patterns has positioning implications since she describes her budgeting in relation to others who, unlike herself, are not able to sustain themselves without the support of charities. Thus budgeting and coping in times of austerity have relational (vertical) dimensions. Amanda demonstrates this in comparing herself and her success in coping with recession, with others who have been less successful in doing so. Her words betray a moral distancing from less successful others and a sense of pride in being able to manage (her own word) the recession successfully. Costanza copes by distancing herself from the market's temptations (being careful) and by adopting new ways of planning and shopping (comparing prices and no longer buying branded products). As we will see in the next section, Costanza's description echoes the ones provided by other participants, showing how coping with recession involves the application of existing gastronomic skills and competences, all resonant with forms of middle-class cultural capital illustrated in the literature (Willis et al., 2011). Coping strategies have also included the intensification of old practices and adoption of new ones involving a network of friends, family and colleagues. As Caterina observes, her acquisition of vegetables and olive oil relies on alternative forms of exchange between family members outside the market. As we will argue, these alternative ways of

Table 4.1 Participants' profile

Name	Age	Education	Household	Occupation	Partner's occupation
Amanda	35	High school	Living with her partner in their own house	Line manager in a call centre	Temporary job in a petrol station (sudden reduction of his salary by 50% in comparison to his previous job)
Antonella	32	High school	Living with her husband in their own flat	Short-term contracts as senior administrator (unstable income due to the different short-term contracts and unemployment)	Civil servant
Arianna	35	Undergraduate degree in maths and sciences	Living with her husband and two children (four and two years) in their own house	High school maths teacher	Barrister (reduced income from the previous year, estimated by 30%)
Caterina	27	High school with various undergraduate diplomas	Living with her partner in a rented house	Administrative job (part-time) Part-time singing teacher (reduced numbers of working hours per week)	Part-time clerical job in a company (reduced salary from full-time to part-time)
Costanza	37	High school	Living with her husband and two children (four and five years) in their own house	Freelancer in marketing communication (salary reduced by 50%)	Line manager in banking sector

Name	Age	Education	Living situation	Occupation	Partner's occupation
Elena	36	Part-time undergraduate student	Living with her husband and her two-month-old daughter in their own house	Administrator in the public sector	Entrepreneur (building company with 70% of income reduced)
Marina	37	Undergraduate degree in economics	Living with her husband and one daughter in their own house	Part-time senior administrator (reduced number of working hours)	Accountant (reduced income from the previous year, estimated by 10%)
Pamela	41	High school	Living with her partner in their own house	Short-term contracts as clerical assistant (unstable income due to the different short-term contracts and unemployment)	Driver (reduction of working hours; reduction of 1/3 of the salary)
Roberta	36	Degree + various postgraduate diplomas	Living with her husband and her six-year-old daughter in a rented flat	Freelance lawyer (reduced income from the previous year, estimated by 50%)	Barrister (reduced income from the previous year, estimated by 30%)
Valeria	35	Postgraduate Master's degree	Living with husband and her one-year-old daughter in their own house	Supply teacher (unstable income reduced by the birth of their daughter)	Short-term contract in a local company (fixed term 0 hours contract)

acquiring food derive from participants' existing social capital and their implementation and/or intensification of associated practices. These represent participants' efforts to counterbalance their reduced economic capital in their attempt to maintain pre-austerity consumption patterns and lifestyles.

Old game, new tricks: gastronomic competences and knowledges in everyday shopping

For all participants, acquiring food is part of their everyday responsibility for feeding the family (DeVault, 1991), putting the children first and being a good mother and/or wife (May, 2008). These women's stories of their daily efforts to feed their families echo previous work which highlights that doing and displaying motherhood is a matter of feeding children 'properly' (Bugge & Almås, 2006; see also Davis, Marshall, Hogg, Schneider, & Petersen, Chapter 10). It is in unpacking the meaning of 'properly' that we identified a set of class-based skills and competences developed in the course of maintaining a 'proper' diet. Among these competences, the most recurrent are comparing quality and price of food among supermarkets, substituting branded products with supermarket own brands or discount supermarket products, collecting vouchers and doing the shopping in more than one retail outlet. There are also new skills and competences that participants admit having developed only recently, including the ability to select the best deal on the spot, change their shopping plan in case of an unexpected special offer or the increased price of a product, and to avoid 'tempting' purchases.

> Recently I am trying new supermarkets, like last week I went to Penny Market, which as a discount supermarket, that allows you to spend very little money. It is far from home, but nearby there is only Conad, which is very expensive. I am experimenting with discount supermarkets trying products that I can gradually substitute [....] Cheeses and yogurt are not bad, I buy them there now. Same for tins, all my tins comes from there, like tuna, beans, chickpeas ... at the end of the day brands are all the same and the fancy brands are too dear.
>
> (Valeria)

> The aim is to continue buying the same things but spend less money. The secrets are special offers! I collect the leaflets from the Coop and Esselunga, I compare their offers and then I decide where to go shopping. [...] I collect loyalty cards and I collect points from Coop and Esselunga and from the pet shop.
>
> (Elena)

Elena and Valeria seem to adopt a similar strategy of investing time in experimenting with the various alternatives available in the marketplace. This process of trial and error involved an in-depth and up-to-date knowledge of marketplace offers and a process of constantly selecting, comparing and substituting. These women do not justify their success in maintaining the same consumption pattern, as a matter of their in-built creativity and crafting attitudes towards food consumption, as some of the consumption literature seems to highlight as the main qualities of the middle classes (Campbell, 2005). Their pragmatic attitude towards maintaining a 'proper' meal is the result of substituting expensive dishes with more economic ones (fish based dishes are substituted with meat dishes), introducing cheaper dishes considered 'proper' (pasta/eggs based dishes), and eliminating items and dishes considered redundant to the overall meal (starters with cold meat and cheese).

> We do not have fresh fish for dinner anymore. It is too expensive. We still have meat, as my husband really likes having meat for dinner, but not every night. I have started making frittata with some fresh vegetables. It's cheap and he likes it. [...] I don't buy cheese and cold meat any more: they are too expensive and they don't fill you up. I can't make a meal out of them ... if I did my husband would think that they were just the starter! (Laughing) I've trained him to eat more pasta, rice, more carbohydrates that fill you up.
>
> (Elisa)

This careful restructuring of the overall meal (from the starter to the centre piece) reflects the well documented middle-class attitude towards meals as 'more of a normative than a rigid construct regulating food consumption' (Marshall, 2005: 81). In fact the ideal of eating 'properly' was considered important but was also subject to broad interpretation reflecting the re-conceptualisation of the 'proper meal' (Marshall, 2005: 81).

Gifting, sharing, swapping and redistributing: the materiality of kinships in austerity times

Participants' reduced family income has meant that they increasingly turn to family and close friends for support. Among these relationships, family is certainly the most prominent one, providing financial and emotional support to participants. Living in a house owned by a family member, inheriting money from grandparents and borrowing money from parents were common in participants' narratives. These resources appeared to largely be dispensed in the guise of gifts.

> Generally speaking we live above our means as we know that our families can help us.... I live in my grandmother's house very close to my parents. We refurbished the house spending a lot of money using a bank loan. My parents helped us a lot giving us some money ... but it is never enough! [...] My parents have a vegetable garden where they grow vegetables and some fruits, they have a few olive trees and they keep

some chickens ... they give me lot of things from there. [...] The other day I went to the local street market and I bought lots of boxes of fresh vegetables ... it was a lot so I divided them between us, my parents and my sister. We spent very little money and the quality was excellent!

(Arianna)

From Arianna we see that gifts received by the family can be extraordinary ones, whose donations consist of a large sum of money or a house, to the more mundane ones like some vegetables and eggs from her parents' allotment. If the symbolic aspects of gift giving are well documented in the literature (see for example Corrigan, 1989) here we want to highlight how these donations are a form of economic support for the family. In fact, Arianna admits living above her means thanks to the help of her family network. Gift giving is not the only type of exchange operating within her family. Sharing is also a key coping strategy adopted by Arianna in redistributing food bought in large quantities at the local market. As others have highlighted (Belk, 2010) sharing is indeed another form of exchange that serves to reinforce family bonding and family collective identity. Here it is noteworthy to highlight the material aspect of this form of redistribution of surplus which, combined with gift giving, creates an intricate net of exchanges of goods within the family.

These exchanges do not simply include family members, but also swapping, gifting, and redistributing resources among a broader network of social relations such as neighbourhoods, friends and colleagues.

Every couple of months we organise a swapping party with friends. Each of us brings some clothes that are not wanted anymore and we swap them. For example I now have far too many shoes so I am going to swap them with some clothes. [...] We started doing these parties a couple of years ago, imitating the initiatives of a vegan association in town.

(Caterina)

[In] the summer my neighbour gives me some vegetables, like rocket salad which I do not buy anymore.

(Amanda)

Another thing that I should do more often is going to Mercafir [a big distribution centre for shops only]. Every Wednesday and Friday afternoons it is open to the public and you can go and save a lot: you can buy big boxes of fresh fruit and vegetables for little money ... the problem is that the quantity is too much. If you go on your own the quantity is too much. The last 3 or 4 times I went with a colleague and it worked out really well. You need somebody to go with you and share the things you buy. You have to go early with a big car and buy big quantity of stuff to be divided with somebody, otherwise you risk wasting money ... the fish and vegetables are really cheap and good!

(Elisa)

Others have highlighted how practices of swapping, sharing and redistributing reinforce solidarities and kinship among the members involved in these exchanges (Belk, 2010; Corrigan, 1989). Without denying the importance of the symbolic aspects of these exchanges for reinforcing the strength of the memberships in these networks, these exchanges are a source of financial support. During parties, expeditions to shopping centres and conversations with neighbours, resources are exchanged in their very materiality (e.g. old clothes, rocket salad), thus these relationships also provide material sustenance. It seems that these exchanges intensify during recession and become fixed appointments that cannot be left to chance, rather they become planned appointments substituting a visit to the local supermarket, a weekly shopping of fresh vegetables and the seasonal visit to a clothes shop. These exchanges become particularly valuable during recessionary times, as women count on them as a way of acquiring food and other goods without monetary exchange. In short, they become part of participants' budgeting strategies.

Discussion and conclusion

In this chapter we have provided an understanding of how Italian middle-class women develop their culinary competence and skills and rely on their social networks to compensate for the drop in their household income. Although budgeting is a new learning process, these women apply skills and competences, which, according to the literature, are typical of their middle-class sensibilities. Their pragmatic attitude to food acquisition, aimed at maximising available resources, minimising waste and indeed producing a satisfying result (a 'proper' and pre-recession diet), echoes other studies in consumer research that highlight the middle-classes' attitude towards minimising risk and waste, and maximising efficiency in all aspects of life (Gershon, 2011; Ong, 2006; see also Närvänen, Mesiranta, & Hukkanen, Chapter 15). We have not investigated the attitudes and strategies of working-class women; as such we cannot claim that Italian women from a less privileged background apply different skills, competences and knowledge. However we can affirm that middle-class women apply and develop competences, sensibilities, skills and network support that are typical of their habitus (Kravets & Sandikci, 2014). These women are not particularly interested in engaging in oppositional consumption practices (Arsel & Thompson, 2011; see also Mourad & Barnard, Chapter 16), or in creatively mixing and crafting products (McQuarrie, Miller, & Phillips, 2013; Campbell, 2005) or in extending their social capital by adhering to subversive groups. They do approach their reduced economic income through a set of shared rules, skills, competences and networking strategies which reinforce their belonging to a middle-class milieu. Therefore these set of shared rules and competences can be seen as collective strategies of the middle class to maintain their pre-austerity lifestyles as far as possible.

Kravets and Sandikci's (2014) study of the Turkish middle classes highlights that adhering to a set of normative practices is critical, as it serves to maintain a sense of unity with social peers in a transforming and prospering society. Our chapter shows how adhering to a set of normative practices, typical of their middles-class identity, is particularly critical for our participants who experience a sense of fracture with their earlier classed sense of entitlement and a more general sense of national decline. Our understanding is that adhering to a set of individual and collective practices serves to maintain a sense of collective identity during the hardest recessionary times since the Second World War.

Theoretically, our study unpacks the relation between the three forms of capitals. It does not show a conversion process between them, as conceptualised by Bourdieu, but rather the compensatory nature of this relation. In fact, we have shown how the significant drop of one capital corresponds with an intensification of skills and resources derived from the other two capitals. Such intensification is addressed at establishing a rebalance between the capitals, which has been disrupted by the sudden loss of economic resources. Participants apply rebalancing strategies, which, as previously mentioned, are framed by habitus, and are aimed at generating some sort of financial support. These commonly shared budgeting practices show how consumers maintain their social positioning, seeking to rebalance their available capitals (see also Ulver & Ostberg, 2014). Such a repositioning shows the centrality of consumption in re-establishing a classed identity. Acquiring and saving practices are not constrained in supermarkets anymore, but they cross the border of social gatherings, leisure times and the learning of new cooking techniques. Quantifying these saving practices is not the main point, here. The issue is that through activating rebalancing strategies, middle-class women manage to perpetuate typical classed values including their positioning above the less successful other (we do not rely on charity for survival), and maintaining links with supportive and similar others. Our study also shows that this process is recursive – a never-ending learning process. More studies are needed to further investigate the relational dynamics between these three forms of capitals, which seem to be less structural and more fluid than has previously been thought.

Note

1 Recent statistics show that Italians have followed this advice, as there is a growing trend in buying from discount supermarkets (10.5 per cent in 2011, 12.3 per cent in 2012 and 14.4 per cent in 2013) (Istat, 2013).

References

Arsel, Z., & Thompson, Craig J. (2011). Demythologizing consumption practices: How consumers protect their field-dependent identity investments from devaluing marketplace myths. *Journal of Consumer Research, 37*(5), 791–806.

Belk, R. (2010). Sharing. *Journal of Consumer Research, 36*(5), 715–734.

Bourdieu, P. (1986). The forms of capital. In J. Richardson (Ed.), *Handbook of Theory and Research for the Sociology of Education*. New York: Greenwood, 241–258.

Bugge, A. B., & Almås, A. (2006). Domestic dinner: Representations and practices of a proper meal among young suburban mothers. *Journal of Consumer Culture, 6*(2), 203–228.

Campbell, C. (2005). The craft consumer: Culture, craft and consumption in a post-modern society. *Journal of Consumer Culture, 1*, 23–43.

Cappellini, B., & Yen, D. (2013). Little emperors in the UK: Acculturation and food over time. *Journal of Business Research, 66*(8), 968–974.

Cappellini, B., Marilli, A., & Parsons, E. (2014). The hidden work of coping: Gender and the micro-politics of household consumption in times of austerity. *Journal of Marketing Management, 30*(15–16), 1597–1624.

Cappellini, B., Parsons, E., & Harman, V. forthcoming (2016). 'Right taste, wrong place': Local food cultures, (dis)identification and the formation of classed identity. *Sociology.*

Corrigan, P. (1989). Gender and the gift: The case of the family clothing economy. *Sociology, 23*(4), 513–534.

DeVault, M. L. (1991). *Feeding the Family: The Social Organisation of Caring as Gendered Work.* Chicago: University of Chicago Press.

Du Gay, P. (1996). *Consumption and Identity at Work.* London: Sage.

Erickson, B. (1991). What is good taste for? *Canadian Review of Sociology and Anthropology, 28*(2), 255–278.

Gershon, I. (2011). Neoliberal agency. *Current Anthropology, 52*(4), 538–555.

Harman, V., & Cappellini, B. (2015). Mothers on display: Lunchboxes, social class and moral accountability. *Sociology, 49*(4), 764–781.

Hollows, J. (2003). Feeling like a Domestic Goddess: Postfeminism and looking. *European Journal of Cultural Studies, 6*(2), 179–202.

Istat. (2013). *I consumi delle famiglie.* Available at: www.istat.it/it/archivio/95184 [Accessed 12 August 2014].

Johnston, J., & Baumann, S. (2010). *Foodies: Democracy and Distinction in the Gourmet Foodscape.* New York: Routledge.

Kravets, O., & Sandikci, O. (2014). Competently ordinary: New middle class consumers in the emerging markets. *Journal of Marketing, 78*(4), 125–140.

Marshall, D. (1995). *Food Choice and the Consumer.* London: Springer.

Marshall, D. (2005). Food as ritual, routine or convention. *Consumption, Markets and Culture, 8*(1), 69–85.

May, V. (2008). On being a 'good' mother: The moral presentation of self in written life stories. *Sociology, 42*(3), 470–486.

McQuarrie, E., Miller, J., & Phillips, B. J. (2013). The megaphone effect. *Journal of Consumer Research, 40*(June), 136–158.

Newman, K. S. (1988). *Falling from Grace: The Experience of Downward Mobility in the American Middle Class.* New York: The Free Press.

Ong, A. (2006). *Neoliberalism as Exception: Mutations in Citizenship and Sovereignty.* Durham: Duke University Press Books.

Silverman, D. (2006). *Interpreting Qualitative Data: Methods for Analysing Talk, Text and Interaction.* London: Sage.

Skeggs, B. (2004). *Class, Self, Culture.* London: Routledge.

Ulver, S., & Ostberg, J. (2014). Moving up, down or sideways? *European Journal of Marketing, 48*(5/6), 833–853.

Warde, A., & Tampubolon, G. (2002). Social capital, networks and leisure consumption. *The Sociological Review, 50*(2), 155–180.

Warde, A., Martens, L., & Olsen, W. (1999). Consumption and the problem of variety: Cultural omnivorousness, social distinction and dining out. *Sociology, 33*(1), 105–127.

Wilk, R. (1997). A critique of desire: Distaste and dislike in consumer behaviour. *Consumption, Markets and Culture, 1*(2), 175–196.

Willis, W., Backett-Milburn, K., Roberts, M., & Lawton, J. (2011). The framing of social class distinctions through family food and eating practices. *The Sociological Review, 59*(4), 725–740.

5 The multi-cultural food market

Grocery stores approaching foreign-born consumers in Sweden

Karin Ekström

Introduction

During the last decades, the Swedish food market has seen a greater selection of food from different cultures. Globalisation and tourism are reasons for a more international food market. For example, Mexican-American Tacos (Pilcher, 2012) can be found all over Europe nowadays, even though there are hardly any Mexican immigrants in Europe. A company called Santa Maria has managed to make TexMex (Texan Mexican) food popular in Sweden. By making ingredients available and easy to cook, a broader group of consumers is reached. Sushi is another example of food that is popular even though there are very few Japanese people living in Sweden.

Another reason for a Swedish food market with a larger variety of food from different cultures is because of its increased immigration. This change in the food market is particularly, but not exclusively, noticeable in countries such as Sweden that traditionally has had relatively few immigrants. Shelves in grocery stores that a few decades ago held one type of cooking oil in two different bottle sizes, half a litre and a full litre, are now filled with a vast assortment of oils in different quantities. The change towards more inter-national food is noticeable in all grocery stores, but particularly in residential areas where many immigrants live.

Consumers who move from one country to another are likely to change their eating habits, but to various degrees. It is common that people keep their original food culture, especially if they are not forced or pressured to set it aside. However, this varies widely with degrees of acceptance and the import-ance of food to a person's identity in their country of origin (Ray, 2004). The extent to which food consumption changes and adapts differs and depends on individual factors such as personality, experience and habits, as well as contex-tual and structural factors. To what degree are foreign-born consumers' food habits acknowledged in the new culture, for example in restaurants and grocery stores? Is it even possible to find brands or ingredients from the home country? Does the attitude of the host country towards migrants make a differ-ence? The purpose of this chapter is to increase the understanding of how grocery stores in Sweden approach an increasingly multi-cultural food market.

Global food culture in Sweden

The global trend of interest in cooking, reflected in television programmes, radio-programmes, newspapers, magazines and books, is noticeable also in Sweden and mirrored by an increased selection of international food in grocery stores. Another reason for increased interest in global cuisine could be that Swedes in general are extremely well travelled. In 2012, nearly 13 million holiday trips were made by Swedes,[1] a country with only 9.5 million inhabitants.

As mentioned earlier, another major reason for a greater assortment of food from different cultures is increased immigration. Sweden has immigrants comprised of around 200 nationalities[2] who represent heterogeneous food cultures. Immigration has increased, in particular during the last decade. In 2012, Sweden had nearly 1.5 million foreign-born citizens,[3] corresponding to about 15 per cent of the population, which is high from a European perspective. The percentage of foreign-born residents is higher in large cities such as Stockholm, Gothenburg and Malmö. In 2012, the most common countries of origin for immigrants were, in descending order: Finland (11.1 per cent), Iraq (8.7 per cent), Poland (5.1 per cent), Yugoslavia (4.7 per cent), Iran (4.4 per cent), Bosnia-Hercegovina (3.8 per cent), Germany (3.3 per cent), Turkey (3.1), Denmark (3.1 per cent), Somalia (3 per cent), Norway (2.9 per cent), Thailand (2.4 per cent), Chile, (1.9 per cent), Syria (1.9 per cent) and China (1.8 per cent). About half of these immigrants are born in Europe and about a third in Asia. Many Finnish people came to Sweden during the Second World War and in the 1950s. Iranians emigrated to Sweden after the revolution during the latter part of the 1970s. Immigrants from Yugoslavia and Bosnia-Hercegovina moved to Sweden during the 1990s. Recent turbulence has seen increased immigration from Iraq and lately Syria and Somalia.

Even though the number of immigrants has increased in Sweden, there is a lack of studies of their consumption patterns and of how retailers view them. This fact is surprising, since foreign-born consumers have relatively large purchasing power when it comes to food. Food is considered important and cooking is vital for spending time with family and friends. This should make the group interesting for retailers (Fridholm, 2006).

The Swedish food market

There is a strong focus on low prices in Swedish grocery stores. This appears to be a consequence of their strategy, since the 1980s, of advertising special prices to customers who have now come to expect low prices. Quality is taken for granted. All the produce is clean, unblemished and everything is wrapped. The focus on low prices corresponds with economic theory where price is determining exchange (Eklund, 2010). In order to offer low prices, there is a need to focus on the sales and turnover of large quantities of produce, as profit margins on grocery products are very low. This has resulted in structural changes leading to fewer and larger grocery stores (Kylebäck, 2007) that have the capacity to purchase goods in bulk. The few grocery store chains dominating the Swedish market can be described as an oligopoly. The market share during 2015 is as follows: Ica 50.8 per cent, Co-op 20.5 per cent, Axfood 15.8 per cent, Bergendahls 7 per cent, Lidl 3.6 per cent and Netto 2.3 per cent (Bränström, 2015). The development of larger entities in the marketplace is not unique to Sweden, but noticeable also in many other countries such as Great Britain, France and Spain.

There have been some recent changes in the Swedish food market. Low price international chain stores such as Netto and Lidl have led to increased competition and they are often located in areas where foreign-born consumers live. New entrepreneurs have also entered the market. These entrepreneurs are immigrants who specialise in selling ethnic food in general, or specialise in food from certain countries, such as China and India. There are some larger stores of this type, but most of them are small businesses. Even small mom and pop stores that sell foreign food and a limited variety of Swedish food have been established, in particular in areas where foreign-born consumers live. Despite the fact that this development has led to a somewhat more diverse food market, the market is still dominated by a few chain stores.

There is a lack of studies of immigrant retailers in Sweden. Imbruce (2006) studied the Chinatown food system in New York and considered this an alternative global food system that helps sustain the cultural practices of new and old inhabitants. From an international perspective, small grocery stores and restaurants have been key parts of most immigrant communities. Owning a business, rather than working in an office or factory, is highly valued in many of the countries and cultures where immigrants are coming from.

Another recent change is the fact that, in the last few years, Sweden has become famous for its gastronomy. This has led to an increased interest in quality and the origins of food and resulted in more entrepreneurs producing high-quality food that is sold in farm shops, certain marketplaces or stores. However, despite these changes, the focus on low prices is still very prevalent in the majority of the Swedish food market.

A multi-cultural market

The concept of multi-culturalism is used in this chapter to illustrate the existence of many cultures flourishing alongside a dominant culture. It means recognising the legitimacy of minority cultures and respecting their way. Peñaloza (2004: 89) defines market multi-culturalism as: 'the array of cultures within a nation, with an emphasis on relations between various cultural groups as they impact consumer behaviour and market practice and structure'. Foreign-born consumers in Sweden represent, as mentioned above, a range of countries with different food cultures. The major food retailers try to reach consumers with different cultural backgrounds in order to achieve high and profitable sales.

Concurrent with the increased immigration in Sweden, it has become more common for food retailers to recognise religious holidays. One example of this is Ramadan. During this holiday, Muslim consumers fast during the daytime but eat special meals after the sun goes down, sharing food with family and friends. More food is consumed than at other times of the year, and involves the consumption of meat, chicken, bread, vegetables, fruit and nuts. Consumption of sweets and pastries is also high. There are celebrations and banquets associated with the end of Ramadan, often referred to as Eid al-Fitr. Another important holiday among many immigrants is the Persian New Year, Nouruz,[4] when food and meals with friends and family also play an important role.

Food dishes from the immigrants' countries of origin are sometimes likely to be adapted to local conditions, for example, when replacing ingredients that cannot be sourced locally. The principle of creolisation (Hannerz, 1987) is used to illustrate the blending of various food traditions and adapting global food according to local availability of ingredients. Apart from immigrants adapting their food into a local context, traditional Swedish food is also likely to be changed by different spices or vegetables that are introduced by immigrants or discovered when Swedes travel. It could, for example, be new recipes of traditional herring served with garlic or lemongrass.

Wilk (2011) discusses appropriation as a local culture taking cultural elements from abroad, and in so doing transforming it into something familiar without the local culture losing its identity. The example he gives is Japan, a country that for thousands of years has taken in imported food without losing its identity. There is an inherent power in the local. In Sweden, food such as potatoes, tomatoes, spices and exotic fruit have, throughout history, been imported and introduced into Swedish dishes. Spaghetti and meat sauce, pizza and Thai food have also been introduced and transformed into local meanings. Wilk (2011: 42) thinks there is no incompatibility between being global and being local and states: 'whatever the global milieu, we are happiest when we are embedded in communities we know well'. He argues that globalisation is not new and that isolated static cultures are relatively rare. Instead, globalisation and localisation are interdependent and part of a single system. This includes the transfer of food across borders, which has influenced and will continue to influence our food practices and make them multi-cultural (see also Julier, Chapter 6).

Peñaloza (2004: 99) advocates a multi-cultural perspective: 'Important in recovering the elusive nature of consumption is sidestepping our discipline's fixation on cultural universals to redirect attention to the wide range of lived social groupings of consumers and how these groups interact within the marketplace.' She prefers to look at ethnic minority communities as communities that consume rather than as subcultures. Even though consumption is important, ethnic minority communities have their primary agency in community rather than consumption. Meals are sometimes eaten as they used to be eaten in the country of origin and sometimes they are influenced by traditions in the new country. In a study of Haitian immigrants in the United States, Oswald (1999) illustrates that both American and Haitian food is eaten and that traditions are blended. Peñaloza (2006: 548) writes:

> As more and more societies in the world are multicultural and as markets gain ground as cultural institutions, it is increasingly important that studies of ethnicity and consumption take a good look at patterns of social relations between mainstream and marginal groups, and how such social relations are played out in markets.

By studying how grocery stores approach an increasingly multi-cultural food market, we will be able to uncover how foreign-born consumers are viewed as customers in relation to Swedish-born customers.

Food practices and food acculturation

When studying food, it is necessary to recognise that food consumption is often strongly routinised (Warde, 1997). The processes for how practices emerge, develop and change (Warde, 2005) are particularly relevant to consider when studying transitions such as consumers moving to a new country. It is the practice, in this case the practice of moving rather than individual desires, that creates wants (Warde, 2005). It can involve finding new food and preparing new meals in the new country, but also keeping or adapting food from the country of origin to the new culture. Warde (2005) discusses that practices and their performance will depend on past experience, opportunities, learning, available resources etc. He suggests a close examination of how understandings, values and procedures of engagement are acquired and adapted to performances.

Many practices and traditions are learned through the process of socialisation (Bourdieu, 1977). A common definition of consumer socialisation in marketing is Ward's (1974: 2): 'the process by which young people acquire skills, knowledge and attitudes relevant to their functioning as consumers in the marketplace'. Consumption patterns, such as food traditions, that are learned at an early age are sometimes kept throughout life. Behaviours also change as consumers learn about food practices throughout life (see Molander, Chapter 11 and Truninger, Chapter 7). When moving to a new country, foreign-born consumers need to learn about products and consumption patterns in their new country. Oswald (1999: 314) writes: 'In the unsettling business of migration, ethnic consumers use products to negotiate differences between home culture and host culture while forging an identity derived from those differences.' In particular, first-generation immigrants need to negotiate conflicts between their earlier and present lives (Oswald, 1999). Second-generation immigrants that are children may interact in different social spheres and introduce to their parents new products and consumption patterns. This may result in a behaviour like 'keeping up with the children' (Ekström, 2007), similar to 'keeping up with the Joneses'.

While consumer socialisation (for an overview see Ekström, 2006a; John, 1999) focuses on learning to become a consumer in an existing culture, acculturation deals with learning and change when moving from one culture to another. However, it should be recognised that acculturation has sometimes been used in the sense of assimilation, not allowing immigrants to be bi-cultural, and is therefore a word that some researchers avoid. Peñaloza (1994: 33) defines acculturation as: 'the general process of movement and adaptation to the consumer cultural environment in one country by persons from another country'. Peñaloza (1994) expected three different outcomes of consumer acculturation in her study on Mexican immigrants: assimilating the culture of immigration, maintaining the culture of origin and expressing a hybrid culture. The first two outcomes were found, but rather than a hybrid culture, she found resistance and segregation. In another study, Peñaloza (2004) found that Mexican-Americans in South Texas, born in the USA of Mexican descent, are still crossing borders, implying the maintaining of Mexican culture, fostering Mexican customs in the marketplace and living somewhat apart from the Anglo mainstream. Acculturation is not a static process that occurs just once, but something that continues over time (Peñaloza, 2006).

Oswald is critical of the idea of assimilation (1999: 316): 'attempts to assimilate the ethnic self into a one-dimensional "melting pot" ideology reduce cultural difference to more of the same'. She uses the term 'culture swapping' in her study of Haitian immigrants, emphasising that ethnic consumers swap cultures by swapping goods and move between multiple worlds instead of blending the worlds into a homogeneous identity. She gives the example of an informant who celebrates her son's birthday at a fast-food chain with American children and then later at a barbeque with the family. Adjustments to the American culture are made by the immigrants without assimilating or differentiating their cultural identity from the mainstream (Oswald, 1999).

Practice theory will allow us to understand how food practices and traditions are learned (Bourdieu, 1977). Practice theory can be seen as sets of habits and predispositions that fit together, often along with particular material culture. For example, peeling potatoes is a practice – in some places with a knife, in other places with a rotary machine. This implies that immigrants would need to adopt things in sets rather than in small random bits. For example, making a meal such as a Swedish smörgåsbord would require a whole set of new ingredients, tools and actions. Warde (2005) discusses how understandings, orientation and knowledge transmigrate across boundaries and that it is of interest to see how different practices affect each other. This is highly relevant to consider when studying grocery stores approaching an increasingly multi-cultural food market, but also foreign-born consumers' adjustments to the Swedish culture.

Design of the study

In order to understand how grocery stores approach an increasingly multi-cultural food market, it felt necessary to study both grocery stores and consumers. Rather than considering them as independent, they are seen as interdependent. Consumers rely on grocery stores and grocery stores depend on consumers. Both consumers and retailers create cultural meaning(s) of consumption.

The study represents a multi-sited ethnography (e.g. Ekström, 2006b; Marcus, 1998). Rather than focusing on one location in a city, multiple sites were chosen. The study originated in an area, in one of the largest cities in Sweden, having a high percentage of foreign-born persons. The first interviews were conducted in the major traditional grocery store in this area. We interviewed the store manager and three employees. Consumers in the area were interviewed and it was discovered that they only made complementary purchases in this particular store and instead did their main shopping in many different grocery stores. We therefore conducted interviews with three managers at three other traditional grocery chain stores they were shopping in. Observations were made in all the chain stores at the time of these interviews. An observation was made one Saturday morning in another traditional chain store that has a food section called 'Food of the World'. A store manager for a large store where foreign-born customers made up a high proportion of the store clientele was interviewed and further observations made. Observations were also made in four mom and pop stores targeting foreign-born customers. The store selection was based on the stores used by the foreign-born customers we interviewed.

We also interviewed representatives of The Consumer Cooperative Society in Western Sweden (Konsumentföreningen Väst in Swedish) to understand how they work towards the multi-cultural food market. We conducted observations in public places where Eid al-Fitr (celebration of the end of Ramadan) and Norouz (the Persian New Year) were celebrated. The interviews took place during the autumn of 2009 and the early beginning of 2010. The study of Eid al-Fitr took place on 20 September 2010 and the study of Norouz on 16 March 2010.

Consumers with a Muslim background were approached, since we initially were interested in studying how the retailers targeted Ramadan. However, the interviews showed that not all of the Muslims interviewed celebrated Ramadan. The consumers interviewed were first-generation immigrants from Iran, Iraq, Lebanon, Syria, Palestine, Bosnia and Somalia. Five interviews were conducted with individual consumers (two men and three women), and one with a focus group of five women. Overall, we experienced difficulties in finding foreign-born consumers to interview. We therefore got in touch with associations for immigrants asking for assistance in finding foreign-born consumers to interview. The contact with one immigrant association resulted in the opportunity to come on a bus trip to the largest department store in

Figure 5.1 Photo of Norouz.

Scandinavia, Gekås Ullared, one which emphasised low prices in their marketing (Ekström, 2015). There could be several reasons for the difficulties we had in finding consumers to interview. First of all is the fact that the foreign-born area we focused on was one of high unemployment and low income. Low-income consumers might feel a sense of shame when talking about their food consumption (Hjort, 2004). A Nordic study (Bonke, 2005) found that low-income households described a feeling of being burdened by the demands of consumption, to consume like everyone else. Furthermore, the consumers might not have had previous experience of research. They might fear a lack of integrity if being asked questions about their consumption. This could be the case in particular if they have been obliged by authorities to explain their consumption patterns or worry that information will be given to the government (Hjort, 2004). Yet another reason could be language difficulties.

All the interviews conducted followed a semi-structured interview guide and lasted about one hour. All except two with bad sound were recorded and transcribed. Notes were taken during observations.

The results

Since the focus of the study was on grocery stores targeting an increasing multi-cultural market, the results presenting the views of the store managers and employees will be presented before the results from the interviews of the customers who led us to the stores.

The traditional chain stores

The store managers and employees in the chain stores found foreign-born consumers valuable, since they spend a lot of money on food. The ones with a difficult socio-economic situation also spend a high share of their money on food. We were informed that the foreign-born consumers in general spend a lot of time shopping and comparing prices.

Instead of segmenting the market into different ethnic groups, the traditional chain stores had chosen to reach out to the entire market. The interviews indicated that the established chain stores had a rather vague idea of the needs of their foreign-born customers. They did not conduct any market surveys. It appeared as if they lacked a strategy for finding out what the market desired. The quantities of sales determined which goods were on offer, in other words, goods with high demand were prioritised. Since self-service scanning is increasing in grocery stores, it also means less interaction between employees and customers and hence less feedback regarding both satisfaction and dissatisfaction (even though cheese, seafood and meats still often have specialist attendants). A few stores had asked employees from different cultures to give suggestions for products to adopt into their range. The store managers appreciated their cultural backgrounds (foreign-born or second-generation immigrants) when planning the selection, especially during holidays. However, no strategy to employ people from certain nationalities existed.

Varieties and product assortment

Observations and interviews indicated that several of the chain stores had international food placed on shelves intermingled with Swedish food, for example beans, dried tomatoes in cans, and rice. One exception was a cooperative chain store that had developed a section in the store called 'The food of the world', containing dry or preserved international food, for example, bulgur, dried olives, coconut milk, sauerkraut and stuffed cabbage rolls.[5] The Consumer Cooperative Society in Western Sweden had contacted immigrant associations to ask for advice regarding which international food to include in this section. The society also sponsored some associations that helped out in the cooperative chain stores, demonstrating cooking during special holidays. The society also participated in the celebration of the Persian New Year, Nouruz, selling baklava in 2010 and the previous years also pomegranate and pomegranate juice. Our limited observation of 'The food of the world' indicated that it attracted not only foreign-born consumers, but also a broader group with a tendency towards younger consumers. Products that sold successfully were later taken from the 'The food of the world' section to be included in the regular range of produce on the shelves, intermingled with Swedish food. Examples given during interviews were American food such as peanut butter and marshmallows.

The chain stores appeared to use a trial and error strategy when launching an international product. Having a high volume of sales was the criteria for being successful. Therefore, it was not sufficient for the chain stores to sell products merely to foreign-born consumers, but to sell to other consumers as well. Very few items targeted foreign-born consumers exclusively, for example, sauerkraut from the Balkans bought by people from the Balkans, and Finnish bread bought by Finnish people. The chain stores made continuous attempts to find new international products to sell in larger quantities. Bakery products such as cakes and pastries were mentioned as an area that could be improved upon. Observational studies of shops geared towards foreign-born consumers, discussed below, indicated that they had a large selection of bakery products.

The traditional chain stores had difficulties carrying some of the products that foreign consumers wanted, for example, an assortment of large packages of rice. There were several reasons. First of all, there are many types of rice and to know which varieties to buy requires particular knowledge. Second, they did not have suppliers that could fulfil their demands. Third, a large assortment of big packages demands quite a lot of space, and that was not available in the stores. Instead, stores targeting foreign-born consumers offered such bulk products. In general, chain stores have a pre-determined variety of food that is centrally controlled. However, it appeared as if all but one chain store had some leeway in contacting suppliers themselves.

Stores targeting foreign-born consumers

The domination of food chains in Sweden, such as Ica, Co-op, Axfood, Bergendahls, Netto and Lidl, is starting to be challenged by individual newcomers. If these new stores are a large size, many of the foreign-born consumers do their weekly purchases there. These stores have a large assortment of, for example, rice and oil in large packages and a large selection of bakery products. An interview with a manager for such a large-sized ethnic store oriented towards a variety of immigrants indicated he listened to the needs of the customers, for example by adjusting the assortment to their needs. For a particular product, the store attempted to offer a variety of brands, hence differentiating quality and price. A strategy to employ employees of different nationalities representing the customers also existed, for example, to employ Somali employees who can speak to customers in their own language.

Interviews and observations confirm that larger-sized ethnic stores also target Swedish-born consumers, but Swedes consider them as complementary shops rather than being considered their main shops. They do not have all the goods Swedish-born consumers demand, such as pork and beer, and they only sell halal meat. We learned during the study that the second-generation immigrant consumers, having learned to eat Swedish food (for example, in school), are more likely to buy their groceries in the traditional chain stores and visit the larger ethnic stores targeting foreign-born consumers for supplementary purchases. This could be a sign of assimilation or hyphenated identity.

Even though the new entrepreneurs of today are often seen as complementary stores, they may become competitors to traditional chain stores as they broaden the varieties of produce they have on offer. The large store, with a high proportion of foreign customers, has built an attractive fruit and vegetable section (high quality) that attracts new customers. The store advertises in the newspaper to become more visible to all consumers, not only those foreign-born, and has also started a restaurant that allows them to spread their knowledge of foreign food to a broader audience. Observations indicate that overall the ethnic stores, to some degree, also seem to be important social spaces as well as retail spaces.

Vegetables and fruit are often the basis for mom and pop stores in areas where many foreign consumers live. The vegetables and fruit are attractively displayed and the shops are visited often, sometimes daily. The shops are visited by immigrants for complementary purchases (rather than large weekly purchases). Immigrants coming from countries lacking a long tradition of refrigeration or room for storage might also be used to doing their shopping daily. Furthermore, some consumers put a high value on freshness and therefore shop more frequently. These mom and pop stores often offer fruit and vegetables that only keep for a few days so as to provide cheaper prices. It is price that attracts the foreign-born customers, but also food provisioning practices involving regular shopping to access fresh produce.

The new entrepreneurs that are targeting foreign-born consumers have a competitive advantage in having contacts with suppliers selling brands that foreign-born consumers are accustomed to and prefer to buy. The larger ethnic store we visited also had its own wholesale business.

Foreign-born consumers' views

The interviews with the foreign-born consumers indicated that they were satisfied with the selection of foods on the Swedish market. The ones who had been living in Sweden for a long time emphasised that the selection of foreign food had increased significantly during the last two decades. One immigrant, who came to Sweden in 1989, expressed how the assortment had changed a lot: 'There is more to choose from [today]. There were no Arabic bread when I came to Sweden, there were no pita bread, there were no falafel. There were neither kebab roll. It is a big difference.'

A focus on low price

The foreign-born consumers indicated an interest in finding low prices on groceries. Many families spent a lot of time trying to find the best offers, visiting many different shops. It was common to make weekly purchases when travelling to a larger chain store offering lower prices. The ones who did not own a car travelled with relatives or friends. Complementary purchases during the week were made in local stores, often so-called mom and pop stores geared towards foreign-born consumers.

One reason for the focus on low prices could be that the families had low incomes and that they often included many family members. They cooked most of their food themselves and it was the women who were in charge of cooking. One family mentioned that they sent money back to their country of origin to support family members living there, which was one reason they had to cut down on expenses. Gentry and Mittelstaedt (2010) discuss that the remittances from immigrants in developed countries to their families back home are substantial. Another reason for the high level of price consciousness among the foreign-born consumers interviewed could be that they have been consumer socialised to this behaviour when living in their countries of origin. Another study focusing on foreign-born consumers in Sweden (Brembeck, Karlsson, Ossiansson, Shanahan, Jonsson, Bergström et al., 2006) indicates that price is important when shopping for food. The observations on the trip with the immigrant association to the department store Gekås Ullared, mentioned above, lends further support to the degree of price consciousness. The participants on the trip purchased many goods and talked continuously about the good deals they had made. Furthermore, our study indicated that those families who found their low income restrictive spent time looking for low prices and bought food in large packages that were less costly than small packages. Another Swedish study of low-income families showed that the families would like to be less restrictive when shopping (Ekström & Hjort, 2010).

Quality of produce

Even though low prices were emphasised, quality was still important. This was particularly true for fruits and vegetables. Some of the interviewees criticised mom and pop stores and open markets for selling cheap fruit of low quality. Established chain stores were considered to have higher quality fruit and vegetables. Quality was associated with freshness, but in particular durability, implying food staying fresh longer. The interviewed consumers seemed unaware of organic production and fair trade. Maybe it is considered a luxury to purchase such food when living with scarce resources? In one of the families interviewed, a child said that she told her mother about organic food when shopping.

The interviews with foreign-born consumers indicated that they were interested in buying new products and cooking new meals. It could involve products they were not familiar with as well as new innovations. It was often the children who introduced new products to their parents. Influence was both direct and indirect (Ekström, 2010). The interview with the Consumer Cooperative Society in Western Sweden indicated that they visited and informed schools about organic food. Children can become a gateway to their parents or even intentionally used as such, something that is not uncontroversial (Ekström, 2007). The role of schools in introducing information about factors such as health and nutrition remains an area of study that deserves more attention in research.

The interviews indicated that the interest in Swedish brands was limited. The interest in famous international brands such as Kellogg's and Coca-Cola were greater, in particular among the children. Food or brands from the country of origin were of interest mostly because they represented earlier experiences and food habits (Jordan, 2015; Sutton, 2001). Quality was, among the foreign-born consumers interviewed, rarely associated with food or brands from the country of origin. The consumers seemed to have limited knowledge of the established chain stores' own brands, so-called private brands. This is similar to the findings by Brembeck et al., (2006). While quality was, as mentioned above, associated with durability, that is, food staying fresh longer, it was also described as expensive and something many cannot afford.

Ramadan

Food is an important part of religious holidays such as Ramadan, which is important for foreign-born Muslim consumers. The interviews with the consumers indicated that consumption of food was higher during this holiday than during the rest of the year as meals are shared with family and friends. Food had to be fresh every day, no leftovers were served and consumption of sweets, nuts and pastries such as baklava was high. One of the consumers expressed:

> You eat more of everything. You eat a lot of sweets. You eat food that originates from where I come from. You must have soup, you must have salad. It is two dishes that Muslims must have daily. Then you have to add food, it can be chicken. I mean that when it is a month that is not Ramadan, you can cook food to eat for two days. During Ramadan, it does not happen, it is fresh food every day.

An increased assortment of nuts, dates and sweets on attractive shelves in the stores were noticed in many grocery stores during Ramadan. It was, in particular, the specialist stores selling ethnic food and international chain stores that attracted most immigrant consumers during Ramadan and at the end of it, when Eid Al-Fitr is celebrated. A manager for an ethnic store expressed: 'some [customers] are here daily and several times per day and they shop two bags at a time. How many families do really you have? No, I have one family. But you eat like ten [families].'

The chain stores had also started to recognise other holidays such as the Persian New Year and Ramadan in their varieties of produce. These holidays are celebrated by a majority of the people who immigrated to Sweden during recent years. However, the recognition of these holidays was somewhat limited.[6,7]

Conclusion

The aim of this exploratory study has been to increase the understanding of how grocery stores in Sweden approach an increasingly multi-cultural food market. The foreign-born consumers are a heterogeneous group with a variety of food cultures and different practices, routines and traditions. Still, they have one thing in common, namely that food plays an important role in their lives. They spend a lot of time shopping, cooking and eating food. Their purchasing power is large, as indicated by the grocery store managers interviewed as well as through observation. The interviews with first-generation immigrant consumers as well as grocery stores confirm that the foreign-born consumers are price-conscious, continuously trying to find low prices on food. This focus on low prices creates practices both in considering how groceries are acquired and how meals are prepared. The foreign-born consumers interviewed spent a lot of time trying to find the best offers, visiting many different shops. Apart from being sensitive to grocery pricing, they are not ready to negotiate on the quality of fruits and vegetables.

Food retailers are starting to realise the importance of foreign-born customers and use a variety of strategies to reach out to them, such as low prices and large quantities, providing the brands and products to which they are accustomed and that they prefer to buy. Since offering low prices has become a tradition in the Swedish food market it also creates practices for how grocery stores run their businesses. The Swedish food market is dominated by a few large chain stores and a high volume of sales is important for them in order to cut prices. Therefore, they try to figure out which foreign goods sell successfully. They also offer fruits and vegetables of high quality to attract consumers. Recently new entrepreneurs targeting foreign-born consumers have entered the market. These stores have contacts with suppliers selling international brands and brands from the foreign-born consumers' country of origin that they are accustomed to and prefer to buy. It is a competitive advantage.

Another strategy to reach foreign-born consumers is to bring in suitable goods for religious holidays, such as the Persian New Year and Ramadan. This is something that the traditional chain stores have started to recognise, but, in particular, stores selling ethnic food and international chain stores attract many immigrant consumers during these religious holidays.

The study has shown that the new entrepreneurs know the market of foreign-born consumers better than the traditional chain stores. Traditional chain stores have a rather superficial picture of the foreign-born market and their consumption patterns, and do not distinguish between different groups of foreign-born consumers. There might be several reasons for this difference. New entrepreneurs in this grocery market are often immigrants themselves and they often offer good service involving interaction with their customers. In the traditional chain stores, there is a move towards more self-service scanning and a greater reliance on a high volume of sales serves to drive the product range. Furthermore, even though the chain stores have employees of different cultural origin, the new entrepreneurs have a strategy to hire employees representing the cultures of their customers.

The chain stores and the new entrepreneurs see each other as complementary. One reason for this is that the traditional chain stores sell mainly to Swedish consumers or second-generation immigrants and the ethnic stores sell mainly to foreign-born consumers. However, this situation might change over time. The traditional chain stores are trying to broaden their customer base to also include the foreign-born consumers. The ethnic stores try to broaden their customer base to include more second-generation immigrants and Swedish-born consumers. In order to succeed they need a range of products that can attract a wide range of consumers. In general, the chain stores today offer Swedish and international brands while the ethnic stores offer international brands and brands from the foreign-born consumers' country of origin.

Barriers and opportunities, gradual convergence and potential conflicts in the Swedish food market deserve more attention in future research. As more Swedish grocery retailers discover the purchasing potential of immigrants and competition increases, they will need to learn to be more consumer-oriented, listening to the voice of the consumer. We also need to know more about how foreign-born consumers construct alternative ways to relate to their original food culture and how this varies among first, second and third generation immigrants. This requires more in-depth studies regarding meal practices among foreign-born consumers. Since immigrants represent heterogeneous food cultures, it is important for future research, as well as retailers and other actors in society, to acknowledge the different backgrounds, experiences and living conditions of immigrants.

Acknowledgement

The author would like to thank Associate Professor Lars Norén for his unstinting cooperation during this study, Professor Richard Wilk, the editors and the reviewers for their valuable comments, and The Swedish Retail and Wholesale Development Council for funding the study.

Notes

1 www.vagabond.se/artiklar/nyheter/20130528/sa-reser-svenskarna   [Accessed   4 August 2014].
2 See https://sweden.se/society/sweden-and-migration-in-brief/#start [Accessed 4 August 2014].
3 See   www.scb.se/sv_/Hitta-statistik/Artiklar/Fortsatt-okning-av-utrikes-fodda-i-Sverige/ [Accessed 4 August 2014].
4 It is common to eat seven items starting with the letter S in the Persian alphabet: Sabzeh (wheat, barley or lentil sprouts growing in a dish), samanu (sweet pudding from germinated wheat), senjed (dried fruit of the leaster tree), sir (garlic), sib (apples), somaq (sumac berries), serkeh (vinegar).
5 Since the study was conducted, another chain store has developed a section called 'Food from the corners of the world'.
6 A content analysis of food magazines published by two of the chain stores during 2006–2009 showed that Swedish holidays are commonly featured. Nouruz is only featured once and Ramadan was not featured at all.
7 Since the study was conducted, the traditional chain stores seem to pay more attention to Ramadan. The have started to recognise the market potential.

References

Bonke, J. (Ed.) (2005). *Udsathed og Forbrug i de Nordiske velfærdsstater* (*Vulnerability and Consumption in the Nordic Welfare States*). København: Socialforskningsinstituttet.
Bourdieu, P. (1977). *Outline of a Theory of Practice*. Cambridge: Cambridge University Press.
Bränström, S. L. (2015). Få mataktörer att välja på (Few food actors to choose from). *Svenska Dagbladet*, 27 June.
Brembeck, H., Karlsson, M. A., Ossiansson, E., Shanahan, H., Jonsson, L., Bergström, K., & Engelbrektsson, P. (2006). *Maten och det nya landet* (Food and the new country). Göteborg: Centrum för konsumtionsvetenskap (CFK), CFK-rapport.
Eklund, K. (2010). *Vår Ekonomi. En introduktion till samhällsekonomin* (*Our Economy, An Introduction to Societal Economy*). Stockholm: Norstedts.
Ekström, K. M. (2006a). Consumer socialization revisited. In R. W. Belk (Ed.), *Research in Consumer Behaviour, 10* (pp. 71–98). Oxford: Elsevier Science Ltd.
Ekström, K. M. (2006b). The emergence of multi-sited ethnography in anthropology and marketing. In R. W. Belk (Ed.), *Handbook of Qualitative Research Methods in Marketing* (pp. 497–508). Aldershot, UK: Edward Elgar.
Ekström, K. M. (2007). Parental consumer learning or keeping up with the children. *Journal of Consumer Behaviour, 6*(July–August), 203–217.
Ekström, K. M. (2010). Consumer socialization in families. In D. Marshall (Ed.), *Understanding Children as Consumers* (pp. 41–60). London: Sage.
Ekström, K. M (2015). Conformity and distinction in Scandinavia's largest department store. In A. N. García Martínez (Ed.), *Being Human in Consumer Society* (pp. 103–125). Farnham and Burlington: Ashgate.
Ekström, K. M., & Hjort, T. (2010). *Det blir många nej. Konsumtionens meningar och villkor för barnfamiljer med knapp ekonomi* (*There will be many no. The meanings of consumption and conditions for low-income families with children*). Konsumentverkets rapport.
Fridholm, A. (2006). *Den mångkulturella marknaden. En studie av invandrarnas köpkraft* (*The Multicultural Market. A Study About Immigrants' Purchasing Power*). Stockholm: Timbro.

Gentry, J. W., & Mittelstaedt, R. A. (2010). Remittances as social exchange: The critical, changing role of family as the social network. *Journal of Macromarketing, 30*(1), 23–32.

Hannerz, U. (1987). The world in creolization. *Africa, 57*, 546–559.

Hjort, T. (2004). *Nödvändighetens pris – om knapphet och konsumtion hos barnfamiljer (The price of necessity – scarcity and consumption among families with children)*. Lund dissertations in Social Work 20, Lund: Lund University.

Imbruce, V. (2006). From the bottom up: The global expansion of Chinese vegetable trade for New York City markets. In R. Wilk (Ed.), *Fast Food/Slow Food: The Cultural Economy of the Global Food System* (pp. 163–179). Lanham, MD: Altamira Press.

John, D. R. (1999). Consumer socialization of children: A retrospective look at twenty-five years of research. *Journal of Consumer Research, 26*(3), 183–213.

Jordan, J. A. (2015). *Edible Memory: The Lure of Heirloom Tomatoes and Other Forgotten Foods*. Chicago: University of Chicago Press.

Kylebäck, H. (2007). *Handel, handel, vart är du på väg? (Retail, Retail, Where Are You Going?)* Göteborg: Bas.

Marcus, G. (1998). *Ethnography Through Thick and Thin*. Princeton, NJ: Princeton University Press.

Oswald, L. R. (1999). Culture swapping: Consumption and the ethnogenesis of middle-class Haitian immigrants. *Journal of Consumer Research, 25*(4), 303–318.

Peñaloza, L. (1994). Atravesando fronteras/border crossings: A critical ethnographic exploration of the consumer acculturation of Mexican immigrants. *Journal of Consumer Research, 21*(June), 32–54.

Peñaloza, L. (2004). Multiculturalism in the New World Order: Implications for the study of consumer behaviour. In K. M. Ekström, & H. Brembeck (Eds.), *Elusive Consumption: Tracking New Research Perspectives* (pp. 87–109). Oxford: Berg.

Peñaloza, L. (2006). Researching ethnicity and consumption. In R. W. Belk (Ed.), *Handbook of Qualitative Research Methods in Marketing* (pp. 547–559). Cheltenham: Edward Elgar Publishing Ltd.

Pilcher, J. M. (2012). *Planet Taco: A Global History of Mexican Food*. New York: Oxford University Press.

Ray, K. (2004). *The Migrant's Table: Meals and Memories in Bengali-American Households*. Philadelphia: Temple University Press.

Sutton, D. E. (2001). *Remembrance of Repasts: An Anthropology of Food and Memory (Materializing Culture)*. New York: Berg.

Ward, S. (1974). Consumer socialization. *Journal of Consumer Research, 1*(2), 1–16.

Warde, A. (1997). *Consumption, Food and Taste, Culinary Antinomies and Commodity Culture*. London: Sage.

Warde, A. (2005). Consumption and theories of practice. *Journal of Consumer Culture, 5*(2), 131–153.

Wilk, R. (2011). Consumption in an Age of Globalization and Localization. In K. M. Ekström and K. Glans (Eds.), *Beyond the Consumption Bubble* (pp. 37–51). New York: Routledge.

Part II
Appropriation

6 Appropriation

Alice Julier

> *Different cultural traditions influence each other, acquire a multicultural dimension and cope with its more or less unsettling influence in their own different ways.*
> Bhikhu Parekh (1999: 455)

Consuming couscous

In a recent *Saveur* magazine article, writer Jay Cheshes (2012) explores couscous, a grain product from northern Africa/Morocco, in France. Cheshes writes about returning to a fancy spot he ate as a child in the 1980s:

> It was hardly the most authentic Moroccan spot in Paris, but the restaurant – among the earliest to promote couscous to a non-immigrant clientele – was moderately priced and was so popular among middle-class Parisians that the owners soon opened additional branches. By the time my family and I moved back to the States, couscous symbolized Paris as clearly in my mind as a buttery croissant.

He goes on to document a growing and well-supported Maghreb (northern African) restaurant and food scene in Paris that goes well beyond couscous, and ends up shopping and cooking with cookbook author Fatema Hal. The rest of the magazine features recipes for Moroccan dishes and desserts from these restaurants and from Hal, including a tagine and other stews. In writing about couscous as it connects to Moroccan cuisine, food writers stress that authentic preparation takes 'patience and care', as the grain must be rubbed and moistened slowly (Wright, 2012).

Recently, couscous has become a popular and common food in France, such that polls show that people across age, race, region, and occupation, now consider it a traditional food or dish. Making couscous from scratch is a laborious process, but it is now a mass-produced product, sold in instant versions all across the globe. Indeed, chef and writer Clifford Wright (2012) finds that it is almost impossible to find anything but instant couscous in American markets. Magazines, blogs, websites and cooking shows tout couscous as a perfect everyday staple because of the speed at which the instant version is cooked and its versatility as a malleable starch that can be used in multiple ways. Examples include Mediterranean wraps with chicken and couscous, couscous and paella soup, feta and green bean couscous salad, and 'Moroccan skirt steak', which boasts a ten-minute cooking time and uses cumin and turmeric rub on the meat. Most recipes include the words 'easy' and 'fast' as encouragement for routine use in home-cooked meals. While some play on Mediterranean descriptors, very few situate the starch in a North African or Maghreb style of cuisine, more often incorporating it randomly and variously across cultures and cooking styles. In the last two years, the number of new recipes for couscous in food magazines and blogs has diminished, as quinoa – a South American grain with more protein and no gluten – gets promoted, marketed, and sold with the same ferocity as an everyday component of modern meals.

The above narrative about couscous is what might be called 'appropriation', a process where goods and practices that are created, produced, consumed and given meaning in one culture become incorporated or embedded in another culture (see Ekström, Chapter 5). This shift happens across space and time, and because this kind of consumption is often done by a group with more power than the group from which the item originated, such appropriation is often seen as a negative process. Wise suggests, 'there is no automatic relationship between a reduction in racism and an increase in multicultural eating' (2013: 106). As bell hooks expressed it,

> Currently, the commodification of difference promotes paradigms of consumption wherein whatever difference the Other inhabits is eradicated, via exchange, by a consumer cannibalism that not only displaces the Other but denies the significance of that Other's history through a process of decontextualization.
>
> (1998: 376)

However, appropriation can be seen as a more interesting and complex process when we consider that food, like all commodities, has a biography and that biography is not historically frozen in time or oriented in one direction. Parasecoli rightly points out that the peasant foods that come to represent ethnic, regional, or national foodways, were frequently rejected by more urban and cosmopolitan generations as 'embarrassing and uncouth, being uncomfortably close to rural realities and ethnic groups that are often at the margins of national projects' (2014: 265). Many studies have shown that regional cultures often absorb 'foreign' foods and appropriate them for their own tastes (Wilks, 2006; Watson, 1997). Others have focused on the adoption of new foods, the invention of culinary traditions, and the transference of skills (DeSoucey & Téchoueyres, 2009; Pilcher, 1998). Pilcher goes so far as to name his exploration of the globalisation of Mexican food, *Planet Taco*, suggesting that specific regional and ethnic foods can morph into an entirely new global phenomenon. In that vein, Abrahams suggests that it is not the shifting of ethnic cuisines that matters but rather, 'what the effect of enlarging our food choice has on our basic notions of what culture is and how it operates' (1984: 20). If appropriation is focused tightly on a single instance of adoption from one culture to another, with a presumption of power differentials, it diminishes our capacity to explore the transference, use, reuse, and re-imaginings of cultural forms. This chapter will focus on a few of these processes as they influence and are influenced by domestic consumption in the form of meals at home.

Most significantly, overarching the exploration of appropriation, we need to consider how almost all food production and consumption is filtered through the public and commercial markets. This is also a highly gendered process, where women mediate both the protection and development of culture and its changes, due to neoliberal market forces. Most directly, mothers create families through the production of meals (see also Davis, Marshall, Hogg, Schneider, & Petersen, Chapter 10), even if they are not doing the majority of the cooking (Julier, 2012; Moisio, Arnould, & Price, 2004; DeVault, 1991). Second, the global nature of cultural engagement and the shifting relationships of ethnic, racial, national, and regional identity shape how foods are or are not appropriated. Ultimately, class-based notions of taste, combined with economic capital, shape the cultural repertoires of both public and private foodways.

Global Food, Inc.

The dominance of the food industry, with its multi-billion dollar advertising and marketing as well as its capacity for continuous innovation and production, commodifies global food cultures and agricultural products. This process has an impact on everyone's cooking and eating. The sheer volume of food that is produced outside the household has increased exponentially, such that a huge percentage of the world's citizens are dependent in one form or another on foodstuffs produced by commercial entities. Similarly, the amount of 'eating out' has increased dramatically in the last three decades. While urban residents, particularly those with economic resources, have always had varieties of eateries and consumption sites available to them, restaurants of all types, but especially chains and prepared food venues, have populated the larger landscape, which makes eating out more accessible for those with less disposable income. In the US alone, 48 per cent of all food dollars are spent on food eaten away from home, with restaurant sales climbing from $379 billion in 2000 to $632 billion in 2012 (National Restaurant Association, 2012). According to the US Department of Agriculture: 'Despite the increasing popularity of restaurant and takeout meals, Americans still obtain about two-thirds of their daily calories from food prepared at home' (Guthrie, Okrent, & Volpe, 2013). Cultural contact and commercialisation have a major impact on people's eating habits. Today one in seven 'food dollars' is spent on ethnic foods, with new 'trends' popping up all the time: right now analysts are pointing to the growing market for Muslim and Polish foods in the UK and other parts of Europe. Two-thirds of consumers who eat ethnic foods at home claim that 'authenticity' in flavour is the most important factor in choosing products (Mintel, 2012). The explosion of products available in full service supermarkets is astounding and the food industry recognises the 'home cook who eats ethnic foods' as one of the critical markets of the future. It's interesting that this category is not sorted by whether people are cooking 'their own' or other ethnic foods, but markets are moving more and more products out of a single 'international' aisle and moving them throughout the store. Additionally, products loosely based on ethnic foods (such as wasabi flavoured chips) are positioned throughout stores and not marketed as such. This differentiation has taken place in very recent history. Surveying the market, *Advertising Age* notes:

> Sixty years ago, Swiss chocolate was considered exotic and the standard ethnic food options were Italian pasta and chop suey. This year the organization highlighted something called 'local-global' as a hot trend ... spotlighting a brand named Chulita's Famous, a Latin seasonings company based in Brooklyn that specialized in sofritos.
>
> (Schultz, 2012)

Implied here is that the spice is meant to be used on foods eaten at home. What is interesting is that the commercial food industry continues to create products that presume some level of appropriation and incorporation into household food habits. Despite the plethora of information about what people buy and eat, our knowledge of their cooking, food preparation, and consumption habits at home is still more speculative than solid, often shaped by data from marketing firms supporting the food industry than by observable or experiential knowledge.

The contemporary context for appropriation around meal provision is a global food system that creates more products than the current population can consume, while reinforcing inequitable distribution and access. Quite simply, the food system exacerbates existing inequalities related to material resources and well-being. This system is supported and created by governments and transnational corporations, but given that food is a necessity for survival, it is engaged and enacted continually by people in their everyday lives. We live in an era where, in many parts of the world, people's daily consumption is made possible by a large array of goods grown, processed, and distributed by abstract agents outside the household and local community. The contemporary food system is built upon the workings of a consolidated and commodified market logic and it is difficult, if not impossible, for people, even those living in more isolated sections of the globe, not to be dependent on this system and to interact with it primarily as consumers rather than producers (Hendrickson & Heffernan, 2002). As some analysts see it, we are currently in what may be characterised as a retail-oriented, consumer-shaped food regime that is characterised by 'growing retail power, interest in freshness and naturalness of food, restructured global agrifood supply chains, and a growing financialization of the sector' (Block, 2012: 59).

The modern marketplace encourages ongoing consumption throughout the day, with foodstuffs available even in gas stations, convenience stores, and the like, including advertising campaigns for late night 'fourth meal' fast food purchases. 'Poor diet' is the frequent cause suggested for a large range of global health problems. At the same time, the induced panic around health-related concerns and subsequent consumption-focused solutions drive a second and perhaps related set of ideas about what to buy, what to eat, and what to do. Both present the marketplace of consumer goods as a magic bullet for hunger and health, built on promises of convenience, which translates into an absence of labour to achieve satiation *and* wellness.

That said, many people still extend some effort to prepare at least a portion of their daily food intake, especially in the form of meals. The meal itself, as the most revered form of consumption, holds sway over the patterning and expectations of all other food events (Douglas, 1975). The patterning of such consumption may not match an idealised cultural form, but it is still dependent on the meal as a measure for what is appropriate and acceptable (Meiselman, 2000; Murcott, 2000; Wood, 1995). In particular, in twentieth century Western societies, the 'family meal', was expected to occur on a daily basis in the household, with foods prepared in the domestic setting, and involved social bonding and cohesion among participants. As Murcott has repeatedly demonstrated, only a segment of the population was able to meet these expectations and that achievement was during a short historical time frame. In particular, the lamented loss of the family meal is often tied to other economic and political pressures (i.e. the increase in women in the paid labour force) rather than any demonstrable data about the reduction of the family mealtime (Murcott, 2000). Despite the increase in women in the labour force as well as some general improvement in their income earning, most global analyses of domestic labour find that women do the vast majority of food labours for their households. While some of that labour has been foisted onto the service industry, including the world of commercially prepared food, responsibility for meals and all the expectations around them, from health to child socialisation to community building, tend to remain women's work. Walzer (1998) finds that women in the paid labour force may rely on paid childcare but they 'do' caring labour by thinking about the baby and its needs. This process exists in food labours as well: even if they are not cooking, women handle the vast majority of invisible tasks such as navigating markets and products, dietary needs, social and cultural expectations around foods, and maintaining class-based standards of variety, consumption, and commensality.

Despite the effort and the alternatives offered by the marketplace, people do continue to eat meals at home together on a patterned basis. The data available suggests that, while not quite as frequent as posed by the aspirational myth, shared meals are still worth the effort for at least some patterned occurrence during the week or month. Eating together remains a sociable collective practice despite issues such as shifting temporal pressures, which make the coordination of eating events within households difficult (Julier, 2012; Warde, 1997).

Connected to the notion of meals is the logic of cuisine, which is a set of patterned approaches to cooking and eating, based on a cultural logic and history connected to place, identity, ingredients and flavouring. In the contemporary global food landscape, unless people are tightly rooted in a cultural community, cuisine is often treated as a set of practices from which one can borrow, adapt, and sample, eating sushi one day and barbecue the next. At the same time, there is a trend towards marketing personalised packaged foods, such that even cuisines can be individualised (Gardyn, 2002). In the public marketplace, this is supported by the easy purchase of prepared foods and ingredients as well as the promotion of new goods. At home, consumption is influenced by perceptions of a time deficit, health concerns, the ideological promotion of the family meal, and the need for variety to support modern cultural values (Julier, 2012; DeVault, 1991). Looking at how 'homemade foods' are often seen as a critical piece of family well-being, Moisio et al. (2004: 363) suggest that 'family meals increasingly represent the intersection between the conflicting logics of the nurturing domestic group and the rationalizing global market economy' (Weismantel, 1998; Warde, 1997). Home meals become the frontline for encountering, resisting, and redefining the marketplace.

Adaptation

One critical way that people address those concerns is by relying on but adapting commercial products or 'appropriation'. People who purchase prepared foods for the meal at home end up transforming the foodstuffs in ways that are both hidden and documented. Such adaptations can range from adding in ingredients, eating the foods in a particular sequence or role in the meal, reconfiguring the foods into a different form, or even consuming them at odd times (i.e. pizza for breakfast). Furthermore, while some cuisine continues to be moored to a specific ethnic, regional, and spatially determined logic, more frequently in the global landscape, many cuisines and their elements are incorporated into new modalities and new positions in the configuration of the meal. Condiments and spices, side dishes and organising principles are upended to include new foods. Bentley (2001) demonstrates how Martha Stewart maintains a kind of culinary whiteness, appropriating ethnic foods as a means of complicating the meal by adding additional 'stressed' items such as sauces, condiments, and side dishes. Stewart was merely the precursor to television shows, cookbooks, and blogs that increase the variety and complexity of meal production without significantly engaging with cultural or culinary difference.

People from various social and economic circumstances incorporate commercial foods into their lives, customising them, adapting, converting, and giving them new symbolic meanings in their daily practice of consumption. Some examples include the adaptation of commercially prepared foods, reconsiderations of the meal format in relation to commercial foods, family meals, and ethnic and regional food appropriation, all of which are experienced through a stratified system of gender, race, and class.

Consuming commercial foods

Kopytoff comments: 'What is significant about the adoption of alien objects – as of alien ideas – is not the fact that they are adopted, but the way they are culturally redefined and put to use' (1986: 67). He reminds us that all commodities have a biography and that, as analysts, we need to consider what biographical possibilities are inherent in an object in a particular period and culture. For commercially created food items, that biography includes the story of its use as told by marketers, the company itself, recipes, consumers, and critics. From the very beginning of modern industrial production and marketing, there have been both concerns and contradictions about how such products were to be used in households – and how they were actually used. The story of the development of the commercial food industry and its continued need to create new desires and new markets includes inventing more variety, encouraging additional uses of existing foods, creating new packaging that supports more individualised uses (single serving and on-the-go eating), adapting slow cooking foods to fast and convenience approaches, and marketing health and ethnicity. From the earliest days of commercialised food, companies changed ingredients, packaging, and the like, especially to attract female consumers, who were and are the major purchasing gateway into households. One undocumented story tells of the invention of cake mixes: while most only required water or oil, the myth suggests that manufacturers felt women needed to feel as if they were doing something so mixes included extra additions, such as eggs or butter. In reality, although consumers may have said they wanted to add ingredients, they generally bought the mix requiring the least amount of effort. Historian Laura Shapiro (2005) explores the claims that cake frosting actually was the additive sales item: women felt they were doing something creative by frosting the cake. Some people now claim to have made a 'homemade' cake even if they have used cake mix and prepared frosting. In some taste cultures, these adaptations would need to be covert.

Campbell's soup: convenient and adaptable

There are many kinds of appropriation related to modernisation of the food industry. Starting in 1890, the Campbell's Soup Company was the first successful mass marketing of food, promoting commercial canned soups to consumers through gendered messages about love and convenience. The product has been sold simultaneously as a labour-saving, tasty alternative to cooking that also materially demonstrated women's care of family members. Scholars of the food culture of the twentieth century such as Shapiro (2005), Levenstein (1993), and Parkin (2001) suggest that advertisers played on this contradiction between cooking as a skilled form of nurturance and the desire to be free of such drudgery. Campbell's is one of the most ubiquitous examples, generating a longstanding brand loyalty that inspired the most recognised pop art images of all time. Warhol's use of the iconic soup can is the perfect example of appropriation, incorporating both kitsch and homage. Rather than resist this process, Campbell's now has a contest where it gives out an award to the best student art that incorporates their product, in the spirit of Warhol.

Campbell's original success was partly built on creating a year-round market for what was once a more seasonal product. Capturing what was to become a standard practice in the food industry, Campbell's created more and more varieties of soup, encouraging a general notion that the modern palate required a diverse set of tastes or even 'more exotic soups that no home kitchen could produce' (Parkin, 2001: 57). From the very beginning, Campbell's also provided cooking pamphlets, cookbooks, and recipes that demonstrated how the soup itself could be enhanced or used as ingredients to make other dishes. In the 1950s, television had live commercial breaks sponsored by Campbell's, where dishes made with soup were demonstrated for home cooks. In terms of appropriation, such usage was encouraged, supported, and often created by the very companies who were also marketing convenience and freedom from cooking.

As a product, Campbell's has weathered changes in food trends, where 'freshness' has become constructed as something found in the refrigerator case and not in a can. Canned foods are not at the top of cultural hierarchies now, since consumers demand 'freshness', which is associated with refrigeration (Friedberg, 2010). Currently, frozen and cold stored foods are more in demand, with supermarkets increasing the energy expensive refrigerator display cases to handle foods that are not required to be kept cold by food safety regulations. Highly processed foods, such as ultra pasteurised almond and soy milk in shelf-stable containers, are placed in the cold section because consumers equate it with freshness. Similarly, although supermarkets often use canned soups 'behind the scenes' for their prepared 'to go' foods section, consumers deem these hot soups to be 'fresher' because they are not in a can. For Campbell's, this has meant focusing on product differentiation and new packaging options. While the brand has strongest appeal among certain regional and demographic groups, it still continues to own more than half of the soup market share.

Many critics tend to construct the use of commercial foods in domestic cuisine as a sign of culinary and cultural decline, the end of civilisation and the reason for most health problems. But this approach misses (a) the patterning of meals as significant and (b) the ways in which people contend with mass culture, making it relevant and useful to their lives. Warde suggests that scholars of consumption are often remiss in

> recognizing the way in which mass-produced commodities can be customized, that is appropriated for personal and private purposes.... Groups of people buy a common commercial product then work on it, adapt it, convert it into something that is symbolically representative of personal or collective identity. That it was once a mass-produced com- modity becomes irrelevant after its incorporation into a person's house- hold, hobby, or life. In one sense, all cookery is of this nature: labour is added, and by transforming groceries into meals social and symbolic value is created. That is the currently legitimate labour of love.
>
> (1997: 152)

Warde's description applies most clearly to an iconic dish created with Camp- bell's soup, the green bean casserole. First developed and demonstrated by women test cooks who worked at Campbell's, the Green Bean Casserole included canned fried onion rings and Cream of Mushroom soup, and rapidly became so iconic for Thanksgiving that the recipe remains the most requested of all time and sales of that soup are generally believed to be for use in the recipe rather than for consumption in its intended form. In considering the appropriation of commercial foods, this is deeply significant. Thanksgiving is the most important – or in Douglas's terms, 'stressed' – among the annual patterning of meals that make up American culture. While ethnic traditions and regional specialties may adapt some parts of the menu, certain aspects are fixed. It is the one holiday in US culture that has such consistency, particu- larly as a holiday where the expectations are on families cooking and provid- ing homemade food rather than going out to eat or getting prepared foods. Given the changes in people's lives and the mass marketing of prepared prod- ucts, what one means by homemade may have changed. Illustratively, in an interview about feeding friends and family, one middle-aged woman pointed out that her career trajectory away from cooking and household chores was limited by Thanksgiving, where her grown children expected to come home to a meal that she cooked. She admitted to purchasing almost all of the dishes as prepared foods at an expensive supermarket and hiding the boxes so her family wouldn't know (Julier, 2013). The reality of Thanksgiving as a home- made meal and the existence of so many prepared products on the shelf suggest that beliefs and practices about cooking are not always consistent.

However, as a particular dish in a sequence of patterned meals, with Thanksgiving being one of the highlights of that pattern, the green bean cas- serole, with its genesis from corporate marketing, has now become central to many people's required menu for holiday food. The example of Campbell's soup captures the relationship between the food industry and consumers. On the one hand, the industry creates a product that is designed to reduce and alleviate home cooking while simultaneously promoting two particular ideas about home food consumption: one, that women are engaged in caring labour by providing food (whether they 'cooked' it or not); and two, that modern meals are built upon a greater expectation of variety.

Ethnicity: from difference to variety

In countries that have shifted from homogenous cultural dominance to multi-cultural and multi-racial populations, ethnicity and race have always provided the grounds for most contested arguments about appropriation. With foods, such contestations are ongoing and connected more deeply to the commercial marketplace than ever before. Gabaccia (1998) suggests that many ethnic foods were originally the product of immigrant entrepreneurs whose businesses did well independently with both ethnic and non-ethnic markets until they were purchased or copied by larger food companies. Most recently, Campbell's, with its claim to many varieties of soup, has lost a fraction of its market share as the 'ethnic soup market' with companies such as Goya, Progresso, and Manischewitz brands have gained popularity. Interestingly, Progresso may have begun as an Italian-focused brand, but its product line mirrors the varieties in Campbell's, such that they incited a recent marketing battle focused on which company's products contained MSG (monosodium glutamate). Parodying the 'soup war', comedian Stephen Colbert jokingly derided Progresso as 'some European company' and exhorted his audience to support the 'American' company. Given the assimilation of Italian–American foods, it is difficult for Americans to consider this kind of commercially produced minestrone an 'ethnic food'. Similar to the shifting taste cultures created by couscous, Italian and Italian–American foods are assimilated as everyday items in Western cuisine.

The contemporary example of the relationship between public and private, homemade and commercial foods comes in the form of a different soup – ramen. Ramen is an Asian noodle soup. While noodle soups existed throughout Japanese and Chinese regional cuisines, the invention of instant wheat noodles in 1958 made ramen widely available to people in homes as well as in street food and noodle shops. Specific brands of ramen noodles ('Top Ramen' made by Nissin, the company owned by the instant noodle inventor) with 'flavor packets' were sold globally. Inexpensive, filling, and easy to make, ramen became a staple food across Asia but also in many other countries. At the same time, there are many examples, narratives, and conversations among people about how they modify, enhance, or personalise ramen for their own consumption. Adding ingredients such as meat, scallions, spices, egg, or vegetables is common and has seemingly endless variation. Youtube videos demonstrate how to make grilled cheese, pizza, gnocchi, and other foods out of ramen.[1] This demonstrates appropriation and adaptation of both a commercial and an ethnic commodity.

In a shift back into public taste cultures, chefs have returned ramen to a restaurant experience. While not among the highest status restaurants, ramen bars in the US are seen as culturally cutting edge places where customers must 'know' something about the types of ingredients one adds or the names of the more famous ramen chefs. Newspaper food columnists describe 'hunting' through Asian enclaves for 'good ramen' (Wells, 2014). Knowing about ramen begins to seem like a new form of cultural appropriation, as aficionados of ramen shops are often young non-Asian men who compete over 'chowhound' information. In many cases, one version of a food item (peasant, homemade, or commercial) fosters its opposite alternative (artisanal, upper class, haute cuisine) and the demographic segments adopt competing versions.

Public eating shapes private consumption. The history of ethnic restaurants suggests a complicated trajectory where some restaurants were originally only for the migrants and immigrants from within their own group and others always catered to other populations when possible, finding affinities in similar but also exoticised culinary patterns. Tuchman and Levine (1993) describe the multiple reasons why Eastern European Jews in New York were so taken with Chinese food and restaurants, including food that did not 'seem' to cross dietary rules, the appearance of sophistication that one gained by eating ethnic, and the similarities in cooking techniques. More recently, Lee (2003) and others document the reversal, where Chinese immigrants gravitate towards Eastern European Jewish foods, particularly those that were invented in the United States, such as bagels. Using interviews with Chinese Americans in the restaurant business, Davis (1999) documents historical changes in the cuisine served, suggesting that such shifts are:

> a representation of Chinese and Chinese-American culture which is both 'unauthentic' fabrication and the product of an 'authentic' cultural adaptation. The accommodation of Chinese cuisine to the American market and palate are the result of a process of negotiation and transformation carried out by Chinese-American restaurateurs.

The experience of adaptation was not just through public consumption. In the 1920s–1950s, New Yorkers incorporated Chinese foods into their everyday cooking via cookbooks, newspapers, and magazines that made adaptations less intimidating, less complicated, and more practical – once foreign, still exotic, yet everyday.

Although today the food industry is dominated by a small, consolidated number of companies, many more food entrepreneurial ventures are small and owned by women and ethnic racial minorities. According to Gabaccia: 'Ethnicity in the marketplace was not the invention of corporate demographic marketing strategies' (1998: 160). She points to the belated corporate recognition of already thriving enclave markets and their attempts to compete with the already existing 'enclave entrepreneurs'. Big business food corporations 'discovered' the selling power of ethnic and regional diversity after the Second World War, when there had already been a long history of successful smaller food producers, often from ethnic and racial groups, promoting products to both enclaves and the larger public market. Today, this process is ongoing.

Rather than focus exclusively on the impact of the capitalist market as it absorbs and sells various cultures, we need to examine how people in various groups act, collide, and collaborate in this cross-consumption. To suggest that 'eating the other' is a form of colonialism or bad appropriation simply by cooking foods outside one's ethnic, regional, or experiential background misses the impact of the commercial marketplace on such choices. The boundaries of cultural groups have been commodified and de-contextualised in many ways – the question is whether or where this diminishes the culture in question. Many moves to create place-based designations and restrictions on foods may help maintain the unique techniques of production or the raw goods in their 'natural' habitat. However, it is not clear that they have the kind of intended impact on consumers, especially when considering how people eat at home and in shared meals. An apt example is lobster. Small-scale research with US mid-western consumers demonstrates that people associate good quality lobster with Maine, based on travel and tourism. However, when asked if they would purchase Maine lobster to consume at home, most balked due to a lack of cooking knowledge, suggesting that preparing and eating whole lobster was something they could not incorporate into their daily routines (Yovino, 2014). Eating a whole lobster required the skill and setting of Maine and could not be appropriated, even by skilled cooks.

Conclusion

Rather than viewing people as mindless consumers who fulfil their mealtime needs directly through the marketing discourses that surround them, it is worthwhile to consider the multiple ways in which such a relationship between market and meal is imperfectly conceived and variably enacted. Even when purchasing foods in the marketplace, the act of cooking and preparing at home means variation and specificity in the 'home made' meal. Wise sums it up well when she concludes that 'there is nothing implicitly communal or disjunctural about food as it crosses cultures. Food can produce both borders and commensalities' (2013: 106). Although almost everyone partakes of the commercial marketplace of food, contemporary social critics push people to 'cook more' at home. Commentators like Michael Pollan[2] and Mark Bittman[3] make a plea for a return to skilled home cooking as a way of improving the food system and the overall health and wellness of citizens. However, like many food reformers before them, these commentators have been criticised for imposing middle- to upper-middle-class white taste culture on a reluctant population. Recent studies find that working-class and poor mothers find the burden of meal preparation to be so great as to create constraints and stress in other aspects of their lives. Additionally, these critics often reject the improvements and enticements of the commercial marketplace that are often necessary and useful. These dichotomies of cultural boundaries and commercial versus homemade food cause observers and researcher to miss or ignore the potential uses and innovations that people create through appropriating and adapting commercial foods at home. While not to say that all culinary crossings and appropriations are good for cultures, communities, and well-being, the suggestion of this essay is that these processes are ongoing and often liberating and should be considered part of the pantheon of human cultural and culinary practices around providing meals.

Notes

1 Various examples can be seen at the following links:

www.youtube.com/watch?v=dze9LRkM9bI
www.youtube.com/watch?v=S_7hKfQS_Cw
www.youtube.com/watch?v=kYheOeEIMmI

2 Pollan, M. Cooking: FAQ & Useful Links. Available at: http://michaelpollan.com/resources/cooking/ [Accessed 4 December 2015].
3 Bittman, M. (2014) The Truth About Home Cooking, *Time Magazine*. Available at: http://markbittman.com/the-truth-about-home-cooking/ [Accessed 4 December 2015].

References

Abrahams, R. (1984). Equal opportunity eating: A structural excursus on things of the mouth. In L. K. Brown, & K. Mussell (Eds.), *Ethnic and Regional Foodways in the U.S.* (pp. 19–36). Knoxville: University of Tennessee Press.

Bentley, A. (2001). Martha's food: Whiteness of a certain kind. *American Studies Quarterly, 42*(2), 89–100.

Block, D. (2012). Food systems. In A. Bentley (Ed.), *A Cultural History of Food: The Modern Age* (pp. 47–67). London: Berg/Bloomsbury.

Cheshes, J. (2012). Maghreb Cooking in Paris. *Saveur*. Available at: www.saveur.com/article/Travels/Maghreb-Cooking-in-Paris [Accessed 20 July 2015].

Davis, N. (1999). We Don't Serve Chop Suey!: Chinese-American Resteranteurs Serving the 'Other'. Paper presented at the annual meeting of the Association for the Study of Food and Society, Toronto.

DeSoucey, M., & Téchoueyres, I. (2009). Virtue and valorization: 'Local food' in the United States and France. In D. Inglis, & D. Gimlin (Eds.), *The Globalization of Food* (pp. 81–95). Oxford and New York: Berg Publishers, 81–95.

DeVault, M. (1991). *Feeding the Family: The Social Organization of Caring as Gendered Work*. Chicago: University of Chicago Press.

Douglas, M. (1975). Deciphering a meal. *Daedalus, 101*(1), 61–81.

Friedberg, S. (2010). *Fresh: A Perishable History*. Cambridge, MA: Belknap Press.

Gabaccia, D. (1998). *We Are What We Eat: Ethnicity and the Making of Americans*. Cambridge, MA: Harvard University Press.

Gardyn, R. (2002). What's cooking. *American Demographics, 24*(March), 28–35.

Guthrie, J., Lin, B., Okrent, A., & Volpe, R. (2013). Americans' food choices at home and away: How do they compare with recommendations? *Amber Waves,*

USDA Publications. Available at: www.ers.usda.gov/amber-waves/2013-february/americans-food-choices-at-home-and-away.aspx#.VaVr8uuNf3M [Accessed 23 September 2014].

Hendrickson, M., & Heffernan, W. D. (2002). Opening spaces through relocation: Locating potential resistance in the weaknesses of the global good system. *Sociologia Ruralis, 42*(4), 347–369.

hooks, b. (1998). Eating the other: Desire and resistance. In R. Scapp, & Seitz B. (Eds.), *Eating Culture* (pp. 21–39). Albany: SUNY Press.

Julier, A. (2012). Family and domesticity. In A. Bentley (Ed.), *A Cultural History of Food: The Modern Age* (pp. 145–163). London: Berg/Bloomsbury.

Julier, A. (2013). *Eating Together: Food, Friendship, and Inequality.* Champaign: University of Illinois Press.

Kopytoff, I. (1986). The cultural biography of things: Commoditization as process. In A. Appadurai (Ed.), *The Social Life of Things: Commodities in Cultural Perspective* (pp. 64–91). Cambridge: Cambridge University Press.

Lee, J. (2003). *The Fortune Cookie Chronicles.* London: Twelve Books Press.

Levenstein, H. (1993). *Paradox of Plenty: A Social History of Eating in Modern America.* New York: Oxford University Press.

Meiselman, H. (Ed.) (2000). *Dimensions of the Meal: The Science, Culture, Business, and Art of Eating.* Maryland: Aspen Publishers.

Mintel. (2012). Ethnic Food UK, report, September 2012.

Moisio, R., Arnould, E., & Price, L. (2004). Between mothers and markets: Constructing family identity through homemade food. *Journal of Consumer Culture, 4*(3), 361–384.

Murcott, A. (2000). Is it still a pleasure to cook for him? Social changes in the household and the family. *Journal of Consumer Studies and Home Economics, 24*(2), 78–84.

National Restaurant Association. (2012). *Facts-at-a-Glance.* Available at: www.restaurant.org/News-Research/Research/Facts-at-a-Glance [Accessed 23 April 2014].

Parasecoli, F. (2014). *Al Dente, A History of Food in Italy.* London: Reaktion Books.

Parekh, B. (1999). *Rethinking Multiculturalism.* London: Palgrave MacMillan.

Parkin, K. (2001). Campbell's Soup and the long shelf life of traditional gender roles. In S. Inness (Ed.), *Kitchen Culture in America: Popular Representations of Food, Gender, and Race* (pp. 51–68). Philadelphia: University of Pennsylvania Press.

Pilcher, J. (1998). *Que Vivan Los Tamales!: Food and the Making of Mexican Identity.* Albuquerque: University of New Mexico Press.

Schultz, E. J. (2012). How America eats today fast, fresh, flavorful: Marketers are adapting to the new demands of a rapidly changing food world. *Advertising Age.* Available at: http://adage.com/article/news/marketers-adapt-rapidly-changing-world-american-eating/238222/ [Accessed 26 May 2014].

Shapiro, L. (2005). *Something from the Oven: Reinventing Dinner in 1950s America.* London: Penguin Books.

Tuchman, G., & Levine, H. (1993). New York Jews and Chinese food: The social construction of an ethnic pattern. *Journal of Contemporary Ethnography, 33*(3), 382–407.

Walzer, S. (1998). *Thinking About the Baby.* London: Temple University Press.

Warde, A. (1997). *Consumption, Food and Taste.* London: Sage.

Watson, J. (1997). *Golden Arches East: MacDonald's in East Asia.* Stanford: Stanford University Press.

Weismantel, M. (1998). *Food, Gender, and Poverty in the Ecuadorian Andes.* Long Grove, IL: Waveland Press.

Wells, P. (2014). Ramen's Big Splash, *New York Times* (4 March 2014). Available at: www.nytimes.com/2014/03/05/dining/ramens-big-splash.html?_r=0 [Accessed 4 March 2014].

Wilks, R. (2006). *Home Cooking in the Global Village: Caribbean Food from Buccaneers to Ecotourists*. London: Berg/Bloomsbury.

Wise, A. (2013). Moving food: Gustatory commensality and disjuncture in everyday multiculturalism. *New Formations, 74*(1), 82–107.

Wood, R. (1995). *The Sociology of the Meal*. Edinburgh: Edinburgh University Press.

Wright, C. (2012). What is couscous? Available at: www.cliffordawright.com/caw/food/entries/display.php/id/58/ [Accessed 24 March 2014].

Yovino, H. (2014). Marketing and branding of the Maine lobster: Case study in Pittsburgh, PA on taste of place perceptions. MA Thesis, Food Studies, Chatham University.

7 Appropriating Bimby on the Internet

Perspectives on technology-mediated meals by a virtual brand community

Monica Truninger

Introduction

It was Christmas day when an intriguing news piece about a kitchen technology was published in the Wall Street Journal in 2013 (Kowsmann, 2013). Immediately after, the piece went viral in the Portuguese (social) media (TV, blogs, press). It reported an odd 'obsession' of Portuguese consumers with a pricey German-made kitchen appliance – the Bimby[1] (Figure 7.1) – during a difficult period of 'painful budget slashing in return for an international bailout'.

The news piece served to unveil the irony: how come 'Western Europe's poorest country' could afford such an expensive technology 'that outsells high-end iPads [...] and is more popular on Facebook than the country's best-known rock band?' The journalistic piece advanced explanations for this technology craze: 'But the Portuguese love gadgets and seem determined, despite hard times, to maintain their tradition of regularly getting together for dinner'.

In this explanatory attempt, Bimby is portrayed as an intermediary that opens up the possibility for thinking about meal practices in a particular way, in this case, linking nation and meals through ideas around commensality.

Figure 7.1 Bimby.

Whether these commensal narratives about Portuguese foodways are enacted in practice remains to be seen. A propos, there is much discussion on the demise of a Mediterranean food diet and culture in southern Europe (Truninger & Freire, 2014). Yet, such a news piece made visible the capacity of food technologies to communicate, translate and frame possibilities for enacting meal practices in particular ways. But what exactly is this kitchen technology that has conquered space in the kitchens, pockets and hearts of many families? In the official Vorwerk UK site the most recent Bimby model (TM5) is described as follows:

> Thermomix TM5 combines twelve appliances in one with functions that include weighing, mixing, chopping, milling, kneading, blending, steaming, cooking, whisking, precise heating, stirring and emulsifying. Whether your goal is healthy eating or expert levels of culinary skill, the Thermomix TM5 will help you by acting like a second pair of hands in the kitchen.[2]

This appliance is marketed through direct sales,[3] by means of a commercial demonstration that is arranged by personal reference, held in the home of the host with family and friends. In the demonstration, the vendor explains this technology and how it can be incorporated into daily meal practices. In this event, a set of dishes is cooked and tasted by participants, and with it an informal and friendly atmosphere develops (Truninger, 2011). In this chapter, I move away from the demonstration site to address the processes of appropriation that take place once users acquire this appliance from the demonstrators. By taking an informed practice perspective the chapter focuses on a particular Internet site – the Forum Bimby. The forum resembles a virtual brand community (Sicilia & Palazón, 2008; Cova & Pace, 2006; Kozinets, 1999) where users can learn about appropriating this appliance in a 'proper' way. Such interactions with other fellow members encourage the use of the product and devise 'proper' uses of Bimby to accomplish the practice of the meal. In what follows, this chapter revolves around three objectives: first, to understand how Bimby affected the organisation of the meal in forum members' everyday lives; second, to grasp what conflicting views about meals and propriety were triggered by Bimby in forum members' families; and third, the learning arrangements, skills and competences that a virtual brand community enabled around meal preparation and cooking with Bimby.

Meal practices, technologies and virtual brand communities

Research on meals is abundant and diverse, and it is looked upon from different disciplinary perspectives. According to the comprehensive work edited by Meiselman (2009) a key conclusion is that meals are indubitably complex and vary across groups, nations, cultures and societies. From a broad literature on meals I identify three important debates: First, working mothers and meal practices; second, domestic technologies and the construction of the family; and third, virtual brand communities and meal competences.

As to the first debate, some studies have concluded that domestic technologies rather than being considered time savers in meal preparation can be portrayed as 'time machines' that help 'ordering, scheduling, co-ordination and timing' of meals (Shove & Southerton, 2000: 313). In the case of working mothers, who navigate across dynamic (and demanding) working and domestic arrangements by adapting working hours to fit around family meals, a domestic technology that facilitates the 'ordering', 'scheduling' and 'co-ordination' of such arrangements may be deemed as a need (Brannen, O'Connell, & Mooney, 2013). In this case, I advance the hypothesis that the need for such domestic technologies emanates from the mother's capacity to orchestrate eating practices in everyday life. That is, given that lack of coordination of time schedules (or lack of synchronicity) and time pressure are constituents of working mother's everyday experiences (Brannen, 2005); a technology that promises to tap into the problem of timing can be very alluring, even more so when it allows achieving the culturally valued and socially desirable 'family meal' – eating a 'proper' meal together at the table with loved ones (see Molander, Chapter 11).

This opens up another important debate that is recurrent in meals research: what is or not appropriate to include in a meal and how that propriety may lead to understandings of good quality standards by the food provider in feeding the family (or guests) and in caring for the family (DeVault, 1991). As Julier (2013: 343) points out: 'eating meals together is a particular enactment of family life although grounded in a more general set of expectations about how families behave'. Moreover, to be seen to perform the practice of the meal according to expected conventions, and by showing good command in such a performance is an important source of inner goods (e.g. self-esteem, pride, fulfilment, well-being) (Warde, 2005). Domestic technologies can be an important vehicle to show such good command of the practice of the meal, by showing competence in its use. Plus, as some studies indicate (Marshall & Anderson, 2002), meanings of eating properly go beyond an understanding of the 'proper meal' reduced solely to the components of a dish – one meat and two veg (Murcott, 1982; Douglas, 1972) – and stretch over towards other aspects of the meal embedded in a particular context and collective (Marshall, 2005). Thus, what, how and by whom the ingredients of the meal were bought, who participates or is left out of the meal, how it is cooked and by who or what, where is the meal taking place, and so on, are all part of the ingredients that integrate a flexible interpretation of meal propriety. If popular discourse and some social research deem the family meal as a vehicle for 'togetherness' and 'harmony' in the family (Brannen et al., 2013), other studies show how it can also be a locus of conflict and disruption (Coveney, 2006). Given that meal propriety can be extended not only to what ends up on the plate but how it was cooked, prepared, by what or whom, one can advance the hypothesis that domestic technologies can trigger family disruptions. Similar disruptions in couples because of domestic technologies were well demonstrated by Kaufmann (1998, 2010).

Finally, it is also relevant to look at a less scrutinised aspect of meals that is becoming increasingly relevant: the proliferation of social media platforms in the food world (Rousseau, 2012). Food and social media have the potential to develop competences in the practice of the meal, through virtual communities around particular branded kitchen appliances. The development of virtual communities around a particular brand is seen as an important marketing tool to strengthen customer loyalty. According to Sicilia and Palazón (2008: 257) a virtual brand community is 'a group of individuals with common interests in a brand who communicate with each other electronically in a platform provided by the company which supports the brand'. There may also be virtual brand communities that are independent of the brand (e.g. a voluntary fan-based community), but that can still fulfil the same values as the ones of a brand sponsored website. Such values encompass functional (e.g. offering advice, information and expertise on the uses of that brand), social (e.g. friendship, emotional support, self-esteem, social status, social enhancement) and entertainment values (e.g. relaxation, fun) (Sicilia & Palazón, 2008: 259). These virtual communities can also work as virtual 'communities of practice' (Wenger, 1999) where members learn ways of doing and approaching things that are collectively shared. In this sense, learning is not something that reflects acquisition of certain forms of knowledge but it is instead an outcome of social practice. Learning is conducted in situations of co-participation, and that means to be 'active participants in the practices of social communities and constructing identities in relation to these communities' (Wenger, 1999: 4). In this way, in order to perform the practice of the meal mediated by a particular domestic technology (such as Bimby) in an appropriate way, several users resource to virtual brand communities (e.g. the Forum Bimby). Such communities resemble Wenger's communities of practice that work as an additional supplement to the sole demonstration offered by the vendor.

Underpinning all three debates is a common denominator that views the meal as composed of a set of social practices. This view stresses the routine, collective and conventional aspects that cut across meals. According to Schatzki (2002: 106), 'practices are intrinsically connected to and interwoven' with technologies, it being important to grasp what role they have in facilitating or disrupting the orchestration of meals in everyday life. In this perspective, practices are routinised behaviours composed of several elements interconnected and interwoven with objects, which are carried out by individuals in the course of their normal everyday life (Shove, Pantzar, & Watson, 2012; Reckwitz, 2002). In tune with this theoretical framework, meals should not be considered as only performed by individuals but as an outcome of the injunctions, sequencing, coordination and synchronisation of many other practices (Shove et al., 2012).

Methods and data collection

The virtual community – ForumBimby.com – despite not being brand spon-sored by the company Vorwerk, was selected for data collection and content analysis given its popularity since it opened in 2006. For years the site gained a large affluence of new members and strongly competed with the brand sponsored virtual community (www.mundodereceitasbimby.com.pt). As of 1 May 2015, ForumBimby.com was composed of 15,881 members, of which 15 per cent were men and the remainder women.[4] In order to explore the online Bimby community the core method employed was netnography. Kozinets (1998: 366) described it as 'an interpretive method devised specifi-cally to investigate the consumer behavior of cultures and communities present on the Internet'. According to the same author this method is a com-bination of the techniques of cultural anthropology, wherein ethnography is undertaken online, among online communities. In this research I employed observation and participation, at different phases of engagement with this virtual community.[5] The empirical material used for the purposes of this chapter was mostly retrieved in 2013. That year, I returned to the site and made an online compilation of texts using the search engine of the forum by selecting members' messages according to the keyword – 'meals'. After clean-ing the database, 40 chains of texts (sequences of posts and replies) were com-piled, totalling 2013 texts. Text analysis involved reading its contents and coding according to specific themes that emerged from the data. In order to protect and reduce harm to the Forum Bimby members when conducting research online, I have followed the Ethics Guidelines for Internet-mediated Research (British Psychological Society, 2013). Thus, permissions to use online data were sought and granted by the administrator of the Bimby forum.

One of the advantages of observing interactive talk about meal practices in forums is that they are displayed without being filtered by respondents in a similar way to when they answer a questionnaire or when interviewed face-to-face by the researcher. Although some members may carefully craft their posts in a forum, many are under the online disinhibition effect (Suler, 2004), where people are less guarded about their feelings, emotions, or what they do in everyday life. They feel secure behind the screen, under an anonymous persona. Talking about cooking and preparing meals with Bimby is seen as a non-threatening topic, and people feel at ease and disclose personal informa-tion. This allows the observer to get a glimpse of the ebb and flow of routi-nised behaviour and the dynamics of interaction of sayings about doings in the lives of the members without them being (fully) aware of being observed by total strangers. It somehow grants the observer easier access to routinised behaviour that is slightly more difficult to get in the context of an interview (wherein people are encouraged to get conscious about routinised food prac-tices that often are 'not readily open to reflection' (Brannen et al., 2013: 421)). Given that undisclosed observation took place on a second phase of data collection, even if it was in a public domain site, anonymity and confidentiality protection of members' data was secured. All the quotes were anonymised in order to protect the identities/pseudonyms of the members. Moreover, I have also translated the material from Portuguese to English to prevent messages (and their authorship) from being traced back to the forum archive.

The practice of the meal in the AB age

There is a general consensus in the forum that the arrival of Bimby in the home significantly transformed everyday life, particularly cooking practices and meal preparation. Members distinguish two important periods in their lives: 'BB' and 'AB' ('Before Bimby' and 'After Bimby', playing with the calendar expressions AD and BC). Such periods are associated with a particular way of cooking and meal preparation, more traditional (BB) or more modern or scientific (AB).[6] Thus, for many members the period BB is associated with repetitive and monotonous meals; the need for various kitchen utensils (e.g. pans and pots, wooden spoons, scales, grinders, blenders, stoves); washing and cleaning dishes; a feeling of boredom in daily cooking; stress when preparing meals for a big party in order to satisfy different tastes; a lack of technical cooking skills which were more visible and prevented more adventurous cooking; less appraisal and positive comments from family and friends regarding cooked meals; demanding time coordination of different practices, leaving a feeling of being harried at all times. As explained poignantly by two members in the chain text 'Bimby changed my life':

> I never had an aversion to cooking but during 'BB' I felt I was losing too much time on useless tasks (chopping onions, tomatoes, stirring pots) and always ended up cooking the same dishes.
>
> (Female, unknown age, one child)

> The time Before Bimby (BB): The mashed potato – there was no patience to make it, not even with an electric food mill. The Jam – how many hours standing up, stirring with a wooden spoon and the dangers of burns! The crème brûlée – always stirring to avoid burning, the milk spilling out and the dirty stove; always crying when chopping onions; the chopped garlic and the smell in the hands; the Choux dough! The dishes unwashed! An endless list of annoying and time-consuming tasks.
>
> (Female, 46 years old, married, two teenagers)

On the contrary, the AB age is considered a happy and pleasurable one, where cooking and preparing meals is effortlessly done. Some of the features that characterise the AB period are the variety and diversity of recipes and meals taken; the eagerness to experiment more and produce meals that were considered too skilful, time consuming or complicated before Bimby;[7] the possibility of handling many other practices at the same time (e.g. children's bathing; doing the laundry; posting messages and pictures in the forum; walking the dog; watching TV) because Bimby does not require close supervision – when a step in a recipe is accomplished, it warns the cook by beeping; encouraging creative cooking; increasing self-esteem as cooking skills are praised by family and friends. As one member points out:

> Everyone is pleased with the arrival of Bimby! Every day we come together for a good long meal, the conversation flows. These moments with the family around a table are just as important! We eat better, a full meal, from starters, juices, soup to dessert. I have more time to do what I like and everybody is willing to help. Sometimes while we have dinner Bimby is making a dessert.
>
> (Female, 46 years old, married, two teenagers)

The possibility for increased simultaneity and synchronisation of several practices while preparing or eating meals is one of the most mentioned advantages by Bimby users. Many allude to the fact they have more time to do other things while Bimby is cooking their meals. Thus, practising with Bimby makes time, and for that reason, many members associate it with labour-saving technology as it releases time for competing practices, some of these involving spending more quality time with children. This is aligned to Southerton's (2006) study where domestic technologies are used to reorder and resequence hot spots (busy times at work or at home) to create space for 'cold spots' (quality time with family and children) (see also Truninger, 2013: 91).

Moreover, despite many women in the forum using Bimby in their daily practices to help them juggle harried everyday lives – and several justify this feeling as they have to work a 'second shift'[8] – some comment about the existence of paradoxes in Bimby time-use. This technology does not always open up a space for quality time spent with children, and sometimes it even demands more time:

> The entry of 'magic' [refers to Bimby] in my life made all the difference. I increasingly like to cook and experiment new dishes. The problem is that sometimes so much culinary dedication steals time to play with my daughter, but as we don't live from air I have to cook the food.
>
> (Female, 48 years old, one daughter)

> I can't say I have gained time because now I spend a lot more time in the kitchen. But with great pleasure! I am eager to experiment everything, specially the recipes posted in this forum. My kids have been also influenced. I can only say that there is definitely a life before Bimby and another one after Bimby, like before and after Christ.
>
> (Female, 35 years old, two small children)

In this sense, and following similar findings on the relations between time, technologies and practices (Shove, Trentmann, & Wilk, 2009; Shove & Southerton, 2000) Bimby helps to create temporal order while scheduling, re-sequencing and coordinating meal preparation and cooking (serving as a *compass* that orientates meal practices), but, simultaneously, it can be interpreted as an object that consumes time. As Southerton claims 'practices come with sets of requirements necessary for competent and meaningful engagement' (2006: 440). Bimby has this double capacity of producing and consuming time, depending on how it is incorporated into particular dynamics of social practices that, undoubtedly, vary across disparate forum members' households. As another woman in the forum reports:

> I do not think I decreased the time I spent in the kitchen:) I think that the time is the same but the difference is that instead of doing one fast meal while hanging my clothes up, tidying up the fridge, and setting up the table.... I do everything calmly now … with much more time … and still make a soup, a meal, juice and a dessert!) So for me the time in the kitchen did not change. I just make 3 more dishes, calmly and without getting worried about stirring pots and control the clock.
>
> (Woman, unknown age)

This kitchen appliance enables the fragmentation of practices into their component parts and the insertion of more tasks in one block of time, without triggering a feeling of harriedness, but instead one of calm and relaxation (Truninger, 2013). Thus, and according to Shove, Trentman and Wilk (2009: 6):

> Rather than seeing material objects as a distracting presence that injects stress and temporal frenzy into our lives, then, it is helpful to see them also as communicators and stabilizing devices which people employ to attain, reproduce and challenge temporal identities.

The appropriation of Bimby for preparing and cooking home meals also triggers a set of views and expectations about what is a meal and how it should be cooked, as will be described in the following section.

Meal expectations, propriety and conflict

The entry of Bimby in the family home can be a stabiliser of meal routines or it can open up spaces of disruption, tension and conflict around family meals, due to different conceptions of what a meal should be and how it should be cooked. The forum has an entire section dedicated to these tensions and conflicts within the family. One woman in her introductory post opens her heart and describes how she lacks in motivation to cook with Bimby, given constant clashing with her husband over what constitutes meals and cooking.

In this specific case, the Bimby purchase never had the entire approval of her husband, and meals prepared with the Bimby were snubbed and criticised by him.

> My husband did not agree that I bought the machine but because I was really keen to buy it he agreed to share half of the costs in our wedding anniversary.... I gave half of the money and he put the other half, but he has always been very critical of Bimby and nagging me for a bad purchase … he doesn't like the meals, always complains, he only likes the rice.
>
> (Female, 44 years old, two teenagers)

Several other members, who replied to the original post, confessed to have the same problem with their husbands, due to a different understanding of what a meal is and how it should be cooked. These differences arise from meanings and conceptions of what is a 'traditional' way of cooking – with the help of pots and pans – where meals are cooked from scratch and by hand and take longer, compared to a modern or 'scientific' way of cooking – with Bimby – where meals are prepared quickly, inside a sealed container with less 'human' intervention. Husbands' complaints revolve around food taste, which is considered different when food is cooked with Bimby.

> My husband also complains about Bimby, with the exception of bread and cakes that he likes. He says that food in Bimby has a different taste … but I actually don't agree as I add my own seasoning as I usually do when I cook in a pan. My advice is that you should make the food in Bimby but don't tell him it was cooked in it, sometimes I do this myself.
>
> (Female, 42 years old, married, young child)

However, there were also husbands who were initially against buying a Bimby but eventually got totally hooked to it, as this young man reports:

> I am one of those husbands who did not want to buy Bimby because of the price. But fortunately my wife convinced me to buy it and I now love to 'bimbar' [to cook].
>
> (Male, married, 28 years old)

However, for those struggling with their husbands' approval several strategies were used. These included pretending that meals were cooked in pots and pans and deliberately placing dirty pans in the sink as 'evidence', or 'winning by the stomach' and preparing their husbands' favourite dishes in the Bimby.

> There are men who are a little 'jealous' when Bimby comes into our home. It happened to me as well. My advice is to try to make some simple dishes they usually like, such as beefsteak with fries and a fried egg

on top or roast chicken with potatoes in the oven. Then back to do some cooking with Bimby, again simple dishes that always work like a Portuguese stew or beans stew with meat and chorizo ('feijoada'). And simple desserts such as puddings. You will see that resistance to Bimby will decrease and with some persistence he will begin to accept more elaborate dishes. And positive thinking, because if he likes the food you make in a pot it is because he values you as a cook, and this is very good!

(Female, 47 years old, married, two teenagers and a baby of 22 months)

Concerns to please their husbands, children, friends and other family relatives with their meals were brought up many times by the members. It was important to cook a meal with Bimby that was fully appreciated by their loved ones. The recognition of their Bimby mastery by loved ones increased self-esteem among women in the forum (but also among the few male members) and created a sense of achievement for well-accomplished cooking practices and a feeling of pleasure for feeding the family appropriately. This confirms that mechanisms of living up to ideals of motherhood, domesticity and family life are still very much present among middle-class working mothers, as previous studies have reported more than 20 years ago (DeVault, 1991). What is considered a 'proper' meal, a 'proper' way of cooking with Bimby was monitored daily, based on the feedback received from family and friends after the meal. Both criticism and praise were crucial to calibrate quality standards (conventions of propriety) and revise or develop skills and competences in the practice of cooking and preparing meals with Bimby. As described in the following section, skills and competences were developed while seeking advice in the Bimby forum.

Competence and virtual brand communities

The Bimby forum was a crucial platform to improve competences and provide feedback, praise and advice to their members, encouraging them to continue the development and reproduction of meal practices with the help of Bimby. The forum was at times used as a source of knowledge regarding proper handling of Bimby but, importantly, was also a source of gratification and self-esteem reinforcement (matching both functional and social values). Several tips, tricks and the testing of recipes pervaded many topics and posts in the forum, where a true virtual community of practice emerged. Given that many of the users had to learn how to use the Bimby, a number of members used the forum to clarify doubts, understand the use of some functions, and revise and correct some of the recipes in the official Bimby recipe book (some recipes in the book, when tested, did not work in practice). Many members also looked for recipes in the forum as a source of inspiration to prepare something different from their routine meals. Often women were with their laptops in the kitchen (see Denegri-Knott & Jenkins, Chapter 8) while cooking with Bimby, looking for recipes on the forum, asking questions to clarify a step in a recipe, posting pictures of their meals, or encouraging other women to face off their fears of failure while trying to master Bimby. The posting of pictures was an important step to gain confidence in being competent in preparing meals with Bimby, but also as a source of gratification. Each time someone posted a good recipe or a picture of their meals, and after having posted more than 50 messages, they were entitled to receive points from other members. As points (or rotations) accumulated, members would step up the ladder of prestige within the forum, being recognised as 'experts' in the use of Bimby.[9] Thus, the forum was far beyond a mere platform for technical clarification:

> What I did not expect after purchasing Bimby was to gain a new world of interests and friendship when I found out about this forum. It was in April that I discovered this forum and with it my life changed a little bit more. It was after finding out about this forum that I started using Bimby more often. And because of this I found out a new passion and hobby: cake decoration. Well done to all the women who are here and contribute to our well-being, to increase and improve our self-esteem as cooks, and above all, as women.
>
> (Female, 25 years old, recently married, no children)

Conclusions

In this chapter I was able to demonstrate that Bimby is a thought-provoking technology useful to examine how its users appropriate it to prepare meals, how it helps to coordinate but also disrupt the practice of the meal, and the significance of virtual brand communities in both developing competences and reinforcing inner goods associated with Bimby cooking practices. By looking at the forum accounts of this virtual brand community I have shown that this kitchen device has the capacity for both producing and consuming time, depending on how it is incorporated into the particular dynamics of social practices that vary across members' households. The use of the Bimby also triggered different conceptions and understandings of meal preparation and cooking, sometimes opening up harmony and togetherness within the family but at other times provoking conflict and tension.

Evidence of alliances between Bimby and other technologies was also exhibited in the analysis of the forum. For instance, the successful use of the Bimby was many times enhanced by the use of laptops. The latter employed to clarify doubts in the forum, look for recipes or post pictures of the final outcome of dishes produced with Bimby. Although virtual brand communities do not give access to the 'actual' meal practices or uses of Bimby, they offer a glimpse into the ebb and flow of routinised behaviour around meals, mediated by this technology. As mentioned in the introduction to this chapter, the Bimby had the capacity to communicate, translate and frame possibilities for enacting meal practices in particular ways.

One important aspect this study sheds light on is the fact that the meal may perhaps be better analysed as the outcome of an orchestration of several practices in everyday life. In this vein, technologies may either help or disrupt such orchestration, depending on how they are incorporated into everyday life and appropriated by its users. Therefore, future research could focus on the uses of this technology for meal preparation, namely in offline contexts, it being important to understand the consequences of grasping the practice of the meal as composed of a plethora of participants: technologies, humans and other animals (e.g. pets).

Notes

1 This kitchen appliance is made by the German company Vorwerk and it is called Bimby solely in the Portuguese and Italian markets – elsewhere it is known as Thermomix – due to copyright protection of an earlier appliance with the name Thermomix in these two southern European markets. The price of this appliance is considerably high compared to other kitchen gadgets (the most recent Bimby model (TM5) launched in 2014 is officially sold for €1109 Euros or around £925). The previous model was TM31 (shown in Figure 7.1) launched in 2004, this is the model that features in many Portuguese homes given the increase of sales in the country over the last ten years.

2 See http://thermomix.vorwerk.co.uk/what-is-thermomix/ [Accessed February 2015].

3 In the last few years a grey market has emerged driven by customers who want to sell this kitchen appliance, either because they need the cash or they ended up finding it useless. As to the official sales, in 2013 they have increased worldwide up to €800 million (17 per cent rise compared to the previous year). Portugal also increased its sales that year by 5.5 per cent with a volume of €37 million, even though it was being hit by hard economic times (Vorwerk, 2014).

4 An analysis of the topic 'Introductions' where several members introduce themselves describing their socio-demographic profile, among 100 presentations, I found that a majority were working mothers with small children, from the ages of 30 to 40 years old. The ones that revealed their professions described themselves as teachers, journalists, public servants, unpaid domestic labourers ('full-time mothers'), engineers, nurses, social workers, accountants, among others. Thus, most fit a middle-class profile and live in an urban area with easy access to the Internet. However, given this is an Internet virtual community of Bimby fans, it does not characterise in a comprehensive way the Bimby purchaser or user. According to the company representative in Portugal, Bimby cuts across several social classes (see Truninger, 2011).

5 In 2009, I registered as a member of ForumBimby.com with a login username and password. I introduced myself and explained who I was, my affiliation and research aims. I have acquainted myself with the forum, its organisation, structure, language, main topics of discussion, type and number of members, their relationships and existing hierarchy. Repeated online browsing and non-participant observation of the forum took place over three months in 2009 and 2010. I have also conducted six in-depth interviews that lasted between 1 and 3 hours with forum members.

6 In one post a member described having Bimby as 'I have the wonder of science (Bimby)'. Many members in several posts contrasted what they call a 'traditional' way of cooking with a 'modern' way of cooking. The former describing the time before Bimby where pots and pans were used, and the latter as the period after Bimby identified with a 'revolution' in the kitchen. Such revolution implies

gaining new competences to work with the device, skills to decode recipes as they are written using a particular language and symbols that need to be learned (e.g. 10s/speed 9; inverted spoon), speeding up meal preparation, ability to multi-task, less handling of ingredients and further distance from the food-preparation experience (less peeling, chopping, washing) that affects the use and development of particular sensory skills (sound) to the detriment of others (smell). Plus, Bimby is many times anthropomorphised (it is called 'Maria' or is understood as a 'person', a member of the family) and gives rise to a new language: the verb to cook (cozinhar) is transformed into 'bimbar'; new expressions appear such as 'fantastic dinner' (jantar fantástico) that becomes 'jantar bimbástico' (Truninger, 2011, 2013).

7 As reported by forum members, the Bimby has some technical capacities that allow the cook to control the heat with a lot more precision than normal cooking (e.g. stoves), considerably reducing the risk of burning things while preparing food. This enhances the confidence of the cook to experiment with more laborious and adventurous dishes and step out of their comfort zone.

8 The overburdening of women is a well-identified problem in Portuguese society. According to recent data, domestic and care work in that country is among the most gender unequal in Europe (Aboim & Vasconcelos, 2012: 4–5), thus, the 'second shift' (domestic work after normal full-time working hours) is a common trait among married or co-habiting Portuguese women.

9 The Bimby forum allows members to visibly increase their standing relative to others. There are two main indicators of standing: speed and rotations (lingo used in Bimby recipes). Regarding speed, from 0 to 50 posts, members have no stars; from 51 to 100, members get one star, from 101 to 150 they get 2 stars and so on until they reach the top with 6 stars (after 350 posts). Once reaching the top of the scale they are labelled 'Bimbólico' (i.e. addicted to Bimby), which indicates the members' popularity. As to rotations, they refer to the number of points (or 'likes') members get whenever they post something others appreciate (e.g. a good recipe, a helpful technical clarification, or something casual such as a funny episode with the Bimby that makes everybody laugh). Only after 50 posts are members allowed to give or receive rotations. The more rotations the more the member's reputation increases in the forum.

References

Aboim, S., & Vasconcelos, P. (2012). *Study on the Role of Men in Gender Equality in Portugal*. Brussels: European Commission Report.

Brannen, J. (2005). Time and the negotiation of work-family boundaries: Autonomy or illusion? *Time and Society, 15*(1), 113–131.

Brannen, J., O'Connell, R., & Mooney, A. (2013). Families, meals and synchronicity: Eating together in British dual earner families. *Community, Work and Family, 16*(4), 417–434.

British Psychological Society. (2013). Ethics guidelines for Internet-mediated research. INF206/1, Leicester: The British Psychological Society. Available at: www.bps.org. uk/search/apachesolr_search/ethics%20guidelines%20for%20internet-mediated%20 research [Accessed 23 July 2014].

Cova, B., & Pace, S. (2006). Brand community of convenience products: New forms of customer empowerment – the case 'my Nutella The Community'. *European Journal of Marketing, 40*(9/10), 1087–1105.

Coveney, J. (2006). *Food, Morals and Meaning: The Pleasure and Anxiety of Eating*. London: Routledge.

DeVault, M. L. (1991). *Feeding the Family: The Social Organization of Caring as Gendered Work*. Chicago, IL: University of Chicago Press.

Douglas, M. (1972). Deciphering a meal. *Daedalus, 101*(1), 61–81.

Julier, A. (2013). Meals: 'eating in' and 'eating out'. In A. Murcott, W. Belasco, & P. Jackson (Eds.), *The Handbook of Food Research* (pp. 338–351). London: Bloomsbury.

Kaufmann, J.-C. (1998). *Dirty Linen: Couples and their Laundry*. Middlesex: Middlesex University Press.

Kaufmann, J.-C. (2010). *The Meaning of Cooking*. Cambridge: Polity Press.

Kowsmann, P. (2013). Even in straitened times, Portugal loves its Bimby cooking robots. *Wall Street Journal*. Available at: www.wsj.com/articles/SB10001424052702 3044038045792626302057379984 [Accessed 7 March 2014].

Kozinets, R. (1998). On netnography: Initial reflections on consumer research investigations of cyberculture. *Advances in Consumer Research, 25*(1), 366–371.

Kozinets, R. (1999). E-tribalized marketing? The strategic implications of virtual communities of consumption. *European Management Journal, 17*(3), 252–264.

Marshall, D. (2005). Food as ritual, routine or convention. *Consumption Markets and Culture, 8*(1), 69–85.

Marshall, D., & Anderson, A. (2002). Proper meals in transition: Young married couples on the nature of eating together. *Appetite, 39*(3), 193–206.

Meiselman, H. L. (Ed.) (2009). *Meals in Science and Practice: Interdisciplinary Research and Business Applications*. Cambridge: Woodhead Publishing Limited.

Murcott, A. (1982). On the social significance of the 'cooked dinner' in South Wales. *Social Science Information, 21*(4/5), 677–695.

Reckwitz, A. (2002). Toward a theory of social practices: A development in culturalist theorizing. *European Journal of Social Theory, 5*(2), 243–263.

Rousseau, S. (2012). *Food and Social Media: You are What you Tweet*. Plymouth: Altamira Press.

Schatzki, T. (2002). *The Site of the Social: A Philosophical Account of the Constitution of Social Life and Change*. University Park, PA: Pennsylvania State University Press.

Shove, E., & Southerton, D. (2000). Defrosting the freezer: From novelty to convenience – a narrative of normalization. *Journal of Material Culture, 5*(3), 301–319.

Shove, E., Pantzar, P., & Watson, M. (2012). *The Dynamics of Social Practices – Everyday Life and How It Changes*. London: Sage.

Shove, E., Trentmann, F., & Wilk, R. (Eds.) (2009). *Time, Consumption and Everyday Life*. Oxford: Berg.

Sicilia, M., & Palazón, M. (2008). Brand communities on the internet. *Corporate Communications: An International Journal, 13*(3), 255–270.

Southerton, D. (2006). Analysing the temporal organization of daily life: Social constraints, practices and their allocation. *Sociology, 40*(3), 435–454.

Suler, J. (2004). The online disinhibition effect. *CyberPsychology & Behavior, 7*(3), 321–326.

Truninger, M. (2011). Cooking with Bimby in a moment of recruitment: Exploring conventions and practice perspectives. *Journal of Consumer Culture, 11*(1), 37–59.

Truninger, M. (2013). The historical development of industrial and domestic food technologies. In A. Murcott, W. Belasco, & P. Jackson (Eds.), *The Handbook of Food Research* (pp. 82–108). London: Bloomsbury.

Truninger, M., & Freire, D. (2014). Unpacking the Mediterranean diet: Agriculture, food and health. In N. Domingos, J. M. Sobral, & H. Weat (Eds.), *Food Between the*

Country and the City: Ethnographies of a Changing Global Foodscape (pp. 191–206). London: Bloomsbury.

Vorwerk. (2014). *Vorwerk Annual Report 2013*. Vorwerk & Co, KG.

Warde, A. (2005). Consumption and theories of practice. *Journal of Consumer Culture, 5*(2), 131–153.

Wenger, E. (1999). *Communities of Practice. Learning, Meaning and Identity*. Cambridge: Cambridge University Press.

8 The digital virtual dimension of the meal

Janice Denegri-Knott and Rebecca Jenkins

Introduction

In a not so distant future 3D food printers are poised to take over the preparation of our meals, lightening the load of meal preparation by taking on 'the difficult parts of making food that is hard and/or time consuming to make fully by hand' (Foodini, 2014). Similarly, food photocopiers that reproduce the molecular structure of food hold the promise of repurposing leftovers into brand new meals (Electrolux, 2009). This future may be unpalatable to some because it supposes a corrosion of human knowledge and a brutal displacement and reduction of human competence by ever-increasing automation of domestic practices within the home kitchen (see for example Fırat & Dholakia, 1998).

A less extreme, but more present infiltration of technology within the kitchen is that of devices like tablets, smartphones and laptops that are routinely used in preparing meals. Based on a global survey of 7,000 cooks, Allrecipes.com (2013) found that nearly half of respondents used smartphones while shopping for food, while almost a third of American and UK cooks surveyed were said to routinely use their mobile phones to find recipes. Through these devices home cooks can access an array of food-related content including step by step tutorials on *YouTube*, recipes and recipe reviews on specialist foodie websites and blogs, and themed meal ideas on *Pinterest* boards. We refer to these devices as digital virtual (DV) devices in that they open up new spaces and opportunities for the home cook. The integrative ontology of the digital virtual (see Molesworth & Denegri-Knott, 2012; Denegri-Knott & Molesworth, 2010; Shields, 2002) that we use here enables us to navigate and consider how consumers' minds (their imagination, memory and knowledge), the digital virtual spaces located on the screens like *YouTube* and BBC *Good Food* website, as well as the device itself – as a physical artefact, interact in practice. For us, this helps to overcome some of the essentialism that is inherited by perspectives that create clear demarcations between reality and virtuality (for a critique see Denegri-Knott & Molesworth, 2010; Shields, 2002) which deny the presence of constitutive elements of practice, their various locations and how they come into play, in this case, during meal preparation.

While popular, the presence of DV devices in the kitchen may raise concerns about the growing digitisation of meal preparations, which sees technology as driving the transformation of human practices. A way of eliding the technology determinist standpoint, where use of DV devices like tablets is seen as displacing human labour, is by adopting a practice-based language to account for how human and non-human actors come together in configuring practice. Adopting this approach has two key consequences for our understanding of doing the meal. First, it enables us to document in detail the many ways in which meal practices are transformed when knowledges, skills, and competences necessary to carry out practices around meal preparation are not only distributed across enthusiastic home cooks and material artefacts (such as hand mixers, food processors, cookers, freezers, recipe books and instruction manuals) and other people, but also located in digital virtual space. Second, it helps us see the kind of new meal work that is required from the home cook in maintaining the coupling between the cook and their devices.

In this chapter we discuss the intersection between DV devices and food consumption and the resultant practices they configure. Drawing on insights gleaned from in-depth interviews with 29 cooking enthusiasts living in the South of England, we provide an overview of new configurations, placing emphasis on the ways in which various components of practice – knowledge, competence and commitment – are redistributed between our home cooks and their DV devices. While we acknowledge the significance of ultimate goals, which are to be substantiated and attained through meal work, for example the expression of caring parent or competent cook (Molander, 2011; see also Molander, Chapter 11) and work on meal preparation as a meta-practice of love and motherhood, here we focus less on the teleoaffective, or goal dimension of practices to deal with specific meal-related projects and tasks, like knowing how to decorate a pirate chest birthday cake or make gluten free bread. In this way we can better hone in on the way in which the coming together of technology and the home cook produce new forms of doing meal work (see Truninger, Chapter 7).

Theoretical context

Our starting point is that competence is central to carrying out practices, and as Watson and Shove (2008: 77) have noted, competence is best understood as 'distributed between practitioners and the tools and materials they use'. Meal preparation should be approached not only as a human achievement but one that is in effect distributed among a range of appliances, utensils and ingredients.

In their study of DIY, Watson and Shove (2008) propose that product development enables amateurs to tackle jobs that would otherwise be left undone or require a tradesperson to complete. Power tools, for instance, make 'lighter' work of physically demanding tasks. In the kitchen a food processor or bread machine provide the same kind of assistance. Other products have more profound effects, modifying the relation between process and result. In their DIY example, Watson and Shove (2008) note that the development of fast-drying non-drip water-based paints means even a first-time painter can produce an acceptable finish on a panelled door, which had previously been a complicated process requiring a certain level of time, skill, knowledge and experience. Today, paint technologies mean fast-drying non-drip paints 'know' how to go onto a door.

The bringing together of scattered fragments of knowledge enables this task to be completed by a novice. Knowledge within the human, the instructions on the paint tin, the paint itself and the equipment used to apply it come together, such that painting is only achievable in the 'doing'. From this perspective it is evident that competence is not only a human quality but is redistributed between person and technology, such that they become a human non-human hybrid (Latour, 1993). Put differently, in our case, a cook with his rolling pin or food processor has a different set of capabilities than one without them.

Like the fast-drying paint described by Watson and Shove (2008), the role of appliances in the kitchen have more dramatic effects on practice than just reducing the load of physically demanding or time consuming tasks – they reconfigure the way in which the practice of meal preparation takes place and the results that can be achieved (Truninger, 2011). How the practice is carried out is also subject to a practitioner's commitment to the practice, by that we mean, how competent a practitioner an individual wants to become. More specifically, commitment includes the desire to cultivate even more specialised skills and knowledge and their ambition to embark on more challenging projects. Differing levels of commitment create distinctions between practitioners, from novices and amateurs to professionals and experts (Watson & Shove, 2008; Warde, 2005).

In further considering the various tools and materials used in the practice of food preparation, and in line with the concept of the human non-human hybrid (Latour, 1993) enabling individuals to enhance and extend their capabilities, we draw on Clark and Chalmers' (1998) work on the 'extended mind' as a way to account for the cognitive aspects of practice that DV devices enhance.

The extended mind in practice

Just as tools enable a human to perform activities they otherwise wouldn't be able to, so too can 'external features' enhance cognitive abilities. Clark and Chalmers (1998) account for behaviour (change) based on this very notion – i.e. DV devices extend the mind of the cook (as well as the skill level and actual practices engaged in) in the same way that a microwave or food mixer extends the practice. Thus, in the same spirit as the human non-human hybrid in practice theory, we use Clark and Chalmers' (1998) work on the extended mind as a framework with which to view the use of DV devices enhancing the cognitive aspects involved in practice, which subsequently inform and change that practice.

Clark and Chalmers (1998: 8) note that humans have a general tendency to 'lean heavily on environmental supports', that is, humans make use of various external sources as an extension of the mind and this enhances the cognitive abilities of individuals and the practices in which they engage. As Clark and Chalmers (1998: 10) state; 'in a very real sense, the re-arrangement of tiles on the tray [in Scrabble] is not part of action; it is part of thought'. We argue that DV devices form part of this general tendency that, by using DV devices individuals delegate some of the cognitive work that goes into their cooking practices, whether it may be learning a new technique from a *YouTube* tutorial, or being able to 'forget' a recipe because it is safely available online at any time. Thus, commitment to some aspects of meal practices would be redistributed between cooks and their devices.

Similar to Latour's (1993) notion of hybridisation, Clark and Chalmers (1998) talk about external entities (objects) and humans as 'coupled systems'. This coupling creates an extended cognitive system just as the hybrid creates an extended human actor. If we remove the external component (i.e. the rolling pin or DV device) 'the system's behavioural competence will drop' (1998: 8–9) – the practice can no longer be engaged in as proficiently. Like-wise, if external features change, so too will behaviour. Indeed, when such components are removed or unavailable, there is a 'de-coupling' – in these instances, we might assume that the practice cannot be engaged in at all because the internal cognition alone is not sufficient to enact it. When successful, reliable coupling between an individual and an external feature occurs (i.e. it is always 'there' when I need it) they become 'part of the basic package of cognitive resources that I bring to bear on the everyday world' (Clark & Chalmers, 1998: 11). In the spirit of this, we want to explore just how much DV devices have become part of the package of cognitive resources when it comes to everyday meal preparation.

Methods

We conducted in-depth interviews with 29 self-described cooking enthusiasts who used DV devices in their cooking practices during a four-month period in 2014. The people we spoke to came from a variety of backgrounds and cultures but all lived in the South of England. The majority of the people we spoke to were female (see Table 8.1 for details), this was not by design but was indicative of the response to our call for participation – a message posted on the university staff forum and a local school's parents' forum – and a common occurrence in research related to domestic life (Beagan, Chapman, D'Sylva, & Raewyn Bassett, 2008).

Interviews ranged from one to two hours in length and followed a phenomenological approach, focusing on lived experiences (Thompson, Locander, & Pollio, 1989) of cooking and uses of DV devices within meal preparation and related practices. We asked about recent experiences, early experiences, as well as memorable experiences of cooking, both good and bad, with and without DV devices. Such an approach enabled us to focus on concrete experience and get a sense of how DV devices have been adopted and used in relation to cooking and the meal. As much as possible, interviews were conducted in the participants' homes and photographs of kitchens, appliances, cookbooks and DV devices used in cooking were taken to enhance the interview data. Initially, the authors undertook data analysis separately via a detailed reading of each interview transcript in order to generate an idiographic analysis of each interview. Global themes were then identified across transcripts and between the authors (Spiggle, 1994; Thompson et al., 1989).

Findings

In this section we illustrate and discuss emerging configurations where knowledges, commitment and competences necessary to carry out meal practices are not only distributed between enthusiastic home cooks, material artefacts and other people (e.g. Watson & Shove, 2008; Hand & Shove, 2007; Latour, 1993), but now to DV devices. These new configurations make certain meal projects and tasks achievable because DV devices take on or augment our home cooks' knowledge and competence. The devices also absorb some of the commitment in the practice by taking on the role of remembering, storing and producing new ideas for meal projects so that the home cook no longer needs to. However, we also find that the coming together of these configurations is dependent on our home cooks' ability to become competent users of DV devices.

New DV devices and meal practice configurations

Our home cooks made use of DV devices throughout the 'life' of the meal. They turned to DV devices to get ideas for what to cook, to help them achieve broader goals, such as being a good dinner party host or not being wasteful, as well as specific tasks like preparing different components of a themed dinner party menu or finding ways to make use of a glut of apples. Our home cooks also used DV devices as a shopping aid – smartphones were routinely used in the supermarket to locate a specific recipe in order to buy the necessary ingredients. In the kitchen, DV devices facilitate the preparation and cooking process, for instance, locating an instructional video on *YouTube* about how to de-shell scallops. After the meal has been prepared and consumed DV devices are used in a variety ways, from photographing food, sharing it on social media, and as a tool to document the cooking and eating experience for later retrieval and use. Such extensions presuppose that meal preparation is now as much about handling DV devices as it is handling food.

As a new link in the configuration of meal practices, DV devices also produce displacements and re-alignments among other active links in the

Table 8.1 Participants' profile

Pseudonym	Age	Gender	Status	Nationality	Type of cook
Katherine	35	Female	Co-habiting, no children	British	Adventurous, experimental
Gina	35	Female	Married, no children	Polish	Likes experimenting, lacks confidence, prefers 'simple' meals
Sophie	24	Female	Co-habiting (with Richard), no children	British	Prioritises cooking, experiments
Richard	28	Male	Co-habiting (with Sophie), no children	British	Prioritises cooking, experiments
Viv	46	Female	Single, no children	British	Good cook, likes to follow recipes
Nicki	41	Female	Married, two children	British	Hearty, traditional, competent cook. Lacks finesse
Rosanna	31	Female	Married, expecting first child	British	'Cowboy Cook' – experimental (cooks based on ingredients in cupboards)
Hannah	41	Female	Married, two children	British	Adventurous, competent; loves food and cooking
Elizabeth	47	Female	Married, five children	British	Competent cook, 'cheats' when busy
Paula	47	Female	Married, one child	British	Good baker, likes to be inventive
John	45	Male	Single	British	Competent cook
Maria	28	Female	Married, one child (baby)	Columbian	Good cook, better baker. Lacks confidence
Ike	26	Male	Single	Thai	Confident cook, enjoys cooking
Sara	36	Female	Married (to Gino), no children	Italian	Experienced enthusiast, cooks from scratch every day

Name	Gender	Age	Marital status	Nationality	Cooking description
Gino	Male		Married (to Sara), no children	Italian	Experienced enthusiast, passionate about cooking
Angela	Female	23	Single, no children	Canadian	Fairly average cook in terms of skills
Maya	Female	24	Single, no children	Canadian	Proficient baker, less proficient cook, likes to follow recipes
Claire	Female	22	Single, no children	British	Keen baker, good cook. More skilled in baking than cooking
Dave	Male	23	Single, no children	British	Adventurous, wants to develop technical cooking skills
Abby	Female		Single, no children	British	Recent enthusiast
Kristin	Female		Single, no children	American	Adventurous, competent, excited about cooking
Kumi	Female		Single, no children	Japanese	Needs to plan cooking, not creative
Jim	Male	24	Single, no children	Vietnamese	Competent cook, loves cooking
Julian	Male		Single, no children	British	Began training as a chef
Ana	Female	25	Single, no children	Russian	Creative cook
Kate	Female	22	Single, no children	Norwegian	Loves baking, likes to put her own twist on recipes
Lucy	Female	29	Co-habiting, engaged	British	Creative cook, makes use of what she has, doesn't like to waste food
Vicki	Female	25	Single, no children	British	Experimental, doesn't like to follow recipes
Lara	Female	26	Married, no children	German	Careful cook, sticks to recipes

configuration. Cookbooks and magazines are re-aligned, their role re-purposed. While most of our home cooks disclosed a preference for DV devices, this was not always at the expense of cookbooks, magazines, or other hardcopy forms of recipes and related cooking material – indeed, our home cooks often used DV devices in conjunction with other sources (see Hewer, Chapter 9).

Viv is 46 and lives alone. She enjoys cooking and is often looking for healthy meals as she attends a weekly slimming club. Viv described cookbooks as '*a bit like my porn*'; she will happily sit and read them and she enjoys the lovely photography, which gives her ideas and gets her taste buds going. Despite the great amount of pleasure she gets from cookbooks, when actually cooking or planning a meal she prefers to use DV devices, to the extent that she even 'googles' recipes she has in specific cookbooks because it is easier than finding the book and getting it down from the top shelf of the big wardrobe where she keeps them. Here she describes the ease and appeal of the Internet over cookbooks:

> It's a bit more, the books I tend to flick through until I see something I like whereas, perhaps if I'm looking online I'm starting with something specific, I might go off on a tangent but I'm starting with something specific, either the type of event or the type of food that I want to do. So, I don't know, if it's a vegetarian meal or a pasta meal or if it was a birthday cake or something, I have that as much more of a focal point, whereas the books I tend to think 'I'll look at Nigella, Jamie and Gordon', get three or four books down and start flicking through and maybe put those back and find some others, just until something inspires me. But online, everything's so quick, you can bring pictures up so easily you can think 'yes, I'm doing that' and it's a much quicker decision than the books, the books I kind of get a bit waylaid with reading them and thinking 'I like that, I like that, I like that', whereas online is a bit more instant.

This preference for DV devices as being quicker, easier and offering a wider variety than cookbooks was echoed by most of our home cooks. The notion that these devices offer more exciting options was particularly preferred, especially when cooking for other people and wanting to showcase cooking skills. Often our cooks expressed no desire to memorise recipes or come up with their own ideas for what projects to embark on. This we can see as an example of commitment to the practice being delegated to the device – the device is tasked with 'thinking' for and 'storing information' on behalf of the home cook. However, this didn't detract from their determination to become more competent practitioners, rather they bypassed some of the mental work (e.g. remembering a recipe) to focus on the 'doing'.

When asked to reflect on their usage of DV devices in meal preparation, many of our cooks reported that they had substantially expanded the repertoire of meals they now cooked on an everyday basis as well as how they had increased the complexity of the meal projects they took on. A 31-year-old expectant mum called Rosanna eagerly showed us photos of the many creations she had saved in her home computer or posted on Facebook (see Figure 8.1). There were colourful children's cakes, infused chilli oils, kale meatballs and Easter treats for friends. She was particularly proud of a pirate chest cake she had baked and decorated for a friend's pirate-themed birthday party. While she had a general idea of what she wanted her cake to look like, she struggled at first to visualise, and then to assemble it:

> Um, there is going to be 40 children, want something spectacular. So I had gone and searched through and found a really good, I suppose it was less of a recipe and more kind of instructions you know, making your chocolate sponges, use like a chocolate fudge so it's quite thick for your icing and then it just had really good ideas of, you know, just carving out the middle, filling it with gold coins and sweets that look like jewels and you can get the sweets that are bracelets and things and I just absolutely filled it with that and made a lid from another sponge and put little hinges on it. Got some gold icing and made brackets and hinges and a lock and it looked like it did in the pictures. I was so pleased and it was a very simple set of instructions just very clear, this is how you do it, this is the process to follow. And I think he was, when we delivered the cake he was speechless, bless him. It went down really well.

As illustrated in Rosanna's experience, the practice of preparing the cake of course brings together ideas, knowledge, tasks, other people's desires, her appliances, and her level of skill and commitment, which we have seen reported in studies where DV devices are not prominent (e.g. Hand & Shove, 2007; Shove & Watson, 2007), but what is interesting here, is that the very idea of what to cook is delegated to the DV device. In everyday life, such ideas may be constrained by a number of variables such as our home cooks' time constraints, level of competence, the produce they have to hand or the occasions they are cooking for. While such contingencies characterise the use and role of devices in the meal preparation, what is significant is that DV devices are seen as central components of meal work.

Rosanna's story is telling of the ways in which these devices are felt as extending the ability to generate ideas. Rosanna searches for 'something

Figure 8.1 Rosanna's stored photographs of cooking achievements.

spectacular' and finds 'really good ideas' about how to get the carving done and the kind of 'coins and sweets that look like jewels'. The language that Rosanna and other participants used talking about how *YouTube* or an App gave them ideas of what to cook is indicative of the ways in which the device is perceived as extending the mind. Twenty-four-year-old postgraduate student Maya told us: 'if I don't get an idea by myself I will go the Internet and see what kind of recipes were there'. It was also common practice for our home cooks to input the food produce they had available in their cupboards and fridges in the hope that the device would magic up some inspiration – some even had specialist apps like Jamie Oliver's, Nigella's and the Hummingbird Bakery, which 'sort of works out what you want to make' (Maya, 24).

Coupling work

We can see DV devices as extending the minds of our cooks, augmenting the cognitive resources mobilised in cooking, but requiring work on the part of the cook to access and sustain. By 'extending' we mean that the device is active in driving the cognitive process that augments or extends the cognitive capability itself (see Menary, 2010; Clark & Chalmers, 1998). This is seen as a form of epistemic action (Kirsh & Maglio, 1994) which demands that links or 'coupling' between mind and device are made to constitute a new cognitive system and in turn, enable or enhance the practice. The process of coupling is useful here, as it helps us bring into focus the kind of efforts that are needed in linking cooks to their DV devices, and then to other appliances and people involved in the configuration of practice. While the notion of coupling continues to be at the heart of animated debates within the field of psychology (see Menary, 2010) what we report on here are the ways in which our home cooks expressed experiencing such devices as augmenting their ability to think about and do meal projects. Specifically, we found that most of our home cooks felt 'as if' they were linked to their DV devices at all moments of the cooking process – in thinking about what to cook, the prepping, executing and documenting of their results.

One of the home cooks we spent time with was Jim, a young Vietnamese postgraduate student. His kitchen was compact and replete with food and utensils. He had been cooking at a more 'skilled level' since his early 20s when he started to look for new ways of cooking, finding new tips and becoming better at using the equipment he had in his kitchen. He noted how with competence came a desire to upgrade his utensils. At the time of our interview, we noticed how his *iPad* was placed in a prominent location next to the chopping board, alongside food produce and in close proximity to the cooker. When he cooked he *iPaded*. He subscribed to a number of *YouTube* channels, like *Gordon Ramsay* and *Food Wishes*, which he routinely checked to find inspiration for his meals (see Figure 8.2). All these preferred resources had been saved in his *iPad*, many of them were held in apps or 'cooking utilities', like *EverNote Food*, *Foodily*, *Knorr*, and *Cookbook*. In telling us about *EverNote Food* he said:

> Here are some apps like EverNote Food.... I can write down what I have cooked before and record their recipes, the proportions, my feelings after I ate it so that I can keep it for later, try and learn from my previous try.

To Jim the writing and learning from past mistakes was important, he often complained of the many times he had wasted a good piece of steak because of his ineptitude. Ruining steak he explained had been 'such a memorable experience for me when I failed making it. So the following times that I tried making it I usually took note of the things that I need to remember.' When he stated he 'needed to remember', he was referring to a remembering that is performed in conjunction with his *iPad*, or put differently, when his mind was 'coupled' to his *iPad*. All that he needed to remember – cooking times and food handling tips – were carefully annotated in his *EverNote Food* app, such that the *iPad* becomes part of what Clark and Chalmers (1998) refer to as the cognitive resources that he brings to bear on his everyday cooking practice.

Achievement of this redistribution of cognitive capacity hinges on the coupling work, demanded first from Jim, to activate the device as a coupling device as described by Clark and Chalmers (1998). *EverNote Food*, a proprietary software designed to aid note-taking and archiving in particular, was the target of extended coupling work. Jim had three bespoke sections where he documented his meals – what he liked and disliked, adding photos of his achievements, and building recipe books and a diary where he annotated his feelings after eating them. For those that didn't recur to such involved curatorial practices, the coupling process was initiated in an ad hoc fashion. Many simply 'bookmarked' recipes, saved them to 'favourites', pinned them to *Pinterest*, uploaded them to *Dropbox* or reported that it was easy enough to find the recipe you found last time, they simply 'googled' key words and recognised the sources they had initially used.

Figure 8.2 Jim getting ready to chop, watching Gordon Ramsey on YouTube.

It is important to highlight the fact that if DV devices are to be considered as extending minds they must, as Clark (2003, 2010a, 2010b; Clark & Chalmers, 1998) emphasises in his work, be at all times successfully coupled or linked to the people who use them – meaning that they must be reliably available when needed, the information easily retrieved and endorsed more or less automatically (Clark & Chalmers, 1998). So it follows, if our home cooks are to remain coupled to their devices, they needed to establish the link or couple with the device. Coupling work was made up of a series of tasks that the device operated in the automatic, reliable and seamless way described by Clark and Chalmers (1998) – 'bookmarking' content, 'backing up' content to *Dropbox*, pinning recipes and ideas on *Pinterest* and using specialist software like *EverNote Food*.

DV devices and new cycles of discovery

That there is a process through which coupling is made and maintained shifts our understanding of DV devices, not only as the centre of epistemic action (Clark, 2003, 2010a, 2010b; Clark and Chalmers, 1998) but also as 'epistemic objects' (Knorr Cetina, 2001). By that we mean that DV devices as objects to probe with are open ended and complex. Their lack of objectivity and completeness makes them oblique or always partial, which provokes a further cycle of discovery – for instance the search for better, more original recipes, or clearer tutorials.

The search for a recipe opens up the possibility that a new process or ingredient, unknown before, requires the cook's attention and thus ignites a whole cycle of discovery. During the interview process it became apparent that once scrutinised, recipes searched and found threw up new projects and tasks; for instance a simple search for gluten free bread led Elizabeth to a discovery of learning about coeliac and specialist ingredients. Elizabeth, mum of five children and part-time worker at a well-known department store has an ample kitchen with a central island, from where she showed us how she used her *iPad* when preparing meals. Elizabeth had recently entertained a group of friends, one of whom was a coeliac sufferer who she was keen to prepare something special for. She spent much of the interview telling us about gluten free bread she baked for the occasion. The search for a recipe for gluten free bread initiated episodes of discovery, where new leads about how to prepare a proper loaf triggered an unfolding of related questions and searches. She explains:

> Knowing what I like and what I've heard of, sometimes I'm not always very good at using things I haven't heard of or not knowing what things are. It's like with gluten free cooking, there's a lot of talk of xanthan gum, I haven't got it yet and don't even know where I'd go looking for it but I need to start asking the questions because to make a loaf of bread, because that obviously was done with buttermilk, but to make a loaf of

bread with gluten free bread flour and yeast and things like that, a lot of people on the Internet have said use this xanthan gum to bind it more, so I thought I have to go and find out what that is.

Temporary and relatively stable configurations for how meal practices are to be carried out need to be found. Doing so limits the potentially disruptive potential of endless possibilities made available through DV devices. It is also apparent that DV devices as epistemic objects need to be sufficiently stabilised or made known to the user if they are to retain their role as extending cognitive ability. Elizabeth had learned from previous experiences that *BBC Good Food* was a trustworthy source; there she had recognised the names of celebrity chefs whose books she had and whose recipes she had already trialled. She had also learned how to use rating systems to narrow down choices and then read related reviews (see Figure 8.3). She told us:

> I think what I'd done was, I'd put 'gluten free' and it came up with BBC Good Food and that was one of the things that had come up on BBC Good Food, if you click on that it comes up with about 20 recipes you see, that's where I got the bread from, though it only had a 3 rating but if you read it, if you go down here, some people have sort of said … I kind of, I read that and I know it sounds silly but when you read a review you look at the language that's used and it gives you an indication, I know it sounds silly and it might sound a bit snobbish, but you kind of get an indicator to who's cooking and I think that, I do take all that into consideration, who's cooking it, how they might've done it. Quite a lot of negative there where everyone around her or him was saying lovely things, nobody was saying anything bad really, I mean yes it says 'soggy, none of us could eat it' but to me that sounds like it hadn't been cooked long enough, it goes like moussey because it's buttermilk, when you mix it looks like a mousse and when you pour it in I was thinking 'oh my God what's it going to be like?', but you can smell it as it's cooking and it's delicious and it was very soft when it came out so I just thought I'd leave it to stand and it is a very soft texture.

Note how Elizabeth picks a recipe with a general rating of 3, because she attributes this relatively poor rating to ill-informed comments, judged so because she 'gets an indicator of who's cooking' and 'how they might have cooked it', that is out of step with others' comments. Her own cooking knowledge is mobilised to explain how a negative reviewer hadn't baked the bread long enough, noting how the bread goes 'like moussey because it's buttermilk' and therefore a premature bake would produce a soggy result. The chosen recipe was saved in her *iPad* and subsequently revisited when she wanted to bake it again for her family to enjoy. The same procedure was also repeated with tutorials she found and trialled on *YouTube*. This again, was done by way of not having to remember recipes by heart, knowing that they could be easily retrieved.

Figure 8.3 Elizabeth's bookmarked gluten–free sundried tomato bread.

Conclusion

In these emerging configurations, the DV device operates as an 'extension of' our cooks' minds (Clark & Chalmers, 1998), augmenting their capacity to come up with meal ideas and retain meal preparation knowledge (recipes, dinner party ideas) and reducing the cognitive load involved in meal preparation. Devices like laptops, tablets and smartphones extend our cooks' cognitive processes (imagining and remembering) and rely on the successful coupling between devices and cooks. This, as we found, required substantial investment from our home cooks who had to continuously gauge the value, relevance and trustworthiness of the meal preparation knowledge they came across. It is this concept of coupling that we see as instructive in helping us account for the complex configurations that result from the integration of DV devices in the practice of cooking. We also note how, in these emerging meal practice configurations, devices absorb or take over tasks previously undertaken by cooks and other material artefacts, causing displacements and re-alignments. While we purposefully did not focus on the teleoaffective dimension of practice or the role of other people in them, we encountered plenty of evidence to indicate they were important links. Future research could bring to the fore this social dimension, highlighting how DV devices make present new social links in the meal practice, for instance providing an audience for successful meal projects that are showcased on social media, and sourcing inspiration from other people connected to DV platforms. Interaction with DV devices often presupposes a high level of interaction with others through these devices, which are little known and deserving of attention.

References

Allrecipes.com. (2013). Allrecipes surveys thousands of cooks worldwide to capture global digital food trends. Available at: http://press.allrecipes.com/press/allrecipes-surveys-thousands-of-cooks-worldwide-to-capture-global-digital-food-trends/ [Accessed 23 June 2014].

Beagan, B., Chapman, G. E., D'Sylva, A., & Raewyn Bassett, B. (2008). It's just easier for me to do it: Rationalizing the family division of foodwork. *Sociology, 42*(4), 653–671.

Clark, A. (2003). *Natural-Born Cyborgs: Minds, Technologies, and the Future of Human Intelligence.* Oxford: Oxford University Press.

Clark, A. (2010a). Memento's revenge. In R. Menary (Ed.), *The Extended Mind* (pp. 43–66). Cambridge: Massachusetts Institute of Technology.

Clark, A. (2010b). Coupling, constitution and the cognitive kind: A reply to Adams and Aizawa. In R. Menary (Ed.), *The Extended Mind* (pp. 81–100). Cambridge: Massachusetts Institute of Technology.

Clark, A., & Chalmers, D. (1998). The extended mind. *Analysis, 58*(1), 7–19.

Denegri-Knott, J., & Molesworth, M. (2010). Concepts and practices of digital virtual consumption. *Consumption, Markets and Culture, 13*(2), 109–132.

Electrolux. (2009). Interview with Nico Kläber (Moléculaire) Electrolux Design Lab finalist. Available at: http://group.electrolux.com/en/interview-with-nico-klaber-moleculaire-electrolux-design-lab-finalist-2040/ble [Accessed 23 June 2014].

Fırat, A. F., & Dholakia, N. (1998) *Consuming People: From Political Economy to Theatres of Consumption*. London: Routledge.

Foodini, (2014). *Company Mission*. Available at: www.naturalmachines.com/press-kit/ [Accessed 23 June 2014].

Hand, M., & Shove, E. (2007). Condensing practices: Ways of living with the freezer. *Journal of Consumer Culture, 7*(1), 79–104.

Kirsh, D., & Maglio, P. (1994). On distinguishing epistemic from pragmatic action. *Cognitive Science, 18*(4), 513–549.

Knorr Cetina, K. D. (2001). Post-social relations: Theorizing sociality in a post-social environment. In G. Ritzer, & B. Smart (Eds.), *Handbook of Social Theory* (pp. 520–537). London and Thousands Oaks, CA: Sage.

Latour, B. (1993). *We Have Never Been Modern*. Hemel Hempsted: Harvester Wheatsheaf.

Menary, R. (2010). *The Extended Mind*. Cambridge: Massachusetts Institute of Technology.

Molander, S. (2011). Food, love and meta-practices: A study of everyday dinner consumption among single mothers. In R. W. Belk, K. Grayson, A. M. Muñiz, & H. Schau (Eds.), *Research in Consumer Behavior, 13*, 77–92.

Molesworth, M., & Denegri-Knott, J. (2012). *Digital Virtual Consumption*. New York: Routledge.

Shields, R. (2002). *The Virtual*. London: Routledge.

Spiggle, S. (1994). Analysis and interpretation of qualitative data in consumer research. *Journal of Consumer Research, 21*(3), 491–503.

Thompson, C. J., Locander, W. B., & Pollio, H. R. (1989). Putting consumer experience back into consumer research: The philosophy and method of existential-phenomenology. *Journal of Consumer Research, 16*(September), 133–146.

Truninger, M. (2011). Cooking with Bimby in a moment of recruitment: Exploring conventions and practice perspectives. *Journal of Consumer Culture, 11*(1), 37–59.

Warde, A. (2005) Consumption and theories of practices. *Journal of Consumer Culture, 5*, 131–153.

Watson, M., & Shove, E. (2008). Product, competence, project and practice: DIY and the dynamics of craft consumption. *Journal of Consumer Culture, 8*(1), 69–89.

9 Fraught contexts and mediated culinary practices

Ontological practices and politics

Paul Hewer

> *The modern world is a 'runaway world': not only is the pace of social change much faster than in any prior system, so also is its scope, and the profoundness with which it affects pre-existing social practices and modes of behaviour.*
>
> (Giddens, 1991: 16)

> *I'm so excited that you're stepping into the world of 15-minute meals. The promise of this book is simple: delicious, nutritious, super-fast food that's a total joy to eat and perfect for busy people like you and me.*
>
> (Oliver, 2012: 8)

Introduction

This chapter stages anew a set of ideas made over a series of papers on the importance of food and cooking as a site for the understanding of contemporary practices (Brownlie & Hewer, 2010, 2011; Brownlie, Hewer, & Horne, 2005). Practice theory is currently on trend, a ready-made staple to restate the importance of social theory for the understanding of contemporary contexts. A key theorist of practice is Pierre Bourdieu, but theories of practice transcend Bourdieu and can also be traced to alternative sources. This chapter reviews the work of such alternative sources, namely Giddens (1991) and de Certeau (1984; see also de Certeau, Giard, & Mayol, 1998) to explore the key insights which such works deliver. The chapter seeks to explore the value of turning to celebrity chefs to better understand the forms of worlding which they offer up. In this manner it considers celebrity chefs as cultural intermediaries who are worthy of analysis for the cultural tales and myths that they offer up for rethinking practices, routines and conventions. Moreso, it suggests that part of their appeal lies within the cultural responses they articulate and make explicit to the shifting and troublesome contexts we inhabit.

The landscape of global culinary culture shifts and turns with rapid abandon; cooking has always been big business and a thoroughly mediated experience at that. A while back we wrote of walking into a bookshop (Brownlie et al., 2005); now a tour of the mega-mall that is Amazon is more likely, or clicking on an app through which we can glimpse and buy into all manner of culinary delights brought to life through the efficiencies and affordances of technology. TV programming has moved on too, from the Food Network with its staple of *30 Minutes Meals* and *Quick Fix Meals*, to the UK 8 o'clock timeslot, with tales of *Mastercheffing* and the domestic pleasures of the *Great British Bake Off*. Cooking is a screened spectacle at its most rhythmic; televisual, performed and choreographed to keep at bay and ameliorate the troubles of contemporary living: of emerging wars on the horizon, of civil unrest, racial tensions and the streets ablaze with disaffection and disbelief, of the squeezed middle, of class wars around culture, of pay freezes and food bank living, of poverty and domestic abuse on the rise. Food programming in such troubled contexts has a necessary predictability and familiar rhythm to its screened pleasures and fictions. *Bad News*, as the Glasgow group of media studies once termed this phenomenon, opens up a space for compensation and respite. To take seriously what Silverstone terms the *mediation of everyday life*: 'the fundamentally, but unevenly, dialectical process in which institutionalized media of communication are involved in the general circulation of symbols in social life' (2007: 109). In this manner, if the cookbooks of yesteryear (Brownlie et al., 2005) were about stylisation over substance, or what Cappellini and Parsons (2014) term 'stylish food for all', cookbooks and their multiple appeals must take on a number of emergent and compelling forms to stage anew audience appeal in increasingly fraught contexts. This chapter seeks to outline some of those appeals.

Screening the practice of the meal

The practice of the meal is thoroughly medialised (Halkier, 2012), to draw our attention to the importance of representations, images and their canned delights, and to better understand them, not as mere froth or necessary distractions and fictions but as critical for understanding people's relations with themselves and each other. Perhaps the most obvious is the cult of personality and celebrity that has always been paramount in the world of TV chefs. Think only of the machismo of Gordon Ramsay, the laddishness of early Jamie Oliver (Brownlie et al., 2005), or the beauty and allure of Nigella Lawson (Brownlie & Hewer, 2010). The screen grants such mortals presence, charismatic authority and the promise of imagined worlds of consumption for us all to dwell within if only for an hour or less. But, in a world of austerity where the clamouring pressures of duty and responsibility reign supreme, such baubles of affectation, such images of taste and status, can however quickly lose their appeal so tales must be rethought, re-spun and re-crafted to take account of changing circumstance, import and context. Such changes hint at what Giddens refers to as 'deeply structured changes in the tissue of everyday life' (1991: 17). From the moment of stylised cheffing to a counter-world of provisioning, caught in this shift are the supermarkets that are quickly losing their appeal (e.g. Tesco, Sainsbury's), and the switch to price consciousness where the likes of Lidl, Aldi and the newly revamped Netto[1] speak of contrasting market solutions in a climate in which pressure drops are all too necessary. From appearances and the stylisation of TV chefs in culinary contexts, to a renewed faith in necessity and austerity at all costs, supermarket loyalty is therefore recalibrating and notions of loyalty on the wane; why be loyal in a world that lacks commitment? Price comparisons are everywhere and now shopping around for whatever recipes life has to offer is on trend and encouraged by the supermarkets themselves. For as Giddens suggested:

> Modernity is a post-traditional order, in which the question, 'How shall I live?' has to be answered in day-to-day decisions about how to behave, what to wear and what to eat – and many other things – as well as inter-preted within the temporal unfolding of self-identity.
>
> (1991: 14)

By this token, cultural intermediaries such as celebrity chefs, while easy to dismiss as irrelevant to the rituals and conventions of food as lived (Marshall, 2005), might be worth revisiting for the cultural tales and myths which they offer up for rethinking practices, routines and conventions; for understanding the shift in focus from the festive and celebratory to the everyday and mundane.

Save, save, save new routes for a saved life: need for money, time and speed

> Waste of time is thus the first and in principle the deadliest of sins. The span of human life is infinitely short and precious to make sure of one's election.
>
> (Weber, 2007 [1930]: 104)

If price comparisons are everywhere, the second coming will also be better achieved with a need for speed and the holy grail of saving kitchen time. Grasping time, saving it, regaining it and losing it has always been an existential concern but also a device through which cookbooks can potentially stand out in cluttered markets of choice. For Weber (2007 [1930]), our relationship with time was a critical ingredient of the spirit of capitalism as expressed through our everyday conduct in modern culture. This was most clearly articulated in the writings of the puritans such as Benjamin Franklin where 'Time was money', so that saving time became a route to salvation and the sense of one's own election. Money, time and kitchen life thus have a certain elective affinity.

The message that saving time is all-important can also be gleaned from a quick tour of contemporary cookbooks. Think here of the cookbooks which advertise themselves on the basis of quick-and-easy solutions to tribulations and trials of the everyday. Austerity thus speaks of time paucity as much as financial fasting and the gnawing feeling of indebtedness (see Cappellini,

Marilli, & Parsons, Chapter 4). Survival strategies for contemporary living thus centre on the home front and its ethos of time-space reorganisation. The best starting place for such an argument to be staged is a return to the more recent books published by Jamie Oliver (2012, 2013). Brand Oliver is now worth an estimated £150 million and employing 7,000 people worldwide (Frith, 2014), with its own philosophy and ethos on contemporary life; and in his 2013 offering *Save with Jamie: Shopping Smart, Cooking Clever, Waste Less* (2013) the ontological concerns of the everyday are updated and revised:

> Jamie gets the nation cooking clever, shopping smart and wasting less with his new cookbook, 'Save with Jamie'. This year, I've got the message loud and clear that as everyone comes under bigger and bigger financial pressure, they want help to cook tasty, nutritious food on a budget, so this book was born completely out of public demand. Save with Jamie draws on knowledge and cooking skills to help you make better choices, showing you how to buy economically and efficiently, get the most out of your ingredients, save time and prevent food waste. And there's no compromise − I'm talking big flavours, comfort food that makes you happy, and colourful, optimistic dishes. Our biggest luxury is knowledge, whether times are hard or not, so get kitchen smart and smash the recession.
>
> (Oliver, 2013, backpage)

The ethos of saving time is on the rise with shopping that is smart and convenient the only way forward. Saving time or what Miller (2009) refers to as 'buying time' is that most ontological of concerns, reminding us as Giddens (1991) suggested that identity work 'unfolds temporally' so that nobody can remain immune to its pressures, exigencies and passing. Brand Oliver and its characteristic brand imaginary does not fail in this regard with two recent offerings which address and speak to such doubts over time-scarcity and the lack of time we continue to experience. Here the USP (unique selling proposition) of a celebrity brand can often be understood in relation to its ability to ameliorate, if only symbolically and in the final instance, the contradictions and tensions of contemporary living: or as Brand Oliver prefers: '15-Minute Meals is a frame of mind.... It's fun, dynamic, no-nonsense cooking' (2012: 10). Here the difference between market failure or market success is best marked by the ability to disturb and unsettle the culinary everyday. The dialectic of the celebrity chef brandscape speaks of and through macro forces, changing contexts of austerity and the practices of *shopping smart* and *cooking clever* to hail an audience as 'busy people'. Fast food is the not the only game in town, but the importance of cooking time proves that Brewis and Jack hit the nail on the head when they suggested that the motto of 'faster, *faster*' (2005: 64), or as I prefer the *need for speed* ethic, was emerging as a key cultural sensibility.[2] Life is now lived in metered terms, the metrics of performance surround us all so that merely drifting, simply doing nothing, or wasting time are unsustainable in the short-term for the long haul. Take *Jamie's 15 Minute Meals* (2012) or *Jamie's 30 Minute Meals* (2010), which tackle these issues head on, or as the blurb for *30 Minutes* reveals:

> The 50 brand-new meal ideas in this book are exciting, varied and seasonal. They include main course recipes with side dishes as well as puddings and drinks, and are all meals you'll be proud to serve your family and friends. Jamie has written the recipes in a way that will help you make the most of every single minute in the kitchen. This book is as practical as it is beautiful, showing that with a bit of preparation, the right equipment and some organization, hearty, delicious, quick meals are less than half an hour away. With the help of Jamie Oliver and Jamie's 30 Minute Meals, you'll be amazed by what you're able to achieve.

The art of organisation, preparation and reorganisation thus come to the fore in our efforts to save those most scarce of commodities in contemporary living: time and money. Brownlie et al. (2005) hinted at this dynamic within the Brand Oliver narrative, when they glimpsed the forms of calculative rationality at work, to argue that a particular form of lifestyling and stylisation of life was being practised and offered up in the early incarnation of the *Naked Chef*. But times change, cultural moods shift and a celebrity chef looking for continued market success over market failure in *Liquid Times* (Bauman, 2010) must always be alert to such changes, ready to rethink its positioning, ready to reimagine itself and its recipes for living if it is to stay relevant and on trend. For as sociologists have revealed, the 'harried' consumer confronting a 'time squeeze' is often looking for 'time-shifting devices' (Warde, 1999: 522; see also Southerton, 2003).

Celebrity chefs appear to answer this call. In this regard, recipes for time-shifting come in a range of shapes and sizes but easy solutions for tricky dilemmas and the erasure of ontological insecurities will always resonate. For as Giddens suggested: 'The maintaining of habits and routines is a crucial bulwark against threatening anxieties, yet by that very token it is a tensional phenomenon in and of itself' (1991: 39). The screening of the practice of the meal and its associated cooking practices thus speaks to forms of 'emotional inoculation against existential anxieties – a protection against future threats and dangers which allows the individual to sustain hope and courage' (Giddens, 1991: 39). That is how practices, routines and conventions, while appearing fixed and timeless, resistant and immutable, remain open to the exigencies of shifting contexts, especially when those contexts speak of new forms of vulnerability and poverty and the necessity for forms of pressured release. For, as Cappellini and Parsons suggest, such texts remain critical for identity projects so that their performative and transformative potential must alert us to their functions as 'living things' (2014: 93).

For Simmel, the sociological significance of the meal expresses itself through the social interactions it offers up, that is: 'the meal becomes a sociological matter, [when] it arranges itself in a more aesthetic, stylized and supra-individually regulated form ... specifically with regard to the *form* of its consumption' (1997: 131). Celebrity chefs by this reckoning stylise and aestheticise the mundane and the everyday, market success resides in their ability to re-enchant mundane consumption through the cultural forms they bring to reshaping markets in their own image. To valorise everyday practices and routines remains their goal, to anchor and make meaningful such practices and routines. In this respect it is no coincidence that *saving money and time* and *buying time* are embedded in their logic and market appeal as these remain essential ingredients to the spirit of capitalism in its modern form. For, as Giddens suggested: 'creativity *as* a routine phenomenon is a basic prop to a sense of personal worth and therefore to psychological health' (1991: 41). Well-being and personal transformation in the domestic space of the kitchen are part and parcel of this new recipe for living, and such forms of *hoping* and *feeling* converge with the will for market and brand success.

It was Erving Goffman who in *Gender Advertisements* (1979) best captured this spirit and logic, when he suggested that: 'Advertisers conventionalise our conventions, stylise what is already stylisation, make frivolous use of what is already something considerably cut off from contextual contours. Their hype is hyper-ritualisation' (1979: 84). The logic of hyper-ritualisation appears to be at work when we seek to explain the logic and appeal of celebrity brands, easy to discount as trivial, easy to dismiss as illusions and fantasy beyond the real stuff of everyday life and ritual, but significant perhaps in explaining the culinary imaginary at work through representations and performance. That is how practice demands a *modus operandum*, a recipe for living, if it is to make sense and become common sense widely distributed and available for all. More so, as Schatzki (2001) revealed, practices are best understood as a set of actions, so that folded within practices are states of one's life as expressed as 'one's ongoing involvement in the world' and contained with this orientating are notions of 'desiring, hoping, feeling, believing, expecting, seeing' (2001: 48).

It is perhaps in this manner that we should understand such shifting representations around cooking practices for nestled within such images and culinary tales lies a shifting politics of ontology. Law and Benschop (1997), when discussing *ideas of difference*, are more explicit on this performative quality when they suggest:

> To represent is to perform. To represent is to generate distributions.... To represent is to narrate, or to refuse to narrate. It is to perform, or to refuse to perform, a world of spatial assumptions populated by subjects and objects. To represent thus renders other possibilities impossible, unimaginable. It is in other words, to perform a politics. A politics of ontology.
>
> (1997: 158)

The politics of ontology which Brand Oliver awakens reveals how celebrity brands converge and speak to popular mythologies of the everyday offering up new forms of practical and collective magic, especially geared around *desiring*, *hoping* and *feeling*. Brand Oliver in this regard looks like a simple tale of heroic masculinity, a storying of the celebrity brand and its distribution through all manner of forms of talk, be they those encapsulated in the images, the recipes, the social media posts, the updates, the apps.

The performativity of celebrity brands such as Brand Oliver must be reckoned in terms of their potential for changing and disturbing practices and conventions, not simply to affirm or to absorb the status quo but as 'the gap, the rupture, the spacing that unfolds the next moment allowing change to happen' (Dewsbury, 2000: 475). Perhaps in this way we witness how they might offer up inspiration and new forms of innovation. Domestic culinary tales, as I have sought to argue, speak to troubled and fraught contexts for market success. Here we enter novel territory, how practices such as those around *identity work* and the *idea of difference* may lose their appeal and demand to be recast. How *taste* and *distinction* are sometimes not enough for ontological security and how practices and routines may emerge for an audience looking for solutions for new dilemmas in troubled contexts. Necessities and fictions – sayings and the things we tell ourselves to get by – much like their associated practices and ways of doing are not fixed or merely static but open to change. A perspective which brings us neatly to the labours of the kitchen and the market opportunities therein.

Labours of love and market opportunities

> Good cooks are never sad or idle – they work at fashioning the world, at giving birth to the joy of the ephemeral.
>
> (de Certeau, Giard, & Mayol, 1998: 222)

Theories of practice are many, and theorists of practice come in a range of shapes and hues. So far we have encountered Giddens (1991) but other options remain on the culinary academic menu. Bourdieu (1984) reads the kitchen for *difference*, for symbolic struggle and as a site for classification and *Distinction*. In this telling the habitus occupies a central place as *the space of lifestyles*:

> The habitus is necessity internalized and converted into a disposition that generates meaningful practices and meaning-giving perceptions; it is a general, transposable disposition which carries out a systematic, universal application – beyond the limits of what has been directly learnt – of the necessity inherent in the learning conditions.
>
> (1984: 170)

Bourdieu reads the kitchen like a true social theorist for classification. For Bourdieu:

Taste, a class culture turned into nature, that is, embodied, helps to shape the class body. It is an incorporated principle of classification which governs all forms of incorporation, choosing and modifying everything the body ingests and digests and assimilates, physiologically and psychologically. It follows that the body is the most indisputable materialization of class taste.

(1984: 190)

Whereas de Certeau (1984) and de Certeau et al. (1998) read the kitchen as would a poet or kitchen dweller (Hewer & Brownlie, 2011) for poetics and aesthetic solutions. The practising of the meal must address the kitchen as practised, lived and a techno-saturated space, but also increasingly a marketised space. Here the kitchen is revealed as a prime site for *feeding the family* for provisioning and what Marjorie DeVault (1994) terms the *social organisation of caring*. In this time-space, familiar exploitations (Delphy & Leonard, 1992) of the division and unequal division of labours are harboured. Kitchens by this account are labouring spaces where the washing up and the wall of 'to-dos' remains. A labouring space for the production of the family and the home; a working space for jobs aplenty; a contradictory space; a space from which to anchor oneself and others as much as it is a space to escape from. Kitchens are also techno-saturated spaces (see also Hand & Shove, 2007). Kitchens remain a technological realm par excellence. If you are lucky enough the kitchen is home to a plethora of such devices from the mixers, blenders, coffee makers, kettles, to the heavy duty of washing machines and dishwashers and fridges. And now kitchens come equipped with televisions, radios, or homes to the mobile laptop and phone. By this reckoning, the kitchen houses all manner of techno devices which speak of its organising capacities allied with a range of everyday kitchen practices from cooking to cleaning, and caring to organise and reorganise one's life around (see Truninger, Chapter 7 and Denegri-Knott & Jenkins, Chapter 8).

The kitchen then exists as a laboured, temporal and practised space for anchorage in turbulent times. Think only of the devices which capture and visualise the shifting of time, the fridge that needs defrosting, the oven that demands setting, the egg timer with its familiar beat and rhythm, the kettle which never boils, the clamouring duties of breakfast, lunch, dinner and evening snacks. Marking time and the passage of time are thus endemic to kitchen living. Kitchens are perhaps the most punctuated domestic time-spaces, their timing and rhythm not as pronounced as work spaces but still measured and metered in their use of time, with the spirit of timing as a constant presence within such lived spaces. Not difficult to see then how such a conventionalised and practised space may be in need of a little livening up, a sprinkling of *hyper-ritualisation* as per Goffman (1979) or blatant celebrity brand merchandising, if we are to reimagine its contours and redefine its boundaries. Here lies the market opportunity: that is, how the materials, competences and troubles of kitchen life might offer a point of purchase for a little celebrity marketisation to be at work and find a home for an alternative domestic culinary imaginary. Not a sealed off hermetic space but porous and open to change and possibility; a space where branded celebrity merchandise – be this in the form of pots, pans, or funky knives – become 'touch points' for brand building and strategising.[3] A kitchen space in other words where pots, pans and all manner of techno devices might be enlivened through tools, gadgets and rethinking practices. The penultimate chapter of Michel de Certeau's *The Practice of Everyday Life* is tellingly titled: 'Ways of Believing: Believing and Making People Believe'. For de Certeau (1984), modern times are perhaps best captured through this spirit of waning belief:

> Believing is being exhausted. Or at least it takes refuge in the area of the media and leisure activities. It goes on vacation; but even then it does not cease to be an object captured and processed by advertising, commerce and fashion.
>
> (1984: 180)

Celebrity chefs and their associated brand merchandising thus trade in practised solutions – forms of practical magic to reawaken belief – offering up inspiration and innovation as emergent forms of belief and believing in troubled times.

Conclusion

This chapter has sought to understand the shifting brandscape of the celebrity chef brand that is Brand Oliver in terms of reimaging practices, routines and conventions. It has turned to the contexts of uncertainty that now surround us to unpack the contexts which such brands now operate within. Turning to Brand Oliver we witness its emergent celebrity appeals around innovative solutions for rethinking everyday practices. Saving time and money while sounding contemporary and on trend were revealed to be associated with the ordering and organisational practices of modernity. Celebrity brands like Brand Oliver spin culinary tales of saving time and money for continued market success, and those simple tales speak to ontological anxieties and everyday solutions, what Bauman (2010) termed the 'displacement of fears – from the cracks and fissures in the human condition' (2010: 13). Understanding practices, routines and conventions in such terms thus takes us to the terrain of ontological politics wherein practices are contextualised as a form of cultural politics embedded within the everyday (see Askegaard, Kristensen, & Ulver, Chapter 2). Here practices of transformation, salvation and well-being trade in and seek to perform renewed forms of believing in fraught contexts of disaffection. Culture as screened and practised thus becomes, as Bhabha (1994) intones:

> an uneven, incomplete production of meaning and value, often composed of incommensurable demands and practices, produced in the act of

social survival. Culture reaches out to create a symbolic textuality, to give the alienating everyday an aura of selfhood, a promise of pleasure.

(Bhabha, 1994: 172)

Herein culture, its labours and forms of consuming, becomes akin to 'a strategy of survival'. It is such survival strategies that we glimpse when we witness the forms of magic and practical belief practised by celebrity chefs: commercial success and personal salvation entangled and prescient for the *here and now* of consumption.

Notes

1 Lidl, Aldi and Netto are discount supermarkets in the UK whose fortunes have seen an upturn in the current economic climate. Celebrity TV Chef Nick Nairn has in this regard endorsed Lidl and its products. Available at: https://vimeo.com/29956735. [Accessed 1 July 2015].
2 A tour (22 June 2015) of UK retailer WH SMITH, also reveals that other (male) celebrity chefs have also responded to this call for speed and time-shifting through fast food. For example: Gordon Ramsay's *Fast Food: Recipes from the 'F' Word* (2009); James Martin *Fast Cooking: Really Exciting Recipes in 20 Minutes* (2013): Nigel Slater *Eat: The Little Book of Fast Food* (2013).
3 See http://ukbrandstrategy.com/2013/06/16/brand-touch-points-get-your-hands-dirty/ [Accessed 1 July 2015].

References

Bauman, Z. (2010). *Liquid Times: Living in an Age of Uncertainty*. Cambridge: Polity Press.

Bhabha, H. K. (1994). *The Location of Culture*. London: Routledge.

Bourdieu, P. (1984 [1979]). *Distinction: A Social Critique of the Judgement of Taste*. London: Routledge.

Brewis, J., & Jack, G. (2005). Pushing speed? The marketing of fast and convenience food. *Consumption, Markets and Culture, 8*(1), 49–67.

Brownlie, D., & Hewer, P. (2010). Nigella.com: celebrity brands and gastrocommunities. Paper presented at 10th Conference on Gender, Marketing and Consumer Behaviour, Ambleside, UK, 26 June 2010–29 June 2010.

Brownlie, D., & Hewer, P. (2011). '(Re)covering' the spectacular domestic: Culinary cultures, the feminine mundane and Brand Nigella. *Advertising and Society Review, 12*(2), 7–26.

Brownlie, D., Hewer, P., & Horne, S. (2005). Culinary tourism: An exploratory reading of contemporary representations of cooking. *Consumption, Markets and Culture, 8*(1), 7–26.

Cappellini, B., & Parsons, E. (2014). Constructing the culinary consumer: Transformative and reflective processes in Italian cookbooks. *Consumption, Markets and Culture, 17*(1), 71–99.

De Certeau, M. (1984). *The Practice of Everyday Life*. Berkeley: University of California Press.

De Certeau, M., Giard, L., & Mayol, P. (1998). *The Practice of Everyday Life, Vol. 2: Living and Cooking*. London: University of Minnesota Press.

Delphy, C., & Leonard, D. (1992). *Familiar Exploitation: A New Analysis of Marriage in Contemporary Western Societies*. London: Polity Press.

DeVault, M. (1994). *Feeding the Family: The Social Organization of Caring as Gendered Work*. Chicago: University of Chicago Press.

Dewsbury, J. D. (2000). Performativity and the event: Enacting a philosophy of difference. *Environment and Planning D: Society and Space, 18*(4), 473–496.

Frith, M. (2014). Has Jamie Oliver bitten off more than he can chew, *Telegraph* online, 2 February 2014. Available at: www.telegraph.co.uk/foodanddrink/10610978/Has-Jamie-Oliver-bitten-off-more-than-he-can-chew.html [Accessed 22 June 2015].

Giddens, A. (1991). *Modernity and Self-Identity: Self and Society in the Late Modern Age*. Cambridge: Polity Press.

Goffman, E. (1979). *Gender Advertisements*. New York: Harper and Row.

Halkier, B. (2012). *Consumption Challenged: Food in Medialised Everyday Lives*. London: Ashgate.

Hand, M., & Shove, E. (2007). Condensing practices: Ways of living with a freezer. *Journal of Consumer Culture, 7*(1), 79–104.

Hewer, P., & Brownlie, D. (2011). Articulating consumers through practices of vernacular creativity. *Scandinavian Journal of Management, 27*(2), 243–253.

Law, J., & Benschop, S. (1997). Resisting pictures: Representation, distribution and ontological politics. In K. Hetherington, & R. Munro (Eds.) *Ideas of Difference: Social Spaces and the Labour of Division* (pp. 158–182). Oxford: Blackwell.

Marshall, D. (2005). Food as ritual, routine or convention. *Consumption, Markets and Culture, 8*(1), 69–85.

Martin, J. (2013). *Fast Cooking: Really Exciting Recipes in 20 Minutes*. London: Quadrille Publishing Ltd.

Miller, D. (2009). Buying time. In E. Shove, F. Trentmann, & and R. Wilk (Eds.), *Time, Consumption and Everyday Life* (157–170). London: Bloomsbury.

Oliver, J. (2010). *Jamie's 30 Minute Meals: A Revolutionary Approach to Cooking Good Food Fast*. London: Michael Joseph.

Oliver, J. (2012). *Jamie's 15 Minute Meals*. London: Michael Joseph.

Oliver, J. (2013). *Save with Jamie: Shop Smart, Cook Clever, Waste Less*. London: Michael Joseph.

Ramsay, G. (2009). *Gordon Ramsay's Fast Food: Recipes from the 'F' Word*. London: Quadrille Publishing Ltd.

Schatzki, T. (2001). Practice minded orders. In S. Schatzki, K. Knorr Cetina, & E. von Savigny (Eds.), *The Practice Turn in Contemporary Theory* (pp. 42–55). London: Routledge.

Silverstone, R. (2007). *Media and Morality: On the Rise of the Mediapolis*. Cambridge: Polity.

Simmel, G. (1997). The sociology of the meal. In D. Frisby, & M. Featherstone (Eds.), *Simmel on Culture: Selected Writings* (pp. 130–136). London: Sage.

Slater, N. (2013). *Eat: The Little Book of Fast Food*. London: Fourth Estate.

Southerton, D. (2003). 'Squeezing time': Allocating practices, coordinating networks and scheduling society. *Time and Society, 12*(1), 5–25.

Warde, A. (1999). Convenience food: Space and timing. *British Food Journal, 101*(7), 518–527.

Weber, M. (2007 [1930]). *The Protestant Ethic and the Spirit of Capitalism*. London: Routledge.

Part III

Appreciation

10 Consuming the family and the meal

Representations of the family meal in women's magazines over 60 years

Teresa Davis, David Marshall, Margaret Hogg, Tanja Schneider and Alan Petersen

Introduction

Bourdieu refers to family as a 'social artefact':

> To understand how the family turns from nominal fiction into a real group whose members are united by intense affective bonds, one has to take account of all the practical and symbolic work that transforms the obligation to love.... This work falls more particularly to the women ... this means both the countless ordinary and continuous exchanges of daily existence.
>
> (1996: 25)

Costa (2013) describes how Talcott Parsons normalised the idea of the 'nuclear family' as the ideal form that fitted post-Second World War American society. This particular ideal worked with that era's post-war affluence, suburbanisation of homes and the growth of new consumer goods being manufactured. She suggests that while these idealised forms persist in popular culture, there has been much media writing around the demise of the (nuclear) family. She suggests that while the nuclear family may now seem an ephemeral ideal, the family in newer forms is being celebrated through practice and ritual. Her focus on time-space and emotion as anchors that 'construct' new sociological forms of family is an important one. In the data we present in this chapter, we attempt to identify these changes in the period of 1950s to 2010s as seen in magazine advertising in two magazines in Australia and the UK. While Costa's work focuses on 'family rituals' in a particular way, we examine family food rituals as depicted in the magazine advertising of this period. In particular we examine the role of women in maintaining the 'happiness' of the family through their emotional labour and food work.

This chapter focuses on the depiction of 'emotion work' (Chambers, 2001; DeVault, 1991) by women in 'producing family' through their care practices as seen in magazine advertising over the past 60 years. In particular it focuses on the 'ordinary and continuous exchange of daily existence' (Bourdieu, 1996: 22) that is, what is involved in preparing and consuming the family meal. It draws on a dataset of advertisements from two key popular magazines from Australia and the UK, covering the period 1950–2010.

DeVault (1991) dissects the complex organisation, negotiation and planning involved in the production of family mealtimes and reveals women's efforts as creative and persistent in this context. Much of this effort centres on creative use of food to materialise the idyllic 'happy' nuclear family. Cook (1995; see also Feder, 2007) suggests that mothers are expected to consume responsibly to keep the family happy and healthy. In this chapter we focus on the 'producer mother' who consumes to produce the family. She is the emotion manager, who uses a variety of tools for cleaning, cooking, and creating in order to keep the family smiling. This production of happy families is not an easy process, but is often presented as effortless in popular media (Tincknell, 2005). This chapter examines the particular depiction of women's constant efforts, attention and 'emotion maintenance work' through food, in order to materialise the emotions that reinforce the idea of family (see Molander, Chapter 11).

We situate our work in the context of the family as a site of discourse and practice. Within this field, we study how the gendered practices of feeding and care as affective work are integral to producing the family (Marshall, Davis, Hogg, Petersen, & Schneider 2014; Marshall, Hogg, Davis, Schneider, & Petersen 2014; see also Cappellini, Marilli, & Parsons, Chapter 4). We build on the work of scholars such as Murcott (1982), DeVault (1991), Sheridan (2000), Martens and Scott (2005), Chambers (2001), and Jackson (2009), and we examine how the emotion work of every day food is used to materialise the emotional links within an 'ideal/happy family'.

Women's magazines have long been considered an important cultural intermediary and implicated in actively producing particular feminine subjectivities. Anna Gough-Yates (2003: 5), taking a cultural perspective, suggests that she views 'the processes of production and systems of organisation of the magazine and advertising industries as discursive. These industries carry meanings about how such sites should be thought about and responded to by others.' Since Betty Friedan (1963) and her seminal critique of women's magazines in *The Feminine Mystique*, these magazines have been seen as spaces where femininity is produced and where women are called upon to consume ideal images of body, family, sexuality and food. The advertising within these magazines is not merely a fantasy world separated from the reality of everyday life. Schroeder and Borgerson explain: 'Advertising images are a central part of the experienced visual world. Reality and advertising do not constitute two separate spheres acting upon one another; advertising and the mass media contribute to the visual landscape that constructs reality' (1998: 161). Thus we focus on advertising images as a rich source of discourses about family and its forms.

Data collection and analysis

We chose two magazines because they are influential cultural vehicles that have been established in the UK and Australia for a significant period of time, and whose circulation and reach have made them important cultural influencers. *Good Housekeeping* (GH) has been rated eighteenth in UK magazine circulation, and if the free magazines are not considered, it is one of the top ten paid-for magazines.[1] Similarly the *Australian Women's Weekly* (AWW) is celebrating an eighty-year reign as the 'bible' for Australian women, dating from its launch in 1933. Its website describes it as a cultural icon.[2] Its circulation today stands at 451,235, with a 2.4 million readership (including the online version).

Using advertisements from *Good Housekeeping*, Martens and Scott (2005) showed how the depiction of cleaning changes over the years. Marten and Scott's study illustrated how useful a historical slicing method can be in covering the breadth and range of advertising imagery (Martens & Scott, 2005; Sheridan, 2000). This historical slicing approach is particularly useful for a study of the shifts and movements in discourses over time (Martens & Scott, 2005: 384). We used a similar historical slice sampling strategy for this study. We included advertisements from the first year of each decade from 1950 to 2010 in our dataset. This method allows for a longitudinal view of magazine content, broad enough to see the range of advertisements published over the decades. We included all advertisements that explicitly showed families eating a meal or implied depictions of family and meals. The authors independently coded, with 2 for Australia and 3 for the UK data. Any major discrepancies in the independent coding were discussed and a final code was arrived at by consensus between the coders. The open coding was then collapsed into collective thematic categories, these themes were used to build a larger conceptual picture of overall discourses around family and food within each decade. Finally these discursive themes in each decade were compared to other decades to get a longitudinal sense of shifts and changes if any.

We adopted a broadly Foucauldian visual discourse analysis approach to our dataset of advertisements. Foucault's work is useful in revealing how families are produced discursively. Practices, ideas about and representations of how to be a family are part of such discourses as is the knowledge of 'experts' who instruct us on the daily practice and routinised ways of behaving like a family (Woodward, 1997). Women's magazines represent one such cultural site where such knowledge is produced and exchanged (Odland, 2009; Woodward, 1997).

We approached this analysis as a form of 'visual technology of consumption' (Rose, 1999: 105). We did not rely purely on the visual, but used the visual in conjunction with accompanying textual material, to contextualise and holistically analyse meaning. We viewed these magazines as one cultural site where consumers are shown idealised ways of consuming, living and being (Rose, 2012; Schneider & Davis, 2010; Schroeder & Zwick, 2004).

These images allow consumers to compare themselves to the ideal families depicted in the advertisements and voluntarily accept/reject those ideals as the 'right' or normal way to be. This naturalises certain depictions of family, shaping and producing particular consumer subjectivities around this form. It also suggests specific practices. Cronin (2004) and Moor (2008) both reveal how advertising and branding serve as cultural intermediaries, shaping the consumer's view of production and consumption of products. This industry is therefore an important arbiter of consumption (a key part of the culture). Thus the (visual) discourses built around family and food, in these magazines, are key to understanding shifting discourses over time in these two cultural contexts.

Findings

We see some clear shifts across the decades in both sets of advertising data. The 1950s depict very similar themes of family and food. The family table is central to many of the food advertisements of this decade. The mother as the worker and patient producer of family meals is an unwavering and constant theme. In the latter decades (1980s, 1990s, 2000s and 2010s) the mother is depicted as both the producer of happy family (meals) and the consumer of these produced happy family (meals). This is a major shift that transformed the magazines' production of the mother as an individual consumer, who consumes not just for the family as a collective unit, but as an individual and as a woman.

The 1950s mother

In the 1950s we see the drawn image of the aproned woman, serving her family with a smile, standing by the dining table surrounded by a family delighted by her food work. Her food work has produced the smiles and the 'happy family' around the table. These images have drawings (rather than photographs) of the ideal nuclear family (father, mother and two or more children around the dining table). Typical of this is the Colman's Semolina advertisement (June 1950) from *Good Housekeeping* and the Heinz Tomato Soup advertisement from May 1950 of the *Australian Women's Weekly*. The GH Colman advertisement shows a clearly delighted family clustered around the dining table. Father in a suit (returned from work), the son raising his hands above his head in delight, daughter leaning in and the other son, stretching his hands towards the delicious semolina shortbread that mum has made. The mother facing the reader has just brought her freshly baked short-bread to the table. This picture is drawn in a pencil sketch style and fills the top left-hand quarter of the advertisement. The main headline declares 'trumps at tea time'. The top right-hand quarter of the page contains text that explains how semolina adds taste and flavour to sweets. The bottom half of the page has the brand name in large type.

This image is typical of this period echoed by the 1950s image in the *Australian Women's Weekly* where the Heinz Tomato soup advertisement has a similar 'sketch' drawing image at the top of the page. It only features the heads of the four members of the family. The mother's head appears to ask the question 'tomato soup tonight?' The mother's head is featured to the left of the page looking across the page at the other three members of the family (all of them look delighted at the suggestion). Most of the centre of the page is taken up by a tureen of soup, which is ornate with a lid and a silver serving spoon immersed in the rich red steaming liquid. A small image of the Heinz soup can appears on the bottom right-hand side of the larger image. The final tag line reads 'you know it's good because it's Heinz'. The body text of the advertisement (left of the soup tureen) reads:

> It's good fun for Mother to watch the spoons getting busy when the family tucks into big platefuls of piping hot Heinz Tomato Soup, it's so easy for Mother to give Dad and the Kiddies extra pleasure by asking for 'Heinz' every time she buys tomato soup.

The implication is that the woman/mother depends on her food work to gain vicarious pleasure through her family. Heinz helps her produce that pleasure for her family, and hence indirectly allows her to reinforce (produce) the joy of family.

The separation of the mother from the rest of the family, paying attention to what they want, and then delivering a delicious meal is seen in the Colman semolina advertisement as well. The mother standing at the table having produced food to delight her family, also produces the 'happy family'. In each of these advertisements, and many of the other advertisements of this period, the mother stands off to one side (usually next to the dining table/or the prepared food itself) offering it to the rest of the family. Her role is distinct and clear – she is the producer of the food and of the emotions of joy, happiness and familyness (Chambers, 2001). However her participation in the consumption is less often displayed. Thus the mother as a consumer appears only in the rare Mother's Day advertisement for chocolates or in advertisements for labour-saving white goods or devices that would help her 'produce' the happy family. Bordo (2004) describes this 'weight' of providing for the family while sacrificing herself, the self-denial and self-regulation of women's bodies by themselves, as normalised and even celebrated. This mother, who stands ready to serve her family, who is never seen to eat, but nurtures her family, is idealised.

The 1960s mother

In the 1960s we see few changes. In the GH advertisement for Scot paper towels, we see the 'sketch' figures of mother and daughter in the kitchen. The mother is tearing off a Scot paper towel and is turned towards a counter laden with Christmas food that the mother has prepared. The pudding and other desserts sit on the counter. On a table, behind which stands the young daughter, is a large roast turkey next to a gravy boat. The daughter is scraping the mixing bowl; with pudding mix (presumably) from the Christmas pudding behind her. The main text reads: 'Happy thought for Christmas.... Scot towels take over the kitchen.' It goes on in smaller type to say:

> so much is going on, so much to be done, wiping hands while rushing from preparing vegetables, to stuffing the bird and putting on the pudding, cleaning down the cooker while the turkey roasts ... they won't fall apart when used for jobs like blanching almonds, washing dried fruit or preparing the chestnut stuffing.

It then suggests that Scot paper towels with a towel holder would be a good Christmas present for a friend. No father or male child is seen in the kitchen, so it is clear who does the preparing of all the food. This is detailed in the text, describing the ritual of cooking the Christmas feast. The little girl's presence is clearly linked to the mother's need to socialise the daughter to her female role as food-preparer for the family. This advertisement is remarkable for the detail it uses to instruct the woman on how to use the product, but also on what foods she needs to be preparing for the festival. The separation of the mother and daughter from the father and or male children in the kitchen space (Umiker-Sebeok, 1996) clearly demarcates who carries out the food work, and exactly how it should be done.

The AWW advertisement for Vegemite from July of 1960 shows the Scealy family seated at the table, except for the mother. The advertisement has a picture of the daughter, Diane, 15 years ago as a little girl, with the text declaring that she is now a glamorous model, and still a fan of Vegemite. The text goes on to describe how good Vegemite is for each member of the family. It declares how good it is for mother's 'nerves'. The mother stands serving the rest of the family, father, Diane the daughter, the teenage son and the baby at the breakfast table. The seated family are all looking out of the picture, only the mother faces away from the reader, only the back of her head is visible. While the text in this advertisement includes the mother in direct consumption, the image negates her as an active participant in the consumption of the product. She remains the producer of the happy/healthy family and vicariously consumes through them. The posture here of both subordination (the head 'cant' – the tilting of the head towards the object of submission as described by Goffman 1979) and the licensed withdrawal (again Goffman describes this as a particularly feminised and subordinated depiction of women in advertisements) of the mother's face and body add to the sense of her self-effacement from the rest of the family on whom she focuses her entire attention. Her hand proffers a plate of toast to her son and husband, but the hand holds the plate delicately, in a form of ritualised touching that Goffman (1979) describes as being a form of indicating gender subordination.

1970s mother

In the 1970s we begin to see a shift. The family still appears around or at the dining table, but the mother is seen engaged in similar consumption activity as the rest of the family. In the 'British Bacon' advertisement of GH (February, 1970), we see the top half of the whole page advertisement is taken up by the 'British bacon' logo and an image of a plate with bacon and eggs on it. The main copy reads 'True home cured flavour still yours to enjoy with British Bacon'. The remaining space is taken up with text explaining how British bacon is grown on family farms and cured carefully etc. This is interspersed with small images of the product served in several different ways. One of these pictures shows a nuclear family of father, mother and three children seated at a wooden farmhouse kitchen table with the father getting ready to carve the impressive side of bacon on the table. The children all look at him in anticipation. The mother is to the left and slightly turned away from us. However, despite the slightly withdrawn image, she is, significantly, seated at the table with the rest of the consuming family. She does not seem to be directly 'connected' to the production of all the food on the table; she merely seems to be enjoying the anticipation of eating the food. The significant shift here from the 1950s is that the producer mother has been brought into the consuming circle of the family. She is now a consumer as well as a producer of family meals. The family is still presented in a 'traditional' mode of the nuclear family, yet the woman is not shown in a subordinated mode. The moment of transition is captured in this balance in depiction of the mother as both producer and consumer.

The AWW advertisement from December 1970 shows a different depiction from the GH advertisement. The Dairy Farmers advertisement shows a father carrying one young child, with the mother standing close to him, smiling directly and proudly out at the camera/reader. To her left and the readers' right is a bespectacled older woman (presumably a grandmother) also smiling into the camera. On the extreme end is the young son also smiling into the camera. They all face out, inviting the reader into their home and party (the table in front of them laden with delicious looking cakes etc.). The main headline reads 'gourmet tricks for everyday dessert'. The rest of the space is filled with dessert recipes. This text seems more ambiguous about who in the family it is addressing. The mother in this advertisement seems to be simply part of the family assembled to enjoy the celebratory meal. She does not appear to be singled out as responsible for producing the spread, or serving the family. She is placed in the centre of the group and in control of the occasion. The image is composed like a family photograph.

Thus, in the advertisements from the 1970s we see the mother in a slightly different depiction from earlier decades. She seems to have been brought into the 'circle' of direct consumption from being a producer who could only consume through her food work.

1980s mother

In the 1980s we see a still of the family meal in the April 1980 issue of GH advertising the British Turkey association, where three generations of the extended family are shown around a celebratory anniversary meal (presumably of the older grandparents in the family). The older couple (presumably the grandparents) are already seated at the dining table at the traditional head of the table position and are formally dressed. They both are focused on a large and magnificently roasted turkey being set on the table by a woman (presumably the daughter/daughter-in-law) of the older couple. This woman is in the classic licensed withdrawal pose, as in advertisements of earlier decades (Goffman, 1979), with eyes down cast, and her fingers hardly touching the heavy platter holding the turkey. Next to her stands a man dressed in a shirt and tie, holding a wine bottle and smiling, ready to pour celebratory drinks. On the side closest to the reader and facing their parents (with their backs to us) are two young children. The little boy is seated on a chair, with his older sister standing with an arm on the back of his chair and smiling and whispering into his ear. The main text says 'whatever the occasion, treat them to turkey'. The picture is curiously nostalgic, evocative of holiday dinners of the past, where traditional roast poultry and multiple generations of the family sit down to a meal, with the woman serving the roast she has just brought from the oven. The difference between this image of the family meal and the classic 1950s depiction is that the father appears in a 'serving' pose as well. He stands behind his wife, ready to pour the drinks, smiling proudly and being involved in the production of the meal, not just the key consumer of the meal the woman/mother prepared, yet seems to be removed from the major 'work' involved. Only the oldest and the youngest are seated and anticipating consumption. Even the older child appears to be active, standing rather than sitting at the table.

In the AWW, a much more informal group is depicted in the Sunrice advertisement. This double page advertisement extols the virtues of Sunrice (Australian grown rice) and its uses in any kind of rice dish. It does not identify who the advertisement is targeted at, but is quite gender neutral in its tone. The text mentions the Spanish–Australian family, the Morenos, for whom this is a simple family meal. In the foreground is a huge platter of seafood paella, surrounded by other platters of typical outdoor summer food (salads etc.). The setting is an outdoor, white painted patio, with earthenware platters and a 'Mediterranean' style. The family clustered around the table, all facing outward and smiling at the reader, are of Mediterranean appearance. The father seated at the head of the table raises a glass, his daughter stands behind him with a wine glass in hand. The mother/wife is seated next to the father and turns towards her teenage son and has her arm on his arm, while he smiles out of the picture.

1990s mother

In the 1990s the Filofax advertisement from the January edition of GH shows a very different mealtime. A modern kitchen table is shown with a young child seated to the right of the frame eating his breakfast toast and drinking milk. He is eating while reading an illustrated book/comic. The remains of breakfast are seen at two other places on the table. Just behind the child stands the father, turned sideways facing his wife who is on the other side of the child and speaking into the kitchen phone. The man is dressed as if on the point of leaving for the office, and appears to be trying to say something to his wife (his right hand with a raised forefinger). His wife appears to be annoyed (furrowed and frowning brow) and is speaking into the phone and holding her hand up to stop him interrupting her. Behind her is an impressive array of kitchen equipment. Apart from the washing machine, coffee machine and dishwasher, on the wall appears a complex calendar with many scribbled reminders and notes on it. A notice board is seen on the wall behind the man. The counter behind the woman looks like an office table with books, pens and pin board all displayed centrally. The main headline declares: 'Busy mother seeks secretary, accountant, travel agent, dietician, and linguist to help organise successful family.'

The text goes on to describe the typical middle-class, affluent urban family and its busy life which Filofax helps organise and manage. It claims to be the professional help busy mothers need to manage the children and carpooling, picking up husband's laundry or organising family holidays in foreign lands. Here the mother is a professional, the image of efficiency and business, controlling the complicated organisation that is her family from the nerve centre of the kitchen. It is a 'corporatisation' of the family unit, the meal here is only a single and small part of what she does. In the interests of efficiency, she does not prepare or consume an elaborate breakfast, but is multi-tasking, managing her family's morning meal, while reaching into the outside world over the phone. The rather strained and not very happy family picture presented here, the text implies, can be turned into a successful (happy) one if a Filofax were used by this frazzled mother. The mother has been transformed into the 'manager' of the family organisation. This could be seen as a key shift in the way the mother's work is depicted. A 'professionalisation' of her role and parallels to the 'male role' seems to be the intent.

The headline of the AWW Tegel Turkey advertisement (September 1990) reads 'anything else is just another roast', accompanied by the image of a man dressed in clothes from a bygone era (having overtones of an American Thanksgiving meal). The woman in the advertisement is likewise dressed in a white bonnet and old-fashioned skirt. Their son stands to one side of the man, both mother and son are holding on to the shoulders of the father. All three look delighted and amazed at the platter held by the man of a whole roasted turkey with all the trimmings. The father appears to have produced this meal, not the mother. Here the mother seems to be fully participating in the consumption, but not the production of the meal. The roast itself seems to have been prepared by someone else (possibly the man), showing a possible shift in the responsibility for meal preparation from the female in the family group.

This reversal of roles in food preparation is an anchoring point in the shifting discourse seen in the data.

The 2000s mother

In the 2000s, the AWW Continental (instant sauces and gravies) advertisement shows a page depicting an extended family, posed as if in a photograph. The group has 14 members of the family seated and arranged in a 'photographic' pose. The foreground contains a large plate with a big helping of a roast dinner. The Continental gravy mix container sits next to the food with the headline running through the middle of the picture, reading 'enough delicious gravy for even the biggest meals!' Here the meal is seen as consumed by the family, but the producer of the meal is again ambiguous. It is unclear who the Continental advertisement is actually addressing. The family all appear happy, and seem to have gathered for an occasion. The mother is placed at the centre of the large group (labelled the 'Prescott family, Pennant Hills') and can be read as the manager of the food work and family occasion, rather than directly producing the meal. She is also consumer of the meal and not distinct from the rest of the family, as in advertisements from the earlier decades.

In the GH Galbani Ricotta advertisement from April 2000, the main headline urges the reader to 'love your family the Italian way'. The image that fills half the page shows no depiction of the family; instead the picture shows a plate full of an Aubergine and Ricotta pasta dish. In a smaller three panel image below are images of the dish in preparation, accompanied by the recipe. There is a pair of hands in these images, which could be either male or female. The only reference to family is the main headline, which implies that the Italians show love for their families by cooking with Galbani ricotta. That cooking a meal for your family (with superior ingredients) equals love is a key message that runs through most of these advertisements. However, it is unclear who the advertisement targets. One could assume it is still directed at the female reader, but the explicit portrayal of women in meal preparation is less obvious than in earlier decades.

The 2010s mother

In 2010, the AWW Maggi tender moments advertisements from the November issue has the family back at the dining table with the mother serving the rest of the family, but she is now seated at the table. While evocative of the images of 1950, the family all seem involved in the preparation and consumption of the meal. The text reads: 'Create a tender moment they'll cherish forever ... and let them bake a cake for dessert!' It continues: 'And then bring the family together for a delicious, tasty meal that will have them asking for more.' The mother has prepared the main meal, and the advertisement is addressed to her, but the rest of the family are involved in creating the rest of the meal. The mother's role has become a managerial role. She manages the production process which other family members are engaged in as well. Here we see echoes of the GH 1990s Filofax advertisement, where the mother need no longer be the actual producer of the meal, but is one who coordinates and manages the different elements of the meal, making the production a family moment.

This collective preparation and consumption is implied again in the Leisure range cooker advertisements of GH (November, 2010). The full-page advertisement is split into two halves. The left-hand image is a close up of a baking tray of inexpertly iced cupcakes. The cup cakes are labelled variously as 'fairy cakes made by Joe and Sam' and 'icing by Chloe' and 'washing up by mum'. The title of this image is 'love food'. The right-hand half of the page has an image of a shiny five burner range cooker, labelled variously 'A energy rated ovens and grill' and 'professional wok burner and warming zone'. This image is titled 'love leisure'. In this advertisement, the family cooking together is implied strongly, and the 'love food' implies both the 'love of food' as well as the collective familial preparation of food as being the manifestation of the love within the family. Here, too, the mother manages the process, by having the right equipment and doing the cleaning up.

Discussion

The linkages between food, families and happiness are seen repeated, in different configurations and differing settings in these advertisements over the 70 years of data examined. The enduring consistency of the family meal is reinforced by the depiction of the dining table images of 'familyness' (Chambers, 2001), seen in all these decades. This term as well as 'familism' (2001: 39) is used by Chambers to describe the naturalised and normalised image of the Anglo-Saxon nuclear family of parents and children, usually seen seated around the table, as the representation of core cultural values of the Western world. The post-war affluence immortalised by the Norman Rockwell paintings (*Freedom from want* http://en.m.wikipedia.org/wiki/Freedom_from_Want_(painting) which was inspired by President Roosevelt's state of the union address in 1941) appears to be the model for this idealised depiction. Norman Rockwell himself declared that it had become a model for the family meal in popular media. The aproned matriarch who prepares and brings the meal to the table, around which the happy family gather, came to epitomise the economic prosperity and affluence in the post-war period and a depiction of its cultural values (Oswald, 2003). This appears as a discursive thread across the Anglo-Saxon worlds of advertising beyond the American – in the UK and Australia the effects of this ideal on popular culture were felt.

In the data from the magazines we see this culturally significant imagery used by commercial food marketers to symbolise the link between the 'happy family' and their food product. In the early decades (1950s and 1960s) we see this imagery being used to reinforce a particular form or 'brand' of the white, middle-class, nuclear and patriarchal family as an ideal form and a norm (Chambers, 2001). As Chambers (2001: 26) says:

> the family can be seen as a discursive construct. Political rhetoric, academic knowledge and popular media texts places limits and restrictions on ways of talking about the family as a topic … when the same discourse appears across a variety of texts, institutional sites and sites of practice, they belong to the same discursive formation.

Thus we see how one particular discursive device of the 'family meal' is used repeatedly across two different texts, in a particular traditional form. This patriarchal form of family is depicted by portraying the mother/wife in a subordinated role and responsible for meal and food preparation. Through this food work, she materialises familial bonds and produces the 'happy family'. This image of the 'happy' family is used repeatedly as an aspirational category in the advertisements we see in our data.

In the second part of the data covered (1980s onwards), we see the discursive device of the family meal represented in slightly different ways. Women are depicted increasingly 'at the table' and consuming *with* the family rather than 'through the family'. The vicarious consumption of mothers has changed in the 1980s onwards, showing a certain ambiguity (Robinson & Hunter, 2008) about who the advertisements address regarding meal preparation. The other members of the family appear to be included in the preparation and the mother is 'at the table' as a consumer, not standing 'by the table' as the sole producer of the meal (as depicted in earlier images).

Thus, while both portrayals of the mother as the person who engages in most of the family 'food work' is part of the same discursive formation, we see two slightly different discursive devices being used in the advertisements. The first is of the mother as the sole food worker and producer of family meals and ultimately the 'happy family'. The second device, appearing in the 1980s onwards, is of the mother whose primary work is still to produce the 'happy family', but not by herself. She is seen much more as the 'manager' of the family who all help in producing the 'happy family'.

Ultimately, it would seem that despite the emergence and increasing normalisation of 'alternate' family forms (Costa, 2013), we see that the key aspects of food preparation remain the mother's responsibility as does the everyday work of keeping the emotional links of family.

Funding: This chapter uses data collected from a larger study funded by the Leverhulme Trust as part of an International Research Network Grant F/00158/CS Discursive Families: A comparison of advertising across two countries.

Notes

1 See UK www.pressgazette.co.uk/magazine-abcs-full-circulation-round-first-half-2013 [Accessed 1 July 2015].
2 www.bauer-media.com.au/brands/the-australian-women-s-weekly/ [Accessed 1 July 2015].

References

Bordo, S. (2004). *Unbearable Weight: Feminism, Western Culture, and the Body*. Berkeley: University of California Press.

Bourdieu, P. (1996). On the family as a realized category. *Theory, Culture Society, 13*(3), 19–26.

Chambers, D. (2001). *Representing Family*. London: Sage Publications.

Cook, D. T. (1995). The mother as consumer: Insights from the children's wear industry 1917–1929. *The Sociological Quarterly, 36*(3), 505–522.

Costa, R. P. (2013). Family rituals: Mapping the post-modern family through time, space and emotion. *Journal of Comparative Family Studies, 44*(3), 269–289.

Cronin, A. M. (2004). Regimes of mediation: Advertising practitioners as cultural intermediaries? *Consumption, Markets and Culture, 7*(4), 349–369.

DeVault, M. L. (1991). *Feeding the Family: The Social Organisation of Caring as Gendered Work*. Chicago: University of Chicago Press.

Feder, E. K. (2007). The dangerous individual('s) mother: Biopower, family and the production of race. *Hypatia, 22*(2), 60–78.

Friedan, B. (1963). *The Feminine Mystique*. New York: W. W. Norton.

Goffmann, E. (1979). *Gender Advertisements*. New York: Harper Collins.

Gough-Yates, K. (2003). *Understanding Women's Magazines: Publishing, Markets and Readership*. London: Routledge.

Jackson, P. (Ed.) (2009). *Changing Families, Changing Food*. London: Palgrave Macmillan.

Marshall, D., Hogg, M., Davis, T., Schneider, T., & Petersen, A. (2014). Images of motherhood: Food advertising in Good Housekeeping magazine 1950–2010. In S. O'Donohoe, M. Hogg, P. Maclaran, L. Martens, & L. Stevens (Eds.), *Motherhood, Markets and Consumption: The Making of Mothers in Contemporary Western Culture* (pp. 116–128). London: Routledge.

Marshall, D., Davis, T., Hogg, M., Petersen, A., & Schneider, T. (2014). Making meal times fun: Representation of mothers and family meals over time in Magazine Advertising. Paper in Special Session, Women, Emotion work and Producing 'Family': The Role of Food and Fun, *Association of Consumer Research* (ACR) Baltimore, Maryland, 23–26 October.

Martens, L., & Scott, S. (2005). The unbearable lightness of cleaning: Representations of domestic practice and products in Good Housekeeping magazine (UK), 1951–2001. *Consumption, Markets and Culture, 8*(4), 379–401.

Moor, L. (2008). Branding consultants as cultural intermediaries. *The Sociological Review, 56*(3), 408–428.

Murcott, A. (1982). On the social significance of the 'cooked dinner' in South Wales. *Social Science Information, 21*(4/5), 677–695.

Odland, S. B. (2009). Unassailable motherhood, ambivalent domesticity: The construction of maternal identity in Ladies' Home Journal in 1946. *Journal of Communication Inquiry, 34*(1), 61–84.

Oswald, L. (2003). Branding the American family: A strategic study of the culture. *Journal of Popular Culture, 37*(2), 309–335.

Robinson, B., & Hunter, E. (2008). Is Mom still doing it all? Re-examining depictions of family work in popular advertising. *Journal of Family Issues, 29*(4), 465–486.

Rose, G. (2012). *Visual Methodologies: An Introduction to Interpreting Visual Materials*, 3rd ed. London: Sage.

Schneider, T., & Davis, T. (2010). Fostering a hunger for health: Food and the self in The Australian Women's Weekly. *Health Sociology Review, 19*(3), 285–303.

Schroeder, J. E., & Borgerson, J. L (1998). Marketing images of gender: A visual analysis. *Consumption Markets and Culture, 2*(2), 161–201.

Schroeder, J. E., & Zwick, D. (2004). Mirrors of masculinity: Representation and identity in advertising images. *Consumption, Markets and Culture, 7*(1), 21–52.

Sheridan, E. (2000). Eating the other: Food and cultural difference in the Australian Women's Weekly in the 1960s. *Journal of Intercultural Studies, 21*(3), 319–329.

Tincknell, E. (2005). *Mediating the Family: Gender, Culture and Representation*. London: Hodder Arnold.

Umiker-Sebeok, J. (1996). Power and the construction of gendered spaces. *Review of Sociology/Revue Internationale de Sociologie, 6*(3), 389–403.

Woodward, K. (1997). Motherhood: Meanings and myths. In K. Woodward (Ed.), *Identity and Difference* (pp. 17–26). London: Sage.

11 From harmony to disruption and inability

On the embodiment of mothering and its consumption

Susanna Molander

Theoretical overview

Consuming mothers

Consumption can be seen as a way to construct, express and negotiate identity (Arnould & Thompson, 2005), including the identity of mother. Encoded in advertisements, brands, retail settings and material goods, the marketplace provides the consumer with a broad range of symbolic meanings which she may tap into in the course of constructing this identity (Hogg, Maclaran, Martens, O'Dohohoe, & Stevens, 2011; Scott, 2006a, 2006b). There are, however, different ways to conceptualise the relationship between consumption and motherhood (see Davis, Marshall, Hogg, Schneider, & Petersen, Chapter 10). One important body of research supports the idea that the identity of mother is related to *role embracing* (The VOICE group, 2010a, 2010b; Thomsen & Sørensen, 2006; Hogg, Curasi, & Maclaran, 2004; Jennings & O'Malley, 2003) which provides consumers with existential meaning and guidance in behaviours and actions. Another body of literature sees the identity of mother as a *discursive construct* shaping consumption in forms of representing, interacting and being (Dedeoglu, 2010; Bugge & Almås, 2006; Moisio, Arnould, & Price, 2004; Arendell, 1999, 2000; Lupton, 1996).

Inspired by practice theorist Andreas Reckwitz's view on the individual (2002: 256), identity can also be seen as *an intersection of practices* which, in turn, serve as the bedrock of consumption (Warde, 2005: 144). This approach locates the practices that constitute identity as the point of departure for the analysis. It underlines the embodied aspects of identity – the kind of learned, tacit, routinised knowledge that is a fundamental part of everyday life. In focus here is mothering as a practice, but briefly discussed are also other practices composing identity and which simultaneously influence each other. Even if approaching mothering as a practice is not new in socio-cultural consumer research (Cappellini & Parsons, 2013; Halkier, 2013; Molander, 2011; Cook, 2009) it still deserves further exploration, especially from the aspect of routinisation and embodiment (Warde, 2014). By conceptualising mothering as one of the embodied practices that can constitute identity and that usually requires consumption to be performed (Warde, 2005), this chapter explores different ways in which mothering strives to express love for a needing child through consumption (Schatzki, 1996; Gallagher, 1995; Merleau-Ponty, 1962).

Mothering as a practice and its consumption

Theories of practice have received considerable interest within the field of consumer studies, especially during the last decade (Arsel & Bean, 2013; Halkier, Katz-Gerro, & Martens, 2011; Schau, Muñiz, & Arnould, 2009; Hand & Shove, 2007; Hand, Shove, & Southerton, 2005; Warde, 2005, 2014). While including the reflective and discursive facets of human life, theories of practice put emphasis on the embodied aspects of performances, pointing to a type of knowledge that is unarticulated and tied to the senses, movement skills, physical experiences, intuition or implicit rules of thumb. According to Schatzki (1996), embodiment on the one hand emphasises the experiential and conceptual unity a person has with her body when acting and experiencing – where one *is* a body (Schatzki, 1996). On the other, embodiment is also the recognition of a distinction between oneself and ones' body in cases of breakdown, malfunction, discomfort and incompetence – where *having* a body manifests itself explicitly (ibid.). When in unity with the body, the practitioner acts beyond conscious thinking according to a *body schema* (Gallagher, 1995; Merleau-Ponty, 1962) that sketches out in advance, and so structures, her awareness of the world (Carman, 1999). Disequilibrium, however, causes a shift to the reflective, deliberate mode of thinking. Here the body becomes an object of awareness, something consciously experienced, conceptually understood and emotionally related to – a *body image* (Gallagher, 1995). But if we needed to depend solely on our body image to get around and think through every step we took, our movements would be awkward. Instead, our bodily strivings are to be in equilibrium with the world, to act smoothly according to the body schema (Merleau-Ponty, 1962). To escape feelings of imbalance, incompetence or inadequacy our bodily tendency is, therefore, to either refine our doings or to do something different.

According to theorists like Bourdieu (1977), Giddens (1984) and Schatzki (1996), in the practice perspective social life is based on a number of collective practices which constitute the individual and become part of her body schema. Schatzki (1996) states that the practice consists of a number of interrelated activities in the form of 'sayings and doings', organised through *understandings, explicit rules* and *teleoaffective structures*, which together constitute the practice. Understandings denote knowing what to do, when and how, while the explicit rules refer to interpretations of a practice formulated in writing or expressed out loud. The teleoaffective structure, although usually tacitly entertained, emphasises a practice orientation towards certain ends (teleo) and emphasises why these ends matter (affect-emotion) suggesting simply that certain things make sense to do because they matter to us. Finally, practice-based approaches also consider how *material arrangements* both influence and are influenced by the performances of practices (Hand, Shove, & Southerton, 2005; Reckwitz, 2002). The elements of a practice, that according to Schatzki are understandings, rules and teleoaffective structure, compose the *practice-as-entity*, its structure. But the practice also requires *performances*, in the form of 'sayings and doings', to exist. When performed, the elements composing the practice can be likened to a gestalt coming together and temporarily creating a whole. While guided by the practice-as-entity, every practice-as-performance is situational and unique and also influences the practice-as-entity (Shove & Pantzar, 2007).

My conceptualisation of mothering as a practice has been inspired by feminist philosopher Sara Ruddick's maternal thinking (1995 [1989]). Her philosophy goes hand-in-hand with Schatzki's notion of practices. According to Ruddick mothering is a practice that develops in relation to, and focuses on, a needing child. The relationship does not necessarily entail the child's biological mother or father but can involve anyone prepared to step into it. The practitioners tacitly strive for overall ends like *preserving the child*, *fostering the child's physical, emotional and intellectual development* and making the child *socially acceptable* – ends they find worth striving for, through their *attentive love*, and which keep the practice going (ibid.). Mothering's teloaffectivity is therefore composed of these ends, which in turn can be broken down into a number of projects and activities like the dinner, guided by attentive love. According to Ruddick attentive love is central to mothering and it is what knits the practice together and what makes the mother practitioner see how things are going for the child and how it is developing. It ensures that the practitioner puts the child in focus rather than herself or the community. This love is mediated by the practice. It is a crucial element of the practice and is constructed and understood only within the practice. It can be expressed in many ways such as joy, contentment, frustration, anxiety or something else and indicates how things are going for the practitioner from the perspective of the practice. Rules can include explicit instructions on, for example, how to cook, that come from books, friends, their own mothers and children, or nurses while understandings refer to the practical knowledge of what to do, when and how, oriented towards certain ends such as 'preserving' the child by, for example, making him or her eat healthily.

Consumption is something that Warde (2005) introduces as moments in most practices, forcing us to understand consumption through the logic of practices. According to Warde, it is the practice that organises behaviour and gives rise to wants. The pattern of similarities and differences in consumption that may occur within and between groups in the form of acquisitions, uses and symbolic meanings can thus be seen as a consequence of the way different practices are organised and performed in different situations rather than as an outcome of a personal taste and choice (2005: 137–142). Thus, in line with Warde (2005), consumption in this particular context should be seen as part of the interrelationship between mothering, children and love. This relationship has also been confirmed by other theorists who have pointed out that parents often consume on behalf of their children (Cook, 2009, 2008; Martens, Southerton, & Scott, 2004; Miller, 1998), especially in the form of everyday dinners (Molander, 2011; Lupton, 1996; DeVault, 1991; Charles & Kerr, 1988). From a practice theoretical point of view the dinner project can therefore be seen as an important part of the teleoaffective structure of mothering by serving as a way to express love through (tacitly) striving for preservation, fostering and social acceptance. With special attention to embodiment, and with help of the concepts body schema and body image, this chapter will explore different ways in which mothering may express love for the child through performances related to everyday dinner consumption.

Findings – from harmony to disruption and inability

The findings are based on data from an ethnographic study of the sayings and doings performed during 47 everyday dinner occasions by nine Swedish single middle-class mothers over seven months. I found not only consumption performances that could be interpreted as a mothering practice but also interesting differences that presented themselves through variations in how the performances were embodied. This variety will be illustrated below by three informants: Eva, Camilla and Linda. Eva was typical for most of the informants – a supermom and routinised juggler of pragmatic ideals. The exceptions are represented by Camilla whose body no longer functioned according to her embodied ideals, and Linda, who experienced that what was expected of the mothering practice just was not part of her body schema. The fact that they were single with poor back-up presumably exposed these exceptions more clearly.

Eva – supermom and routinised juggler of pragmatic ideals

Children's voices echoed as usual throughout the kitchen as the local radio station aired its children's program, while Eva in some 15 minutes made what she called, a 'homemade' broccoli soup by warming frozen broccoli with water and two bouillon cubes and mixing it with a hand blender. We were silent and Eva was caught up in her doings without seeming to notice me. Although she never really listened, Eva later told me that she enjoyed the background sound of children and, afterwards, news in Finnish – a language she did not even speak. Eva said that cooking offered a relaxing moment and that she appreciated the solitude. Thanks to former experience she knew that her homemade broccoli soup accompanied with bread and cold cuts was something that the children really liked: 'You have to try … then they realize that it is actually edible,' said Eva. The intense eating mixed with heated discussions during dinner also confirmed this although the dinner turned out to be a relatively quick affair. 'Just being together for a while is important,' said Eva.

(Excerpt from field notes)

Eva's dinner activities clearly played a central role in her mothering in the example above. Her body operated according to a body schema of latent knowledge in harmony with the environment to deliver meaning (Gallagher, 1995) in the form of attentive love for her children related to their preservation, fostering and social acceptance (Ruddick 1995 [1989]) by making sure they ate healthily enough and sat together and talked for a while. The flow she demonstrated was probably due to her being an experienced practitioner who understood what to perform, when and how, engaging in activities that seemed well thought out and tested beforehand according to explicit rules. The body had organised the practice according to its own pragmatic schema (Gallagher, 1995). The food was prepared, albeit minimally, and balanced between ideals and daily resources in the form of time and money. She did what she could and her whole being also manifested that she considered it to be good enough. She was in equilibrium, her body schema was attuned to environmental circumstances.

By studying the example above in the context of intersecting practices we can get an even better understanding of her embodied mothering performances. Eva studied psychology and worked extra hours at a youth housing project with the future goal of getting a full-time job helping troubled adolescents back on their feet. She was an experienced mother who, apart from her two teenagers, also had a 26-year-old grown-up son. The two fathers were basically not involved at all. Despite a hectic life, dinners were the norm and Eva was responsible for them so she had to be extremely effective to bring it all together – in particular because she tried to organise the dinners before the children ran off to their respective training classes. Eva used to do aerobics herself but it had become more or less impossible to combine with their joint dinners, her work, her studies, the children's homework and their training. Instead she usually took a walk in the vicinity of her home after dinner.

Eva did not improvise but followed certain explicit rules. Dinners were usually carefully planned to meet her budget, avoid fuss and ensure that everyone got at least something that was reasonably healthy within the short amount of time available. She had only recently begun to bulk shop together with the children once a month and had a weekly schedule that included a number of what she called 'basic dishes' such as soup, oven pancakes and tacos so that she 'didn't have to think anymore than necessary'. This method was particularly helpful since her daughter Sara was 'picky' and usually avoided new things. Eva knew what worked and what did not, for example, that carrots for some reason seemed to be tastier when served as sticks rather than grated. Eva's goal was that the healthy meals she considered herself to serve would become a natural part of the children's lives, something that they would choose voluntarily in the future as it was in their best interests.

She was also careful about which borders were not to be crossed. To end up at McDonalds, to buy expensive, unplanned, fattening fast foods or sweets went counter to the healthy, future-oriented and rational economising that Eva worked so hard to accomplish. Still, it was usually the sweets, the fat and the processed foods that the children loved and Eva's control also seemed to have its limits. On weekends Eva allowed herself and the kids the Swedish ritual of 'Cosy Friday' which meant 'crash landing' in front of the TV in the living room with 'scrap food'. This was when a certain level of control was dropped, not only regarding food content and cost, but also regarding the dinner situation as such. On Fridays the children were allowed to decide and the mothering practitioner could rest (Solér & Creixell Plazas, 2012).

Overall, Eva appeared to be a routinised juggler of pragmatic ideals and a supermom (Thompson, 1996) who, despite tough circumstances, managed to combine not only studies and work but also mothering in the form of home-cooked dinners (see Truninger, Chapter 7). She let the children participate in the planning and purchasing and was committed to developing them into independent individuals who could choose for themselves. The shared and in her words 'reasonably healthy dinners' around the kitchen table appeared to be holy and were rarely compromised. Still, the economising austerity and disciplined order of the everyday was confirmed by the occasional excesses during the weekends (see Miller, 1998). This hardworking pragmatism combined with letting go was characteristic for most of the informants who just carried on without thinking much about it – an embodied way of performing that was perhaps best illustrated by performances that were not in line with what was expected.

Camilla – high ambitions in a disabled body

> One day when I came home to Camilla, 42, a former IT-consultant and researcher who had been on sick leave for almost 10 years I found a beautiful, golden brown lasagna in the kitchen. 'But I can tell you that I'm done out now. I'm totally exhausted. Completely finished. I almost cried today. […] Yes, it's true. I ought to go to bed really. It's horrible…' cried Camilla. But she calmed down and asked me to stay for dinner. We ate the lasagna that had taken her several hours to make together with her four-year-old daughter Maja. And while content, Camilla asked herself if all the work had been worth it but didn't answer the question.
>
> (Excerpt from field notes)

Camilla expressed a great interest in cooking and willingly tried relatively demanding dishes, all the while her illness limiting her strength significantly. She lived in a rented two-bedroom apartment in central Stockholm with her four-year-old daughter Maja, who also spent time with her dad on some weekends. Camilla herself grew up in a small town with both parents and two siblings and had learned how to cook already as a child. Her mother, with whom she spoke almost daily, had worked as a home economics teacher and was committed to food 'cooked from scratch'. Camilla had taken over this ambition and was also committed to carry it on with her daughter who from time to time in Camilla's words 'helped out' or 'messed around' in the kitchen.

As a result of her bad health Camilla was often tired. She said she felt vulnerable as a single mother on sick leave and that she somehow felt that she incarnated what the government called 'outsidership'.[1] This feeling of 'outsidership' had increased since the government started talking about it and now she saw articles written on the subject every other day about people like her who had to be put back into the workforce. 'Of course you want to work when you have a long education [like I have]. But it has to be feasible. As it is now I have to prioritize being a good parent to my child.' Everyday life was characterised by caring for her daughter and their home including serving dinners. She couldn't cope with much more than that. Camilla feared the authorities who, according to her, would sabotage the routines she had managed to establish by forcing her into the job market. Camilla worried she would collapse with additional requirements that in turn would impede her mothering.

During the time I spent with Camilla and Maja, the everyday dinner appeared to be the rule but the cooking, and especially 'cooking from scratch', was frequently forgone due to colds and fatigue. She often had to back down and instead resort to the exclusive pre-cooked meatballs from Ejmund's farm,[2] 'with 80 per cent meat' that she always made sure she kept in the freezer. Our gatherings were regularly characterised by Camilla's concern and uncertainty about what was going to happen in the future and her focus on being a good mother to Maja.

Rather than just carry on without thinking much about it according to her body schema like Eva, Camilla's body had become an object of her constant scrutiny – a *body image* – that interfered with her daily activities. Still the body image does not interfere with performance of body schema unless something happens (Gallagher, 1995). Camilla's body schema was formed in an environment with high mothering ideals and where working mothers were the rule. Thus, the explicit rules and understandings of what to perform when and how were set high. Her body, however, had suffered a breakdown and lost some of the functions she needed to act smoothly towards the ends she aimed for. Yet, these functions appeared as *phantom limbs*, a presence of a body which should not be felt since the corresponding limbs were not there (Merleau-Ponty, 1962). Camilla's high set ideals were part of the practical attunement of her body to its environment, only to find that the bodily functions needed to deal with these ideals were not there, like in the case when making the lasagna. Her high ideals and former strength were like a previous present that could not commit to becoming a past (ibid.). Before turning ill and becoming a mother, Camilla said she had enjoyed her fast-life pace, including a demanding career and high ideals for the home and cooking. Her 'new' body, however, had difficulty in achieving her ambitious mothering ideals and required her to abandon the desire to be a working mother altogether. Still, body schemas are not fixed structures but dynamic processes that strive for equilibrium (Merleau-Ponty, 1962) and Camilla seemed to have accepted her situation and the fact that work no longer was what defined her.

Nowadays, it was through her mothering, including her cooking, that she found meaning. But she kept her high ideals and expressed worry and inadequacy for not being able to communicate attentive love in the way she found acceptable. Camilla also reacted strongly when she perceived that even part of her everyday life was threatened by possibly being forced to get back to work. Overall, her body schema seemed to be in limbo longing for a lasting direction. Over time, however, she skillfully coped by lowering the bar in small steps towards equilibrium through, for example, going for ready-made meatballs from Ejmund's farm rather than homemade lasagna.

Linda – when the expected just isn't part of the make-up

> It was about 6 p.m. and Linda, 35, an unemployed single mother with an education in environmental science, had spent a good half hour in the toy store at the mall in the centre of Stockholm with her son Leon, 4, with whom she lived alone in an apartment in a suburb close to Stockholm. Despite Linda's initial reluctance to go to the toy store, she was now as committed as Leon to play with Thomas the Tank Engine, Roary the Racing Car and the rest of all their friends. Linda and Leon were completely in their own world, looking, pointing, discussing and trying the different products. But they never bought anything. This was a very popular activity after she picked up Leon from the day care centre. It usually ended with a dinner for some 150 Swedish Krona (some 16 Euro) or more at a café in the mall because if Leon did not eat here it would be too late for him to eat once they came home. Linda, however, felt that they needed to break the habit with the mall because it was too expensive to eat out every day. Besides, she found it embarrassing to spend so much time in the toy store without buying anything. It was past 6 p.m. and getting time for dinner. Linda knew that the mall closed at 7 and wanted to get dinner over with before that. She began persuading Leon and promised that they would return to the toy store as soon as they had finished eating. After a bit of disco dancing on one of the toy store's carpets that made sounds as they danced, Linda and Leon went to their ordinary place where Leon to some irritation on Linda's behalf ended up eating more chocolate biscuit than lasagna.
>
> (Excerpt from field notes)

Linda really struggled with the everyday dinner. Even though she said she wanted Leon to eat a proper dinner at a reasonable cost, she also wanted them to spend time together and play. When performing mothering she prioritised play while the dinner was handled in a way she did not like afterwards. Linda herself had been brought up by her single mother, an associate professor in art history, who more or less never cooked. Instead, Linda often warmed frozen crepes with mushrooms or a slice of pizza in the oven when she was a child. Even though dinners had never become a natural part of Linda's everyday life, had never become a part of her understanding of what to perform when and how, she did express a longing for them through the symbolically charged meatballs that manifested the explicit rules of how to perform mothering: 'When I got pregnant I thought: "Now I'm going to cook real meatballs"… but for some reason it did not happen during the months we spent together.' Cooking seemed too unwieldy to operate. It was hard to fit in and make it a part of her everyday life. Instead, Linda practised a rather large part of her mothering, playing with Leon outdoors in parks or in malls in town. To her, playing with Leon simply seemed more natural than to cook and bulk shop.

Meanwhile, Linda's on the surface seemingly unstructured and spontaneous life was just as structured as the others, but according to a different organising principle. Instead of acting as the competent mother who knew when, how and what the child should eat, Linda was the competent mother who let her competent child decide. All this according to the psychologist Jesper Juul's (2009) principles on 'the competent child' which Linda summarised as children's willingness to cooperate and please their parents and their ability to take responsibility. When practised by Linda, this meant that Leon's wishes became the dominant organising principle. Linda had been brought up in the same way but had mixed feelings about it all the same: 'Maybe I let him decide whether to eat at all rather than when.' She often worried about giving Leon too much responsibility, about him not having a diet that was varied enough, about the costs related to eating out as much as they did and about Leon going to bed too late as a result of their playing and late dinners.

When in a mothering mood, Linda's bodily schema was set to play. Her attentive love was manifested through the play as a way to approach mothering goals like physical, emotional and intellectual development, as well as social acceptance by letting Leon experiment with the social environment in different ways, such as running around, playing identity games and learning how to behave through play. But at the same time Linda's body image interfered with her by manifesting concerns about not really doing what was expected of her. The gaze of others (Ruddick 1995 [1989]) was always present. She worried about everything she felt she ought to do, like homecooked meals, but she still did not seem to be able to deal with these doings. They just were not part of her make-up, or rather, her body schema. Instead of being in unity with her experiences and actions, like when playing with Leon, her mothering at times shifted to a reflective, deliberate mode of thinking, recognising a distinction between herself and her body, a sort of incompetence that, with attentive love as her guide, made her experience discomfort and guilt.

Concluding discussion

Focusing on embodiment and with the help of body schema and body image, this chapter has explored different ways in which mothering expresses love for the child through dinner consumption. As illustrated by the empirical examples, even if performed according to an overall mothering logic, the practitioners had different bodily experiences, were exposed to different situations and adapted their performances accordingly (Warde, 2005). Indeed, every performance is unique and marked by its practitioners, who are also embedded in a complex of other practices that need to be considered in order to fully understand the practice in question. Eva represents the pragmatic working mother majority who repeatedly performed according to a body schema that seemed in harmony with the environment with little consideration. Camilla and Linda, however, represent situations where the body manifests itself explicitly as a body image. Rather than just going on without thinking, the performances shifted to a reflective mode where the body was experienced as behaving in an inexact and awkward way (Gallagher, 1995).

While Camilla constantly reflected over her incapacitated body that hindered her embodied, ambitious, mothering strivings, Linda's mothering was performed more or less without thinking when playing, but was hesitant and uncomfortable in relation to the dinner. Camilla seemed to have been taught a mothering that was unusually ambitious compared to the others, whereas Linda's reflective mode expressed anxiety about play not being enough to accomplish her motherly strivings as well as being unsure about how the practice should be performed. Because even if there are numerous performances that may be involved in mothering, the examples presented in this chapter suggest, along with other studies already mentioned, that those related to food are of major importance. Despite great variety, the importance of the dinner can be understood in light of its ability to contribute to the objectives of mothering on an everyday basis. Products that are constantly used up and recreated may be perceived as more tangible than mothering's long-term goals, which only become clear in the long run (Holm, 1993). The preparations function as a way for the practitioners to singularise mass-produced products (Kopytoff, 1986) by infusing them with love through self-sacrifice, thereby making it a worthy gift for their loved ones (Cappellini & Parsons, 2012; DeVault, 1991; Miller, 1998).

Still, the importance of the dinner should also be understood in the light of explicit rules such as moral ideals and the concern these ideals risk creating among practitioners. As Wilk (2010) underlines in his work on the family dinner, the construction of normative family performances is part of a process that constructs different family types as deviant and delinquent. These normative performances are closely connected to the nuclear family, where the mother is responsible for the family's emotional development and the dinner functions as one of the emotional tools. Wilk's thoughts can be applied to this study by seeing this normativity as part of the practice-as-entity and the performances deviating from this ideal as delinquent. As illustrated by Linda and Camilla, in addition to performing outside of what was experienced as ideal, these delinquencies were also manifested through their body images that expressed feelings of inadequacy and guilt.

But deviating performances also contain seeds of change that influence the more stable parts of the practice-as-entity including its understandings, rules and teleoaffective structure. In line with Schatzki (1996), Merleau-Ponty (1962) emphasises that our bodily strivings have to be in equilibrium with the world to act smoothly. Thus, to escape feelings of imbalance, incompetence or inadequacy our bodily tendency may either be to refine our doings according to the practice-as-entity or, if possible, to change them. Because, as Warde states (2005: 140): 'Conventions will usually be to some degree contested, with some practitioners typically still attached to prior codes of conduct, while others, perhaps of a new generation, seek to replace current orthodoxies with new prescriptions.' However, mothering's idealisation of the dinner has proven to be surprisingly stable ever since the family dinner made its entry into modernity along with the nuclear family (Cinotto, 2006; Holm, 2001; Murcott, 1997) – this despite new generations, new situations and breakdowns among 'supermoms' who are sometimes unable to keep it all together. There are many reasons for this stability. Not only does mothering involve deeply entrenched dispositions on how to act, learned from infancy. As a fundamental part of the social order in most societies, mothering is also deeply embedded in a web of surrounding practices, organised in identity bundles characterised by such aspects as gender, class, age, ethnicity and, in particular, power and prestige which may impede change (Molander, 2011). If at stake, this social order will most likely be defended by those benefiting from it. Within the framework of this study, Linda's alternative mothering and Camilla's bodily breakdown led to disruptions in their practice performances and to body images expressing frustration over their bodies and feelings of inadequacy. How bodily disruptions of different sorts influence the practice-as-entity and the way it expresses love over time is an empirical question in need of further study.

Notes

1 Outsidership or 'utanförskap' was a term mainly articulated by the right-wing Alliance during the election campaign in 2006 and onwards to describe individuals and groups that were depicted as being outside the Swedish society and who for various reasons were dependent on the welfare system to get by.
2 Ejmund's farm is a small-scale local family livestock farm on Gotland, Sweden; they breed their own animals and market themselves as caring for the animals and offering premium quality meat.

References

Arendell, T. (1999). Hegemonic motherhood: Deviancy discourses and employed mothers' accounts of out-of-school time issues. Working Paper 9, Center for Working Families, Berkeley.
Arendell, T. (2000). Conceiving and investigating motherhood: The decade's scholarship. *Journal of Marriage & Family, 62*(4), 1192–1207.

Arnould, E. J., & Thompson, C. J. (2005). Consumer culture theory (CCT): Twenty years of research. *Journal of Consumer Research, 31*(4), 868–882.

Arsel, Z., & Bean, J. (2013). Taste regimes and market-mediated practice. *Journal of Consumer Research, 39*(5), 899–917.

Bourdieu, P. (1977). *Outline of a Theory of Practice.* Cambridge: Cambridge University Press.

Bugge, A. B., & Almås, R. (2006). Domestic dinner. *Journal of Consumer Culture, 6*(2), 203–228.

Cappellini, B., & Parsons, E. (2012). (Re)enacting motherhood: Self-sacrifice and abnegation in the kitchen. In R. Belk & A. Ruvio (Eds.), *Identity and Consumption* (pp. 119–128). London: Routledge.

Cappellini, B., & Parsons, E. (2013). Whose work is it anyway? The shifting dynamics of 'doing mothering'. In S. O'Donohue, M. Hogg, P. Maclaran, L. Martens, & L. Stevens (Eds.), *Motherhoods, Markets and Consumption: The Making of Mothers in Contemporary Western Cultures* (pp. 183–196). London: Routledge.

Carman, T. (1999). The body in Husserl and Merleau-Ponty. *Philosophical Topics, 27*(2), 205–226.

Charles, N., & Kerr, M. (1988). *Women, Food, and Families.* Manchester: Manchester University Press.

Cinotto, S. (2006). 'Everyone would be around the table': American family mealtimes in historical perspective, 1850–1960. *New Directions for Child & Adolescent Development, 11*(1), 17–33.

Cook, D. T. (2008). The missing child in consumption theory. *Journal of Consumer Culture, 8*(2), 219–243.

Cook, D. T. (2009). Semantic provisioning of children's food: Commerce, care and maternal practice. *Childhood, 16*(3), 317–334.

Dedeoglu, A. Ö. (2010). Discourses of motherhood and consumption practices of Turkish mothers. *Business and Economics Research Journal, 1*(3), 1–15.

DeVault, M. L. (1991). *Feeding the Family: The Social Organization of Caring as Gendered Work.* Chicago: University of Chicago Press.

Gallagher, S. (1995). Body schema and intentionality. In J. L. Bermúdez, A. J. Marcel, & N. Eilan (Eds.), *The Body and the Self* (pp. 225–244). Cambridge: MIT Press.

Giddens, A. (1984). *The Constitution of Society: Outline of the Theory of Structuration.* Berkeley: University of California Press.

Halkier, B. (2013). Contesting food – Contesting motherhood? In S. O'Donohue, M. Hogg, P. Maclaran, L. Martens, & L. Stevens (Eds.), *Motherhoods, Markets and Consumption: The Making of Mothers in Contemporary Western Cultures* (pp. 89–103). London: Routledge.

Halkier, B., Katz-Gerro, T., & Martens, L. (2011). Applying practice theory to the study of consumption: Theoretical and methodological considerations. *Journal of Consumer Culture, 11*(1), 3–13.

Hand, M., & Shove, E. (2007). Condensing practices: Ways of living with the freezer. *Journal of Consumer Culture, 7*(1), 79–104.

Hand, M., Shove, E., & Southerton, D. (2005). Explaining showering: A discussion of the material, conventional and temporal dimensions of a practice. *Sociological Review Online, 10*(2). Available at: www.socresonline.org.uk/10/2/hand.html [Accessed 3 April 2014].

Hogg, M., Curasi, C., & Maclaran, P. (2004). The (re)configuration of production and consumption in empty nest households/families. *Consumption, Markets & Culture, 7*(3), 239–259.

Hogg, M., Maclaran, P., Martens, L., O'Donohoe, S., & Stevens, L. (2011). (Re)creating cultural models of motherhoods in contemporary advertising. *Advertising & Society Review, 12*(2). Available at: http://muse.jhu.edu/journals/advertising_and_society_review/v012/12.2.hogg.htm [Accessed 3 April 2014].

Holm, L. (2001). Family meals. In U. Kjærnes (Ed.), *Eating Patterns: A Day in the Lives of Nordic Peoples* (pp. 199–212). The National Institute for Consumer Research, Oslo: SIFO.

Holm, U. M. (1993). *Modrande och praxis: En feministfilosofisk undersökning.* Göteborg: Daidalos.

Jennings, R., & O'Malley, L. (2003). Motherhood, identity and consumption. *European Advances in Consumer Research, 6*(1), 221.

Juul, J. (2009). *Ditt kompetenta barn. På väg mot nya värderingar för familjen.* Stockholm: Månpocket.

Kopytoff, I. (1986). The cultural biography of things: Commoditization as a cultural process. In A. Appadurai (Ed.), *The Social Life of Things: Commodities in Cultural Perspective* (pp. 64–94). Cambridge: Cambridge University Press.

Lupton, D. (1996). *Food, the Body and the Self.* London: Sage.

Martens, L., Southerton, D., & Scott, S. (2004). Bringing children (and parents) into the sociology of consumption. *Journal of Consumer Culture, 4*(2), 155–182.

Merleau-Ponty, M. (1962). *Phenomenology of Perceptions.* New York: Humanities Press.

Miller, D. (1998). *A Theory of Shopping.* Oxford: Polity Press.

Moisio, R., Arnould, E. J., & Price, L. (2004). Between mothers and markets: Constructing family identity through homemade food. *Journal of Consumer Culture, 4*(3), 361–384.

Molander, S. (2011). *Mat, kärlek och metapraktik: En studie i vardagsmiddagskonsumtion bland ensamstående mödrar.* Stockholm: Stockholm University School of Business.

Murcott, A. (1997). Family meals – a thing of the past? In P. Caplan (Ed.), *Food, Health and Identity* (pp. 67–83). London: Routledge.

Reckwitz, A. (2002). Toward a theory of social practices: A development in culturalist theorizing. *European Journal of Social Theory, 5*(2), 243–263.

Ruddick, S. (1995 [1989]). *Maternal Thinking: Toward a Politics of Peace.* Boston: Beacon Press.

Schatzki, T. R. (1996). *Social Practices: A Wittgensteinian Approach to Human Activity and the Social.* Cambridge: Cambridge University Press.

Schatzki, T. R. (2002). *The Site of the Social: A Philosophical Account of the Constitution of Social Life and Change.* University Park, PA: Pennsylvania State University Press.

Schau, H. J., Muñiz, A. M., & Arnould, E. J. (2009). How brand community practices create value. *Journal of Marketing, 73*(5), 30–51.

Scott, L. M. (2006a). Editor's introduction: Young mothers talk back. *Advertising & Society Review, 7*(3). Available at: http://muse.jhu.edu/journals/advertising_and_society_review/summary/v007/7.3editorial_intro.html [Accessed 23 February 2014].

Scott, L. M. (2006b). Editor's introduction: Young mothers talk back. *Advertising & Society Review, 7*(4). Available at: http://muse.jhu.edu/journals/advertising_and_society_review/summary/v007/7.4editorial_intro.html [Accessed 21 February 2014].

Shove, E., & Pantzar, M. (2007). Recruitment and reproduction: The careers and carriers of digital photography and floorball. *Human Affairs, 17*(2), 154–167.

Solér, C., & Creixell Plazas, M. (2012). Integration of ethnic food into Swedish food rituals: The cultural fitness of tacos. *Appetite, 58*(3), 928–935.

The VOICE group. (2010a). Buying into motherhood? Problematic consumption and ambivalence in transitional phases. *Consumption, Markets & Culture, 13*(4), 373–397.

The VOICE group. (2010b). Motherhood, marketization, and consumer vulnerability: Voicing international consumer experiences. *Journal of Macromarketing, 30*(4), 384–397.

Thompson, C. J. (1996). Caring consumers: Gendered consumption meanings and the juggling lifestyle. *Journal of Consumer Research, 22*(4), 388–407.

Thomsen, T. U., & Sørensen, E. B. (2006). The first four-wheeled status symbol: Pram consumption as a vehicle for the construction of motherhood identity. *Journal of Marketing Management, 22*(9), 907–927.

Warde, A. (2005). Consumption and theories of practice. *Journal of Consumer Culture, 5*(2), 131–153.

Warde, A. (2014). After taste: Consumption and theories of practice. *Journal of Consumer Culture, 14*(3), 279–303.

Wilk, R. (2010). Power at the table: Food fights and happy meals. *Cultural Studies ↔ Critical Methodologies, 10*(6), 428–436.

12 The intersection of family dinners and high school schedules in urban China

Ann Veeck, Hongyan Yu and Fang (Grace) Yu

Introduction

I strongly object to this style of education. It destroys children's health. But we have no choice.

(TH, father of 16-year-old son)

As in the US and Europe (Wilk, 2010; Daly, 2001), family dinners in China are often represented as idealised shelters of family life, a time in which the family can relax, commiserate, and draw strength from one another (Veeck, Yu, & Burns, 2009; Veeck & Burns, 2005). Even as working and leisure lives have become busier, the incidence of dinners eaten at home with the whole family present remains high (Shi, Lien, Kumar, & Holmboe-Ottesen, 2005). Yet, when urban Chinese children enter middle school and especially high school, the time students are required to physically spend at their school can increase to up to 12 to 14 hours a day. As a result, two valued rituals of Chinese family life come into direct conflict: the practice of family meals and the practice of education.

Everyday life is composed of a number of practices (e.g. working, studying, exercising, commuting) that have to be ordered and synchronised (see Marshall, Chapter 13). Every individual is a 'unique crossing point' of a multitude of practices (Reckwitz, 2002), each with its own claims and compensations, and governing rules and procedures (Shove, 2009; Southerton, 2006; Warde, 2005; Schatzki, 1996). While studies have examined competing practices within a 'meta-practice' (i.e. Molander's 2011 study of 'everyday dinner') and the temporal organisation of practices (Southerton, 2006), less empirical work has explored the direct encounter of two or more conflicting practices. What happens when practices compete for time, space, and energy? What characteristics of practices affect how the intersecting activities are reconciled?

The purpose of this study is to empirically investigate the mechanisms guiding the resolution of conflicting practices. We are interested in what Warde (2005) calls the 'hierarchy of practices', in which two or more practices are interdependent in fundamental ways, such that one practice profoundly alters or impedes the activities of another (Southerton, 2006). Warde

(2005) suggests that studying the intersection of practices can be revealing in several ways. First, Warde (2005: 149) states that examining more than one practice reveals 'what level of commitment is displayed to different practices'. Second, Warde (2005: 147) proposes that studying the hierarchies of practices 'becomes an empirical question of which specific internal and external benefits accrue to people in particular positions within identified practices'. Third, Warde (2013: 27) postulates that a practice that is 'weakly regulated and weakly organized', such as eating, is vulnerable to domination by other practices. We find all three of these propositions useful for our analysis.

The focus of our study is the intrusion of teenagers' school schedules on family meals. To explore these intersecting practices, we draw on interviews with pairs of high school students and their parents, in which we examine idealised and actual patterns of meals. Our analysis substantiates the notion that, rather than being simply a product of individual and family choice, meal patterns are often intrinsic to the socio-economic and institutional forces in which they are embedded (Halkier, 2012). We develop a framework that, according to 1) the extent of the conflict of the practices in time and space, and 2) the degree of formal regulation of one practice versus another, describes four potential outcomes that can result when one practice is threatened by another: integration, modification, debilitation, and domination. The findings highlight a 'value-action gap' (Blake, 1999), or at least an absence of conscious reflexivity or intentionality, as might be predicted, given the structuring social, economic, and historical context of the actions (Askegaard & Linnet, 2011; Warde, 2005).

In the following sections, we first describe the context of our study – i.e. the educentric lives of urban Chinese teenagers. Next we provide an overview of our method for examining the interplay of family dinners and education in the lives of households with high school-age children. We then introduce a two-dimensional grid that demonstrates scenarios that may result from overlapping practices. In the conclusion, we discuss the dynamics of the interlinked forces that can affect daily behaviour.

Family meals and *Gaokao* preparation

The context of this study is the family dinner for households in urban China that include high school-age children. As with nearly every aspect of daily lives, family meals have been profoundly influenced by the rapid social and economic changes that have occurred in Chinese cities during the last three decades. Daily routines that once allowed most urban residents – including school children and working adults – to return to their living residences midday for a home-cooked lunch and brief nap (Veeck, 2000) have been largely supplanted by long days at work or school. Food systems have evolved to accommodate these new lifestyles, including a rapidly growing processed snack industry and restaurants that cluster around workplaces and schools and will deliver boxed meals to office workers and high school and university students (Veeck, Yu, Yu, Veeck, & Gentry, 2014). Family meals at home now compete with the convenient food options offered away from home.

The biggest challenge to regular family dinners in Chinese cities might be rigorous school schedules, which relentlessly intensify as students advance through grade levels (Veeck et al., 2014). The time required in school reaches a peak the final couple of years of high school as students prepare for the *gaokao*, the national higher education entrance examination whose score largely dictates whether or not a student will attend a high-ranking college, which in turn can determine if a graduate obtains an adequate paying job, or even a job at all, in China's tightening economy. While the pressure for Chinese youngsters to perform well on the *gaokao* has a lengthy history, with roots in the imperial exam used to select government officials (Zhao, 2012), the stress has increased with the advent of the one-child policy, which has led the hopes of a family (i.e. two parents, four grandparents) to be channelled towards a single child (Fong, 2004; Veeck, Flurry, & Jiang, 2003). The one-child policy has recently been relaxed, but the single child phenomenon is projected to continue in urban areas, given the large amount of time and money required to raise a child in a city (*The Economist*, 2014). Increasing the stakes of the outcome of the *gaokao* is the fact that not only are children judged on their *gaokao* scores, but so are their families, their teachers, their schools, and the districts in which they live (Zhao, 2009).

The overall number of higher education institutions in China has increased with the advent of for-profit universities, but the supply of universities that are considered to be of high quality has remained fairly constant, even while demand has risen (Kirkpatrick & Zang, 2011; Wong, 2012). The Chinese media abounds with reports condemning the perceived lack of development of physical, mental, social, and moral health that accompanies intense preparation for the *gaokao* (e.g. Carducci, 2014; Xiao, 2013; Chen, 2012). Research has confirmed a link between education pressures in China and mental and physical impairment (Wang, 2014; Chen, 2012; Hesketh, Zhen, Lu, Dong, Jun, & Xing, 2010; Hesketh & Ding, 2005). Still, recent central government initiatives aimed to reduce the academic pressure on Chinese children have had little traction (Zhao, 2009). Meanwhile, a flourishing market, called the '*gaokao* economy', has developed around the national exam, the beneficiaries of which include tutoring services, study aid vendors, hotels and restaurants near test sites, sellers of lucky charms, and temples that accept donations from hopeful parents and grandparents (Luo, 2013). Our objective is to use this context to explore conflicting family practices.

Methodology

This chapter is part of a larger study of teenager food choices in urban areas of China. For this research, 16 family pairs, consisting of a child in upper-middle (high) school who lives at home and the primary food shopper in his or her household, were interviewed in Changchun, China. The members of the dyads were interviewed in their homes or at a public location of their choice, using a semi-structured interview guide. The child and adult family member were isolated for the interviews. The teenagers were asked to detail the guidelines they believe should be used to make food choices, including what to eat, where to eat, with whom to eat, how much to eat, and when to eat. The teens were subsequently asked what, where, with whom, how much, and when they ate on the previous day. In parallel interviews, the adults were asked to outline the guidelines that they contend should be used to make food choices, then asked to state what, where, with whom, how much, and when they believed that their teenage child ate during the previous day. While the families we interviewed were mainly middle-class families, the experiences they describe, related to the time conflict between family dinner and education commitments, affects virtually all families of adolescents in Chinese cities (Zhao, 2009; Fong, 2004).

Following the data collection, the interviews were transcribed in Chinese and then translated to English, and the transcriptions and field notes were analysed. An inventory of the most important self-defined guiding meals for both teenagers and adults were compiled and compared. Then, the actual food patterns of teens and their external influences were examined. Finally, we identified and analysed incidents in which competing practices encroached upon family meals, iteratively comparing and categorising tensions and strategies that resulted from the conflicts.

Balancing family meals and education

Findings from the interviews reveal that the eating practices of Chinese children are greatly affected when students reach middle and especially high school, as the pressure to prepare for the college preparation examination intensifies and the time away from home increases. Further, the food habits of these children appear to change in ways that are in direct contradiction to what their parents consider to be best practices. When asked to articulate what they believed to be the most important guidelines related to eating, parents' answers could be roughly divided into three tenets. The first tenet might be called 'eat nutritiously' and would include rules such as 'eat lots of fruits and vegetables', 'avoid processed food', 'eat a balanced diet', and 'eat food in season'. The second tenet is 'eat safely', including such rules as 'don't eat at risky places', 'avoid risky food', 'avoid counterfeit food', 'eat at home', and 'observe expiration dates'. The third tenet is 'eat regularly', with rules including, 'eat three meals', 'eat dinner together as a family', 'eat at regular times', 'avoid snacks', and 'don't eat too close to bedtime'.

Most of these parent-defined eating rules are difficult to follow for students who may leave home as early as 6:00 a.m. for their commutes and routinely remain in school until 8:30 or 9:00 p.m., as was standard for our older teenage informants. HY, age 16, described her schedule this way:

Honestly I can't eat three regular meals. In the morning I get up late, I Just wash my hair and face then have to rush to school without breakfast. I have one hour for lunch break, so I can't eat right, just foods like ma la tang (spicy noodle soup).... For supper, I get home at 8:30 p.m. at the earliest, sometimes after 10:30 p.m.

As HY indicates, the education schedule of high school children leaves little room for family meals and instead encourages food consumption patterns for teenagers that often involve eating at irregular times, eating meals from fast food restaurants, and consuming snacks such as potato chips and candy bars. While we encountered 'devotional mothers' (Cappellini & Parsons, 2012) (and some fathers) who are committed to providing well-balanced, tasty dinners for their families, we often discovered later in the interview – when parents detailed what they believed their children had actually eaten the previous day – that the children's school schedule did not allow them to regularly participate in family dinners. It was striking to what extent the actual food patterns of the teenagers deviated from what their parents listed as ideal prescriptions for eating.

A number of relevant intersections between education and eating practices might be examined to understand how parents' purported guidelines for eating become undermined within the context of interest (see Molander, Chapter 11). Eating practices that could be studied, for example, might include teenagers' patronage of restaurants, the purchase of snack foods, and dieting behaviour. For this study, we have chosen to focus on the practice of family meals because of the degree to which they are affected by the secondary education schedules, with all three meals – breakfast, lunch, and dinner – compromised. Since eating lunch at school is normative behaviour for students from an early age, it is not generally perceived to conflict with family meals, as opposed to breakfast and dinner. Breakfast, on the other hand, was often severely undermined by school schedules. The pre-dawn waking time that is common for middle and high school means that the teenagers we interviewed often reported grabbing something convenient, such as bread, to eat on the way to school, or skipping breakfast altogether and eating packaged snacks later in the morning. Ultimately, however, we chose to focus on the family dinner due to its privileged, idealised status, not only in China but in many other places throughout the world (Wilk, 2010; Daly, 2001). In our findings, we found four scenarios that can occur as a result of a conflict between family meals and organised activities: integration, modification, debilitation, and domination. Each of these scenarios will be illustrated via four different families who are balancing family meals and education.

Integration

'Integrations' of practices occur when intersecting practices are not strictly regulated and the practices take place at more flexible times. Younger

Chinese children are generally home from school early enough for their school schedules not to interfere with an appropriately timed family dinner. As such, in younger grades family meals and education might be called integrated. The parents' self-defined guidelines for eating are easier to adhere to under 'integrated' conditions since parents retain control of dinner conditions.

For instance, TJ (aged 46), mother of a 16-year-old son, LW, said that dinner was the most important meal of the day for the family, since her child left the house too early to eat what she considers to be an adequate breakfast and ate lunch at school. As a result, TJ said that their family almost always eats together.

> Our son is growing, so we focus on him. We adults should eat more vegetables. But our son is growing, so we often cook meat and vegetable dishes for him.... Our family always eats together, at the same time, always at the dining room table. We never casually eat whenever we want.... These are ingrained traditional Chinese values. This is just what we should do as a family. It's traditional for Chinese families.

When TJ was asked what time they ate dinner, she responded that there was no fixed time because the family coordinated their meals with their son's school schedule. 'There are no strict rules. We entirely follow our son's school times. If he comes home late, we eat late.' When asked what time was too late, the mother emphasised that they would never eat too late, because that would not be healthy: 'In our family, we never eat dinner after 8:00. Too late is impossible.' In a separate interview, TJ's son, LW, confirmed that his classes end at 6:50 p.m., and that he eats dinner with his parents at 7:30 p.m. after he returns home. In other words, at least at this stage of LW's education, LW's family is able to satisfactorily balance their guidelines for eating and LW's education obligations.

Modification

Modification of practices occurs when the timing of the practices frequently conflict but neither practice has a formal schedule that regularly precludes the activities of another. Chinese freshmen and sophomore high school students have a relatively more relaxed schedule than older students that often allows the practice of a family dinner, although irregular events may mean that the timing of the family dinner has to be adjusted to the child's schedule. As such, rules related to eating meals at regular times may experience minor infractions due to school events, but guidelines related to food practices can generally still be controlled.

The family of YJ (aged 17) is an excellent example of 'modification', since they moved to an apartment that was a five-minute walk from their son's school when YJ was accepted at a top-rated high school, to ease coordination of the family's activities. YJ's father, ZJH (aged 43), stressed that his son has a strict schedule, stating that YJ eats breakfast at home before leaving for school at 6:00 to 6:30 a.m., eats lunch with classmates at school between 11:30 and 12:00 and then eats dinner at 5:00 to 6:30 p.m. The father emphasised the importance of a fixed meal schedule, but said that if their son stayed late at school, then they would postpone dinner to eat with their son. A reason that ZJH felt that family dinners were important was to be sure that his son would have a nutritious meal, stating, 'I worry. Sometimes he skips lunch.'

Separately, ZJH's son, YJ, admitted that he perceives the meals that he eats at home to be more nutritious and safe than those he eats with his classmates:

> It is okay for me to have meals outside or at home, but I prefer to eat at home. It is healthy and safe and I enjoy the family environment. If I have to eat out, I try to choose a clean restaurant.... I like best to eat with my family. I enjoy the family atmosphere, and I feel comfortable and relaxed. When I eat out, it's with my friends.

It is important to note that close physical distance between the apartment and the son's school facilitates regular attendance at family meals while accommodating the school schedule – a choice consciously made by the parents.

Debilitation

When two practices conflict slightly and one practice is regulated strictly, the practice that is less regulated will experience 'debilitation'. In this scenario, the less-regulated practice will continue, but in a compromised form. An example of 'debilitated' family dinners occurs in the case of the family of 17-year-old LG. LG's father, LF (aged 45) has very strong opinions related to nutrition. For example, the father stated that it is important to avoid eating excessive amounts of the food in the evening, which for him means to not eat a large dinner, or in particular, to not eat too late in the evening, the practice of which he said could lead to indigestion and obesity. LF explained that their family adapted their breakfast and dinner times to the school schedule of their son:

> Our meals are always coordinated to our son's schedule. We eat when he goes to school and when he comes home from school. Take breakfast, for example. We eat when my son wakes up.

Later in the interview, LF relayed that his son returns home from school late every evening. This means that, in fact, he and his wife cannot always coordinate dinners with their son's schedule, since that would violate their rule about eating too late. As a compromise, he and his wife eat dinner together earlier but one of them always serves their son dinner when he comes home later and sits with him while he eats. LF explained how he and his wife coordinate dinners as follows:

> In summary, we first consider our son's time, and then our own time. In fact, to maintain a healthy lifestyle the time [between lunch and dinner] should not be too long. We eat lunch at noon, but our son doesn't get out of school until 8:30 in the evening. We usually cook and eat our dinner earlier. One of us will keep our son company when he eats. Why do we eat earlier? Because when you get older, if we eat with our child and then go to sleep, the time [between eating and sleeping] is not adequate and it will be bad for our health.

In short, LG's late school schedule places the family's rules (i.e. don't eat too late, eat at regular times, and eat as a family) in direct contradiction with one another, with the result being a compromised form of family dinner.

Domination

The final outcome of conflicting practices, 'domination', occurs when two practices are so incompatible that one practice ultimately dominates the other. This scenario characterises the family dinners of almost all of the high school seniors, many of the juniors, and even some of the freshmen and sophomore informants. In a typical case, the family dinner had been largely abandoned. The teenagers generally ate dinner with their peers, either on the school grounds or at a nearby restaurant, or ate large snacks in the late afternoon, supplemented by whatever leftovers were available when they returned home, typically around 9:00 p.m. In this case, the main tenets defined by parents to guide food-related choices – eat safely, eat healthily, and eat regularly – were all imperilled.

An example of the 'domination' outcome occurred in the overlap of education and family dinner during the senior year of YK, a 19-year-old male who had recently graduated from high school, completed the *gaokao*, and been accepted to a top-ranked university. When we talked to his father, YXD (aged 47) emphasised the importance of the family dinner, characterising the meal in idealised terms (Wilk, 2010):

> Supper should be tasty – that is the most important part of dinner. It should be good and tasty, and dinner should be plentiful.... All the family comes back. It's the main meal. At noon our family can't eat together. The child is studying in school and the parents are working.... Dinner is when the family gets together after they've all been away. Getting together after being apart all day, everyone will be happy when the food tastes good. The mood of the family will also be very good. In addition, after a hard day of study and work, everyone is tired when they get home and can eat some delicious food. Then everybody can relax,

which makes you have a better mood at the end of the day. This also improves quality of life.... Parents don't get enough chance to communicate with their children, so eating is a good chance to communicate.

Upon an additional query, however, YXD disclosed that, in actuality, this scenario had seldom occurred in recent months:

In fact, in the last year, when our son was preparing for the university-entrance exam, it was difficult for our family to get together for dinner.

In a separate interview, the son, YK, recounted that during his senior year he rose at 5:20 a.m. to reach school by its required 6:50 a.m. start and left school at 8:30 p.m. By the time he reached home, his parents had usually already eaten but left food for him. YK described how he generally ate both lunch and dinner with 15 or 16 of his male friends. Showing us a large pile of restaurant menus, YK explained that he and his friends would select a restaurant, and then sometimes eat at the restaurant or call in a large food order to be delivered to the school gates. YK admitted that these meals are often unhealthy and/or unsanitary.

We like to eat great tasting food but the majority of delicious food is unhealthy.... Near to our school there are a lot of restaurants, but many are unsanitary. It's really common to see a cockroach.... Eating (healthy foods) takes too much time. As a student, we only have 40 minutes to eat. If I took the time to eat healthy foods, I'd be punished in class. I didn't even have time to take a nap. If I put study second, I'd fail.

Asked about his school cafeteria, which would presumably offer healthier and safer food, YK explained:

Nobody goes to the cafeteria. The cafeteria is a rip-off. Freshmen will go because they have a cafeteria card with money that they have to use up. But after that nobody usually goes. The cafeteria food isn't great, and the prices are the same as the outside.

Importantly, YK seemed to take great pleasure in the meals he had with his friends, describing the fun he had selecting food and eating with his classmates. He noted that dinners with his family are not always pleasant: 'Sometimes, for example, my father will say, "Why didn't you get a good grade on this exam?"' While admitting that his meals with his classmates were not as healthy as family dinners at home, YK seemed to receive social benefits from eating with peers.

Discussion: understanding the hierarchy of practices

Our research reveals that, as has been found in studies describing family meals in the US and Europe (e.g. Cappellini & Parsons, 2012; Wilk, 2010; Daly, 2001), a disconnect exists between the normative ideal of the family dinner, as described by parents themselves, and the realised practice for Chinese families with high school-age children. As children progress through high school, increased time requirements are added to the students' academic schedules, with the result that the family dinner is likely to metamorphose from integrated, to modified, to debilitated, and, finally, to dominated in the course of a child's education. For example, TJ, the mother who currently 'integrates' family dinner and education, stated that her family never eats past 8:00 p.m. ('Too late is impossible'). If her son follows the course of the older high school students we interviewed, the mother will inevitably need to choose between the 'impossible' position of eating after 8:00 p.m. or forgoing family dinners with their son altogether. As illustrated in Figure 12.1, conflicting practices can be represented in a grid: the horizontal axis, 'conflict', represents the extent that the practices are in direct contention in time and space, and the vertical axis, 'regulation' represents the extent that one practice is formally regulated versus a second practice.

Studying intersecting practice presents challenges. Presumably, examining how conflicts between practices that collide are resolved should reveal the relative value of each set of practices. Yet, in the case of the conflict between Chinese family meals and the college preparation system, it is not clear the extent to which reflexivity guides these decisions. The father quoted at the beginning of the chapter who claims that the current system of education

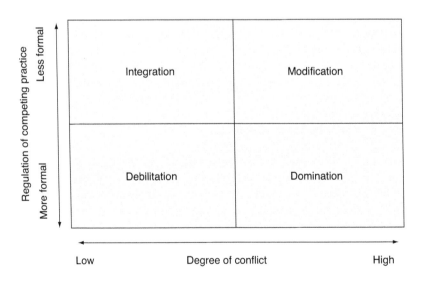

Figure 12.1 Potential outcomes for contested practices.

'destroys children's health' stated that 'we have no choice'. 'We have no choice' was a frequent response of parents when asked how they feel about their children being away from home for long days to pursue their studies. In the current competitive education environment, parents feel that their teenagers must conform to the rigid requirements of the system to be successful, thus ensuring the reproduction of the practice of mandating that adolescent students spend an intense amount of time on high school studies. Given the frequent reports in the popular media that the pressure on teenagers created by the educational system can be harmful to physical and mental health, requiring late night classes at the expense of family dinners, can deliver a message – whether accurate or not – that academic achievement is more important than health.

A close examination of the hierarchy of practices can also reveal the benefits and harms that practices offer to stakeholders (Warde, 2005). As explained in the discussion of the '*gaokao* economy', a number of players benefit financially from China's national exam system. In addition, the convenience stores and restaurants that tend to circle secondary institutions reap direct and indirect benefits from the late hours that children spend in school. Teachers, school administrators, and politicians who are judged by the performance of students under their responsibility will also not be anxious to relax the time their charges spend preparing for the exams. And, most crucially, children and parents, with their futures at stake, feel powerless to renounce a system so entrenched in contemporary Chinese society.

It is also quite possible that a formally regulated practice, such as a school schedule, could be allowed to dominate another practice because of more hidden, less overt values that are not readily accessible. For example, while parents almost universally praised family meals, their teenagers were not as unanimous in their praise. Although some teenagers, such as YJ cited above, seemed to enjoy eating with their parents, several other teenagers, like YK, complained that they were often nagged during meals. While not necessarily sources of good nutrition, the communal meals of high school students may contribute to the socialisation, maturity, and independence of these children (Stead, McDermott, MacKintosh, & Adamson, 2011). Just as family meals reinforce the importance of identity as a member of the family (Cappellini & Parsons, 2012; DeVault, 1994; Charles & Kerr, 1986), eating with peers during late adolescence may reinforce other equally important identities for teenagers (Stead et al., 2011) and offer external social benefits (Bourdieu, 1984).

The increased difficulty in organising family meals due to the infringement of individual participation in structured events by children is certainly not exclusive to China. The Chinese case is simply an extreme example, since the interruption of family dinners by organised education activities reaches near universality in urban Chinese families with teenage children. In North America and Europe, family meal rituals are regularly disrupted by structured and unstructured activities (Harkness et al., 2011; Lareau & Weininger, 2008), fuelling an ongoing debate related to the relative value of family activities, organised activities, and unstructured time (Fiese, Foley, & Spagnola, 2006; Eccles, Barber, Stone, & Hunt, 2003). Organised programmes, particularly ones from which other powerful stakeholders benefit, can impede parents' authority to guide how children spend their time, including what, how, when, and with whom they eat. As this study illustrates, understanding the value regimes that drive the (non)practice of family meals requires analysing the place of meals in the hierarchy of interrelated practices as embedded in the socio-cultural patterns of everyday life.

References

Askegaard, S., & Linnet, J. T. (2011). Towards an epistemology of consumer culture theory: Phenomenology and the context of context. *Marketing Theory, 11*(4), 381–404.

Blake, J. (1999). Overcoming the 'value-action gap' in environmental policy: Tensions between national policy and local experience. *Local Environment, 4*(3), 257–278.

Bourdieu, P. (1984). *Distinction: A Social Critique of the Judgment of Taste.* Cambridge, MA: Harvard University Press.

Cappellini, B., & Parsons, E. (2012). Sharing the meal: Food consumption and family identity. *Research in Consumer Behavior, 14*(1), 109–128.

Carducci, L. (2014). Develop mind but don't forget body. *China Daily* [online] 9 August. Available at: http://usa.chinadaily.com.cn/epaper/2014-08/15/content_18319665. htm [Accessed 15 August 2014].

Charles, N., & Kerr, M. (1986). Eating properly, the family and state benefit. *Sociology, 20*(3), 412–429.

Chen, H. (2012). Impact of parent's socioeconomic status on perceived parental pressure and test anxiety among Chinese high school students. *International Journal of Psychological Studies, 4*(2), 235–247.

Daly, K. J. (2001). Deconstructing family time: From ideology to lived experience. *Journal of Marriage and Family, 63*(2), 283–294.

DeVault, M. L. (1994). *Feeding the Family: The Social Organization of Caring as Gendered Work.* Chicago: University of Chicago Press.

Eccles, J., Barber, B. L., Stone, M., & Hunt, J. (2003). Extracurricular activities and adolescent development. *Journal of Social Issues, 59*(4), 865–889.

Fiese, B. H., Foley K. P., & Spagnola, M. (2006). Routine and ritual elements in family mealtimes: Contexts for child well-being and family identity. *New Directions for Child and Adolescent Development, 111*(2), 67–89.

Fong, V. L. (2004). *Only Hope: Coming of Age under China's One-Child Policy.* Stanford: Stanford University Press.

Halkier, B. (2012). *Consumption Challenged: Food in Medialised Everyday Lives.* Burlington, VT: Ashgate Publishing.

Harkness, S., Zylicz, P. O., Super, C. M., Welles-Nyström, B., Bermúdez, M. R., Bonichini, S., ... Mavridis, C. J. (2011). Children's activities and their meanings for parents: A mixed-methods study in six Western cultures. *Journal of Family Psychology, 25*(6), 799–813.

Hesketh, T., & Ding, Q. I. (2005). Anxiety and depression in adolescents in urban and rural China. *Psychological Reports, 96*(2), 435–444.

Hesketh, T., Zhen, Y., Lu, L., Dong, Z. X., Jun, Y. X., & Xing, Z. W. (2010). Stress and psychosomatic symptoms in Chinese school children: Cross-sectional survey. *Archives of Disease in Childhood, 95*(2), 136–140.

Kirkpatrick, R., & Zang, Y. (2011). The negative influences of exam-oriented education on Chinese high school students: Backwash from classroom to child. *Language Testing in Asia, 1*(3), 36–57.

Lareau, A., & Weininger, E. B. (2008). Time, work, and family life: Reconceptualizing gendered time patterns through the case of children's organized activities. *Sociological Forum, 23*(3), 419–454.

Luo, W. (2013). Businesses benefit from 'gaokao economy'. *China Daily* [online] 7 June. Available at: www.chinadaily.com.cn/m/fuzhou/e/2013-06/07/content_16635811_3.htm [Accessed 21 August 2014].

Molander, S. (2011). Food, love and meta-practices: A study of everyday dinner consumption among single mothers. *Research in Consumer Behaviour, 13*(1), 77–92.

Reckwitz, A. (2002). Toward a theory of social practices: A development in culturalist theorizing. *European Journal of Social Theory, 5*(2), 243–263.

Schatzki, T. R. (1996). *Social Practices: A Wittgensteinian Approach to Human Activity and the Social*. Cambridge: Cambridge University Press.

Shi, Z., Lien, N., Kumar, B. N., & Holmboe-Ottesen, G. (2005). Socio-demographic differences in food habits and preferences of school adolescents in Jiangsu Province, China. *European Journal of Clinical Nutrition, 59*(12), 1439–1448.

Shove, E. (2009). Everyday practices and the production and consumption of time. In E. Shove, F. Trentmann, & R. Wilk (Eds.), *Time, Consumption and Everyday Life: Practice, Materiality and Culture*. New York: Berg, 17–34.

Southerton, D. (2006). Analysing the temporal organization of daily life: Social constraints, practices and their allocation, *Sociology, 40*(3), 435–454.

Stead, M., McDermott, L., MacKintosh, A. M., & Adamson, A. (2011). Why healthy eating is bad for young people's health: Identity, belonging and food. *Social Science & Medicine, 72*(7), 1131–1139.

The Economist. (2014). One-child productivity. 19 July, 40.

Veeck, A. (2000). The revitalization of the marketplace: Food markets of Nanjing. In D. Davis (Ed.), *The Consumer Revolution in Urban China* (pp. 107–123). Berkeley: California University Press.

Veeck, A., & Burns, A. C. (2005). Changing tastes: The adoption of new food choices in post-reform China. *Journal of Business Research, 58*(5), 644–652.

Veeck, A., Flurry, A., & Jiang, N. (2003). Equal dreams: The one child policy and the consumption of education in urban China. *Consumption, Markets and Culture, 6*(1), 81–94.

Veeck, A., Yu, H., & Burns, A. V. (2009). The 'proper meal' and social capital in urban China. *Advances in Consumer Research, 36*(1), 636–637.

Veeck, A., Yu, F. G., Yu, H., Veeck, G., & Gentry, J. W. (2014). Influences on food choices of urban Chinese teenagers. *Young Consumers, 15*(4), 296–311.

Wang, Y. C. (2014) In search of the Confucian family: Interviews with parents and their middle school children in Guangzhou, China. *Journal of Adolescent Research, 29*(6), 765–782.

Warde, A. (2005). Consumption and theories of practice. *Journal of Consumer Culture, 5*(2), 131–153.

Warde, A. (2013) What sort of practice is eating? In E. Shove & N. Spurling (Eds.), *Sustainable Practices: Social Theory and Climate Change*. Oxford: Routledge, 17–30.

Wilk, R. R. (2010). Power at the table: Food fights and happy meals. *Cultural Studies ↔ Critical Methodologies, 10*(6), 426–438.

Wong, E. (2012). Test that can determine the course of life in China gets a closer examination, *The New York Times* [online] 30 June. Available at: http://www.nytimes.com/2012/07/01/world/asia/burden-of-chinas-college-entrance-test-sets-off-wide-debate.html [Accessed 21 August 2014].

Xiao, L. (2013). A social problem on moral grounds, *China Daily* [online] 13 March. Available at: http://usa.chinadaily.com.cn/opinion/2013-03/13/content_16303928.htm [Accessed 21 August 2014].

Zhao, Y. (2009). *Catching Up or Leading the Way: American Education in the Age of Globalization*. Alexandria, VA: ASCD.

Zhao, Y. (2012). Reforming Chinese education: What China is trying to learn from America. *Solutions: For a Sustainable and Desirable Future, 2*(2), 38–43.

13 Meal deviations

Children's food socialisation and the practice of snacking

David Marshall

Introduction

The sanctity afforded to the idea of three meals per day is probably best reflected in an iconic advertising campaign for the Milky Way chocolate bar, screened on UK television in the 1980s which included the famous strapline[1] 'The sweet you can eat between meals without ruining your appetite'. In this chapter I want to examine snacking as part of children's food socialisation and consider how these practices serve as a meeting point between the marketplace and the home. Adopting a practice perspective encourages us to understand how consumption is 'entangled in webs of social reproductions and changes' (Halkier & Iben, 2011: 102). Practices refer to ways of doing things linked through understandings (know what to do), procedures (understand the principles and rules) and engagements (emotionally and normatively) (Halkier & Iben, 2011; Warde, 2005; Schatzki, 1997). I want to show how snacking, with the emphasis on informality and fun, is seen as a legitimised deviation from 'proper eating', with its own rules and rituals, rather than a challenge to the serious practice of meals. As Schatzki (1997: 302) notes, we can only begin to understand associated activities within the context of the practice.

Eating properly

Eating properly is about much more than nutrition, and the shared consumption practice of the meal is often seen as an important site for introducing children to the rituals and regulations of 'eating properly' (Jackson, 2009; Valentine, 1999; Grieshaber, 1997; Charles & Kerr, 1988; Murcott, 1982). Whereas the ideology of the family meal may be very different from the actual practice (see Gram, Chapter 3), eating together remains an important aspect of family life (Jackson, 2009; Marshall, 2005; Murcott, 1982). Moreover, family meals are seen by some as an opportunity to 'discipline' children in a 'normalising' process (Grieshaber, 1997) that prepares them in their transition to adulthood (Ward, 1974). As family decision making becomes increasingly 'democraticised', children are exerting more influence over what families eat (Johansson, 2014; Brembeck et al., 2013; Kerrane, Hogg, & Bettany, 2012; Dixon & Banwell, 2004) and buy (Gram, 2015; Marshall, 2014). By challenging rules around eating, children are beginning to modify the social order and (re)negotiate household food practices around personal preferences (O'Connell & Brannen, 2014; Ochs & Shohet, 2006; Valentine, 1999; see also Molander, Chapter 11). This influence can be seen primarily in small meals and snacks (Cook, 2009; Nørgaard, Brunso, Christensen, & Mikkelsen, 2007; Romani, 2005). However, as Curtis, James and Ellis note 'children's eating practices are marginalised in out-of-family-time and "othered" in relation to the important business of proper family meals' yet managed within 'the ebb and flow of everyday family lives' that reflects inter-generational identity (2010: 301).

Mind the gap

The term 'snack', probably originates from Middle Dutch *snacken,* a variant of *snappen* to snap, and refers to '1. light quick meal eaten between or in place of main meals. 2. A sip or bite.... 5. (*intransitive*) to eat a snack' (Collins English Dictionary, 1986). Yet there is sufficient breadth of interpretation to make the definition of a snack somewhat ambiguous (Chamontin, Pretzer, & Booth, 2003). Johnson and Anderson (2010) argue that the lack of a universal definition is an impediment to the interpretation of research in this area and propose that:

> A snack is composed of solid food(s), including those typically eaten with a utensil (with or without a beverage) that occurs between habitual meal occasions for the individual, is not a substitute for a meal, and provides substantially fewer calories than would be consumed in a typical meal.
>
> (2010: 851)

Snacks have a few simple ingredients, incorporate smaller quantities of food, often using less healthy and usually uncooked items; they are often eaten on the move, alone and do not involve a lot of planning. As Marshall (2005) notes, snacks may include portable, processed or takeaway foods which can be eaten anytime during the day. They do not necessarily involve everyone eating the same food. Snacks include 'self-contained' food items that are often assembled rather than prepared, although the combination of ingredients is not random and the timing of snacks is aligned closely with the mid-morning, afternoon and supper snacks of the past (Yates & Warde, 2015). Young adults associate snacks with eating alone, standing and smaller portions while meals are associated with family eating, larger portions, sitting down, using plates and napkins (Wansik, Payne, & Shimizu, 2010). But what do children make of these eating occasions?

Marketing snacks and promoting 'fun'

[I]n the context of parents' busy lives and a highly marketized food environment, child-led approaches to parenting are likely to result in children's diets being high in 'children's foods', which, in the UK at least, are foods considered 'junk' or highly processed.

(O'Connell & Brannen, 2014: 97)

The UK snack market, comprising three key sectors – confectionery; crisps and savoury snacks; cakes and biscuits – was worth £13 billion in 2012 (Mintel, 2013). Snacking is ingrained in the habits of British children with the majority of children snacking at least once a day and over half snacking continuously, or several times per day. Hunger is cited as the main motivation for children snacking and parents prefer to give children snacks they will eat. Around two-thirds of children have a say in what they snack on; popular snacks include: fruit (72 per cent), crisps (70 per cent), chocolate (58 per cent), sweet biscuits (53 per cent) and yogurt (52 per cent) (Mintel, 2013; YouGov, 2013; Macdiarmid, Loe, Craig, Masson, Holmes, & McNeill, 2009). Children (7–15 years old) who eat healthy snacks (around 58 per cent) are outnumbered by those who eat crisps, biscuits, confectionery or cakes (around 89 per cent) (YouGov, 2013). Despite these concerns about the increase in children's snacking, their preferences and practices appear to extend beyond the heavily promoted snack food categories.

While the relationship between advertising and food consumption is complex (Ambler, 2006; Livingstone & Helsper, 2004; Young, 2003) the majority of food advertising expenditure[2] goes towards the promotion of foods that are less healthy (Cairns, 2013; Federal Trade Commission (FTC), 2012; Boyland, Harrold, Kirkham, & Halford, 2011; Harris, Pomeranz, Lobstein, & Brownell, 2009; Hastings et al., 2003). In contrast, basic foods and staples such as potatoes and rice, meat and fish, fruit and vegetables, receive relatively little promotion from the respective producer or retail bodies (see Gamble & Cotugna, 1999). Much of the promotional expenditure on food goes on high fat, sugar and salt products (HFSS) or 'unhealthy' foods (Hastings et al., 2003). Prior to the 2007 UK advertising ban on HFSS foods during children's prime television, around 20 per cent of all commercials seen by children were for food (Ofcom, 2006, 2013). However, children's viewing is not confined to child time programming slots and even after the ban these core foods remain the most heavily advertised food categories on television and are an integral part of television programmes (Scully et al., 2014). Snack marketing extends beyond the television screen to include the Internet, the retail store, even sports facilities and schools (Boseley, 2014). The extent of this media exposure is reflected in children's ability to recall specific campaigns, slogans and jingles from confectionery, fast foods and drinks commercials, much of it centred on fun (Marshall, Kline, & O'Donohoe, 2006). This idea of food as fun, often underpinned with a promise of nutritional value to appeal to parents, is reflected in the brand names, bright colours and appealing packaging seen on television, on-line (where there is much less regulation) and in store (Cairns, 2013; Elliott, 2008, 2011). Marketing campaigns include celebrity endorsement, animation to attract younger consumers, as well as in store activities that younger children may find attractive but difficult to understand (Kline, 2011; Which?, 2005). Given the much smaller amount spent in advertising healthy foods, one can understand some of the frustration of the health lobby (International Obesity Task Force, 2004; Gamble & Cotugna, 1999). This proliferation of fun foods and marketing activity raises questions about how this alters children's perceptions of eating and their relationship with food more generally (Elliott, 2010; Schor & Ford, 2007).

Snacking as oppositional

[C]hildren are being persuaded to eat particular foods, not on the basis of their tastiness, or other benefits, but because of their place in the social matrix of meaning. As this process expands, branded (i.e. junk) food comes to occupy an increasingly central position in children's sense of identity, their relationship to other children and adults, and the construction of meaning and value that structures their lives.

(Schor & Ford, 2007: 16)

James's (1979) early work on children's confectionery shows that children's worlds, while largely dependent on adults, are nevertheless separate and this dependency is itself subject to a creative process of interdependence. As she notes –

children construct their own ordered system of rules by reinterpreting the social models given to them by adults ... hence the true nature of the culture of childhood frequently remains hidden from adults, for the semantic cues which permit social recognition have been manipulated and disguised by children in terms of their alternative society.

(James, 1979: 83)

She shows how the term 'ket' has come to denote a particular type of sweet (usually a cheaper, unwrapped version) that represents the antithesis of (adult) food with names like Jelly Wellies, Lucky Black Cats, and Fizz Bombs. Moreover, it is not a case of sweets interfering with meals, rather, meals disrupting the eating of sweets[3] (James, 1979: 84). Children's snack consumption marks generational differences and within families children's food practices are often marginalised and their snacks differentiated from their parents in terms of quality and access. While some of the challenges to proper food that snacking represents are offset by delimiting access to certain times and occasions, it remains 'othered' and constituted as morally different, residing outside proper family food. But with this comes a paradox for families – how to manage children's food given their vulnerability to making 'wrong' choices (Curtis et al., 2010). Schor and Ford, quoted above, argue that marketing of branded (i.e. junk) food has led to a shift in perceptions[4] that promotes the 'cool factor'. In their analysis 'junk food' is 'anti-adult' and oppositional to such an extent that 'Ads often transport children to adult-free utopian spaces, devoid of the unwelcomed stresses and pressures caused by adults' (Schor & Ford, 2007: 17). Thus the appeal of sweets and junk food lies in this subversion of, and challenge to, the adult world.

But it is more than anti-adultism. In positioning their products as 'fun' marketers can positively identify with children and take their side, thus empowering them against adults (Cook, 2012: 45). Drawing on the example of Impact Confections, Cook (2012) shows how one company has created a line of interactive sweets (candy) that allows children to create their own flavour combinations and in the process recognises children 'as kids – i.e. as playful consumers who are distinct from adults' (Cook, 2012: 45). As Elliott points out, fun is a key component in food marketing to children and something that resonates with children, but it is not associated with nutrition and may have unintended consequences (Elliott, 2009). Moreover, promoting snacks as fun further differentiates the branded world of sweets and snacks from the domestic meal. Indeed much of the food advertising targeted at children[5] shows them grazing rather than sitting down to meals (Soni & Vohra, 2014) reinforcing the idea of snacks as less formal and fun. This positioning of snacks (children) as distinct from meals (adults) is complicated by the fact that snacking is not by any means exclusive to children although adult snacks may be differentiated in terms of quality (Curtis et al., 2010).

Snacking as practice[6]

The term 'snack' is somewhat ambiguous (Chamontin et al., 2003) and can refer to both specific foods and the eating event. 'Snack foods' might include a wide range of foods from crisps, chocolate and confectionery, as well as sugary breakfast cereals and fast foods that feature in much of the debate around children's snacking through to more wholesome biscuits and cakes and healthier fruit and vegetable items. Some of these 'snacks', usually home made by parents, such as beans on toast, bacon rolls or sandwiches might be better described as 'mini meals'. So snacks include a wide range of foods from the heavily branded to homemade and there is evidence that, despite the promotion of certain snack categories, notably those high in fat, sugar and salt, children make limited reference to brands when talking about food (Elliott, 2009). Snacks are not just about identity (Schor & Ford, 2007) they have a functional role – something to 'fill you up' and 'keep you going' until mealtimes. Children's limited reference to brands, when unprompted, may reflect the fact that popular snacks such as fruit are not branded; or 'homemade' snacks such as beans on toast are largely devoid of branding; or simply that brands are taken for granted by these children and become engulfed by the generic term. But it is the informality of snacking that is most striking and differentiates this practice from that of eating meals. Many of the regulations about eating meals do not apply. This idea that you can run around with a snack, eat it on the move, or while doing other things reflects a different practice from the meal.

Snacking occasions: points of interdependence between children, adults and marketing

There are a number of concerns, as we have seen, around the increased marketisation of snacking and the types of snack food being promoted to both children and adults. Promoting snacks as anti-adult and fun accentuates this distinction between children and adult snacks but children remain reliant on their parents for much of their snack consumption (one survey found 16 per cent of primary school children sometimes bought food or snacks on their way to or from school, compared to 42 per cent of secondary school children (Food Standards Agency 2012)). Rather than seeing marketing as encouraging children to pester their parents we need to consider how parents mediate this influence, in part by regulating what marketing children see on television, on line and in store as well as their access to, and availability of, snacks across different occasions. Similarly, there is the question of how children view snacking.

Children's[7] accounts of snacking show a wide range of practices both inside and outside the home. While meals tend to occur at particular times in the day the perception is that snacking is much more flexible and can take place 'anytime you're allowed'. In practice this usually refers to a mid-morning break at school, a snack at lunchtime, after school or in the evening. But there are general rules about when snacks are 'allowed' that children both understand and adhere to – no snacks before meals; at the start or the end of the day; and not too many snacks at one time. Snacks are eating events that take place between meals thus reinforcing the hegemony of the meal. Snacking at home is seen by children as complementing, rather than competing with, meals. Meals are serious, formal, family events whereas snacks are fun, informal and individual (Marshall & O'Donohoe, 2010).

Snacking is an integral part of children's food consumption experience and encompasses a wide range of snack occasions (Figure 13.1) where children and their parents negotiate the choices offered by the market. Thinking about snacking as an event allows us to reflect on how the occasion impacts on what is eaten and subsequently to think about how and why specific types of snack are permitted at certain occasions. Figure 13.1 offers a conceptual model that locates children's snacking occasion according to 1. where the snack is eaten (inside or outside the home); and 2. the purpose of the snack (to refuel or as a treat). This allows us to categorise different types of snack occasion depending on the location and purpose of the snack, for example watching television with the family might be seen as a treat at home in

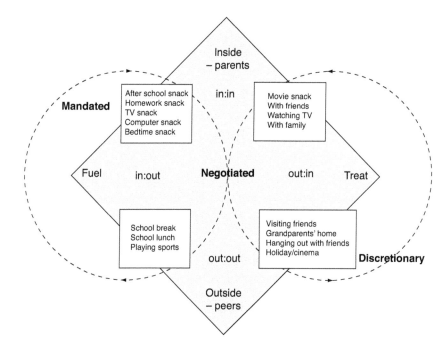

Figure 13.1 Snacking occasions.

contrast to a school lunch which is seen as refuelling outside the home. Where as most snacks are portable they may be prepared and eaten in home (in:in), prepared at home and eaten outside (in:out), prepared and eaten outside the home (out:out) or prepared outside the home and eaten inside (out:in) which will influence the snack selection and the reliance on the market. Children have differing degrees of discretion over what they eat depending on the timing and location of the snack. Much of the discussion around snacking focuses on in-home snacking where parents often regulate and control what their children eat either because the snacks are prepared at home or because the parents regulate what is available (Marshall, O'Donohoe, & Kline, 2007). In contrast, much of the commercial discourse around snacking as oppositional and fun is located outside of the home and under the influence of peers. This allows us to further categorise snacking as mandated, negotiated or discretionary. Children's snacking activity may be mandated, or controlled, by parents, who decide what snacks are available to children both inside and outside the home. As parents are responsible for the majority of household food purchases, including snacks, and because certain types of snack food have to be prepared, for example making sandwiches, toast, waffles, or omelettes, this often means an adult takes responsibility, or at least supervises the child. Even when there is no further preparation, parents often have the final say over what is eaten. In other cases there may be some negotiation over snacks, depending on where the snack is eaten and who is present. This is notable in the case of school snacks or when snacks are used as treats, in these cases children can make specific requests. Alternatively, discretionary snacking involves the child exercising the greatest choice over what they eat because they are using their own money or have found ways to access snack foods. In the following accounts these three different scenarios are presented as distinct types of snacking but in practice there is an element of mandated, negotiated and discretionary consumption across snacking occasions.

Mandated snacking

After-school snacks, homework snacks, television snacks, computer snacks and bedtime snacks tend to be regulated by parents. Most of these snacks are eaten at home with the primary aim of satisfying hunger, for example snacks before dinner are often organised around homework and likely to include small savoury items, sandwiches or toast rather than confectionery. However, this depends on what children have eaten that day[8] and proximity to dinner time. Some children are allowed to eat snacks after their dinner, as a reward for finishing their meal – the snack food becomes the dessert.[9] Where snacks are seen as a treat, for example, movie snacks, or snacks eaten with friends, these occasions are more likely to include confectionery items where the emphasis is on pleasure rather than nutrition. Watching television, for example, is often associated with less healthy snacks (Marquis, Filion, & Dagenais, 2005) although fruits and vegetables are also popular on these occasions (Marshall et al., 2007). Snacks can be eaten alone or shared with siblings, peers or other family members.

Most of this at-home snacking is under the control of parents and access to snacks, especially for younger children, is highly regulated (Gevers, Kremers, de Vries, & van Assema, 2014). Parental sanctions depend on how 'healthy' the snack is and children can identify 'good' (typically fruit) and 'bad' (typically sweets, chocolate, crisps) snacks.[10] While access to confectionery and chocolate is often controlled by parents, fruit consumption is less regulated and actively encouraged; some children claim fruit is their favourite snack. Fruit remains a popular snack among children (Canadean, 2014; Mintel, 2013) although whether this be driven by the parents or the children is not clear. Mandated snacking is arguably least exposed to the market, in part because a number of the snacks prepared at home are unbranded, the exception being the at-home treat where the emphasis is likely to be on fun and indulgence with friends and family.

Negotiated snacking

Negotiations about snacking take place inside and outside the home. Snacking at school includes items eaten as part of the mid-morning school recess (around 10.30 a.m.) and snacks as part of school lunch (around 12.30 p.m.). The mid-morning snack usually comprises one item, whereas the packed lunch can include several snack items; often a savoury item such as crisps, a chocolate bar, or cake, along with some fruit, accompany the ubiquitous sandwich. What is included in the lunchbox is under the control of the mother and involves some internal, and external, negotiation with children (Harman & Cappellini, 2014, 2015). Most of this negotiation centres on 'treats' and a number of these are branded, for example, branded yogurts (Yoplait Petits Filous and Frubes), cheese (Dairylea Cheese Strings and Dunkers) savoury snacks (Smiths Bacon Fries, KP Hula Hoops) and cereal bars (Nature Valley, Kellogg's Squares) along with supermarket own label products (Harman & Cappellini, 2014, 2015). Moreover, children negotiate with other children as they swap food in the schoolyard. While there is no shortage of advice on healthy lunchbox snacks, the availability of highly processed ready to eat meals such as 'Lunchables', targeted at both parents and children, highlight the trade-off between health and convenience. Launched in the US in 1988 under the Oscar Mayer brand, and sold in the UK under the Dairylea brand, these were targeted at working mothers and designed to appeal to children, offering a range of meal combinations including crackers, mini pizzas, hot dogs, burgers, nachos, subs, and wraps, with or without drinks or smoothies, and promoted online to parents as a way to give children the foods they love and to children via a range of games, videos and downloadable apps.[11] The negative press around the highly processed nature of the product has spurned a series of healthy alternatives (Passy, 2014; Moss, 2013) but highlights the increased marketisation of this eating occasion.

At home younger children typically have to ask their parent's permission to get sweets, chocolate or savoury snacks such as crisps and carbonated soft drinks, although there are a range of practices. Some children ask permission and parents get the snacks for their children; other children ask permission and get the snacks themselves; others get the snacks and then ask their parent(s). Regardless, of which tactic is used many kids ask for their parent's permission. Conversely, access to 'healthy' snacks is much less regulated in middle-class households (Marshall, 2010).

Discretionary snacking

The opportunities for independent choice are somewhat limited when it comes to snacking as most snacks are bought by parents. Children appear less willing to spend their own money on snacks and prefer to save their pocket money rather than spend it on confectionery (Marshall et al., 2007). They do have more discretion when it comes to snacking outside the home, for example at a friend's house, visiting grandparents or visiting the cinema (where they will be spending their pocket money or money given to them by parents) or travelling to and from school (if not collected by parents). Snacking at a friend's house, or having friends visit, is often seen as an opportunity to relax some of the rules and indulge. On these occasions children are allowed to eat differently (Curtis et al., 2010). Other occasions where the rules are more relaxed include holiday snacks, for example, Halloween or Christmas 'treats'. In situations where children are unable to 'negotiate' with their parents they may resort to 'covert' attempts to access snacks by taking these without their parent's permission. 'Raiding the cookie jar' brings with it a sense of empowerment[12] and rebellion as children attempt to out-smart their parents; even though some admitted that their parents often knew what they had been doing (Marshall, 2010). It is this area of discretionary snacking where children have more direct influence over what they eat and much of the marketing activity is directed towards this sector. It is here that fun is prominent and the emphasis shifts towards indulgence and the treat, particularly when away from home and parental supervision. Overall, children's snacking appears to be highly mandated and they have fairly limited discretion in how they snack. However, snacking was an integral part of their everyday food experiences and a regular feature throughout the day.

Conclusion

The marketing of less healthy snacks targeted at children is raising concerns in some sectors as the practice shifts from an occasional treat to an everyday reality for a number of children. The informality of this eating event, the smaller portions and the portable nature of the snack are arguably more appealing to children, irrespective of how healthy or unhealthy the food is, especially when compared to the more formal, structured and fixed nature of family mealtimes. The appeal of snacks to children appears to lie in their opposition to the normal rules about eating. Snack occasions have their own rituals and restrictions on what can be eaten and with whom but with an emphasis on fun, rather than nutrition; some see a categorical shift in the ways in which children's relationship with food is being (re)constructed (Elliott, 2011). Yet the variety of snack occasions means that snacking encompasses a range of practices that children can engage in and relate to, depending on where, when, with whom they eat and the purpose of the snack. Some of these occasions are heavily mandated while others involve negotiation and some individual discretion with varying degrees of marketisation.

Children exercise more influence over small meals and snacks (Nørgaard et al., 2007) yet many of these eating occasions remain under the control of parents who purchase the majority of the food and snacks that their children eat (Gevers et al., 2014; Colls & Evans, 2008; Marshall et al., 2007). Moreover, what parents say and do can have an impact on their children's healthy eating (Pedersen, Grønhøj, & Thøgersen, 2015). While snacks provide an opportunity to deviate from the more serious practice of meals, snacking is still predominantly regulated by adults and children's level of discretionary snacking may be relatively limited. Snacking, while remaining distinct from 'proper meals', has been incorporated and accommodated into the family eating pattern, allowing children's food to be managed in a way that does not necessarily challenge the family meal. Snacking simultaneously reflects the interdependence between children and parents while providing an opportunity for children to establish their own meaning[13] and identity, independent from adults (James, 1979; Zeiher, 2001).

In focusing only on the functional and nutritional aspects of snack food we ignore much of the practice around snacking. Although snacking is associated with 'doing other things' and the food is often 'secondary' it provides a break from the serious matter of meals and a respite from the adult table; an opportunity to indulge and enjoy food as fun.[14] Snacking is an integral part of children's everyday food practice and they are aware of the differences between snacking at home and outside home, or between a snack that is to 'keep them going' as opposed to a treat. The simple dichotomy of snacks versus meals fails to account for the myriad of snacking occasions and the different types of experience and practice. Children see snacks as complimenting rather than conflicting with meals and recognise the difference between these types of eating occasions. Examined from a practice perspective they know what to do, understand the principles and rules, and engage emotionally. Snacking is as much part of their identity construction as the food brands they consume and the 'branded (i.e. junk) food' (Schor & Ford, 2007) is more likely to be prevalent in specific types of snack occasion. What I have tried to show in this chapter is that first, while children are given more autonomy when engaged in snacking versus meals, their timing, food choices and other decisions remain heavily mediated by adults and there is a high degree of interdependence between adults and children; and, second, and just as important, snacking is an integral part of children's socialisation in food consumption practices. Despite the rise in snacking there is little to suggest that this poses a threat to family meals and, if anything, increases the symbolic importance of these eating occasions (Curtis et al., 2010). While the original Milky Way advertisement, the one I remember from my childhood, reaffirmed and reinforced the hegemony of the family meal, there is little to suggest that much has changed in this respect.

Notes

1 It was the subject of a complaint to the Independent Television Commission in 1991 by the Health Education Authority who argued that it encouraged children to eat sweets between meals. See http://en.wikipedia.org/wiki/Milky_Way_%28chocolate_bar%29 [Accessed 7 October 2015]. By 1993 the strap line was changed to 'So light it won't ruin your appetite'. When the original 1989 Red Car Blue Car advertisement was re-released in 2009 the race destination had changed from 'Dinner town' to 'Light town' and the strapline to 'Lighten up and play'.

2 Television and the Internet are attractive media for those wishing to promote their products. Of the US$9.65 billion spent on food and drink promotion in the US in 2009 some 18.5 per cent was directed towards 2–17 year olds; down one-fifth on 2006 (FTC, 2012). Fast food restaurants, carbonated soft drinks and cereals

accounted for almost three-quarters of the US$1.79 billion directed towards US children and teens. The Federal Trade Commission looked at cereals, drinks, dairy, snacks, prepared foods, candy/desserts, and fast food restaurants and found some marginal nutritional improvement on average across the products they surveyed between 2006 and 2009. While expenditure on new media was significantly up, by 50 per cent, television remained the primary communication medium (FTC, 2012).

3 James makes a clear distinction between 'kets' as the antithesis of adult food and sweets which, for adults, are metonymic meals. In this sense, sweets are regulated by adults whereas kets are controlled by children (James, 1979: 91).

4 Schor and Ford argue the increase in marketing coincides with the deterioration in the healthfulness of children's diets, with much of the calorific intake coming from energy dense snack foods with increased consumption of soft drinks and fast foods.

5 This work looks at televised food advertising targeted at Indian children.

6 This section draws on a conference paper – Marshall, D. (2010) What's in the Cookie Jar: Young children's accounts of snacking, ANR Colloque international consommations alimentaires, cultures enfantines et éducation Angoulême 1–2 April 2010.

7 This draws on qualitative research on eating with younger children aged 8–12 years, using focus groups in Scotland, New Zealand and Canada (Marshall & O'Donohoe, 2010).

8 In the New Zealand research we found that a number of schools send any uneaten items home in the children's lunchboxes so parents can see what the children have eaten at lunchtime. This is now common practice in UK schools.

9 In some US research the category 'desserts' includes biscuits, cookies and a number of other foods that might be considered part of the meal signifying the end of the more formal eating occasion.

10 Some avoid this moral categorising and argue that no food is inherently good, bad, healthy or unhealthy (Colls & Evans, 2008).

11 This refers to the US website www.lunchablesparents.com/ [Accessed 7 October 2015]. The UK Dairylea website has no information on Lunchables. The Rudd Centre found that only 5 out of 42 varieties of Lunchables met CFBAI nutrition standards for foods that could be advertised to children and suggest that Kraft stop marketing these products directly at children www.yaleruddcenter.org/resources/upload/docs/what/reports/RuddReport_Lunchables_4.14.pdf [Accessed 7 October 2015].

12 Few of the children saw this as stealing.

13 We have much less evidence about what happens outside of the home or in the school environment where eating is increasingly regulated and monitored.

14 It could be argued that snacks are not as central to the children's notion of identity as 'kets' (James, 1979).

References

Ambler, T. (2006). Does the UK promotion of food and drink to children contribute to their obesity? *International Journal of Advertising, 25*(2), 137–156.

Boseley, S. (2014). *The Shape We're In: How Junk Food and Diets are Shortening Our Lives*. London: Guardian Books.

Boyland, E., Harrold, J., Kirkham, T., & Halford, J. (2011). The extent of food advertising to children on UK television in 2008. *International Journal of Pediatric Obesity, 6*(5), 455–461.

Brembeck, H., Johansson, B., Bergström, K., Engelbrektsson, P., Hillén, S., Jonsson, L., Karlsson, M., Osslansson, E., & Shanahan, H. (2013). Exploring children's foodscapes. *Children's Geographies, 11*(1), 74–88.

Cairns, G. (2013). Evolutions in food marketing, quantifying the impact, and policy implications. *Appetite, 62*(March), 194–197.

Canadean. (2014). Fruit is top of the tree among UK kids snacks. 11 August. Available at: www.canadean.com/news/fruit-is-top-of-the-tree-among-uk-kids-snacks/ [Accessed 23 August 2015].

Chamontin, A., Pretzer, G., & Booth D. A. (2003). Ambiguity of 'snack' in British usage. *Appetite, 41*(1) 21–29.

Charles, N., & Kerr, M. (1988). *Women, Food and Families*. Manchester: Manchester University Press.

Collins English Dictionary. (1986).

Colls, R., & Evans, B. (2008). Embodying responsibility: Children's health and supermarket initiatives. *Environment and Planning A, 40*(3), 615–631.

Cook, D. T. (2009). Semantic provisioning of children's food: Commerce, care and maternal practice. *Childhood, 16*(3), 317–334.

Cook, D. T. (2012). Pricing the priceless child: A wonderful problematic. In A. Sparrman, B. Sandin, & J. Sober (Eds.), *Situated Consumption: A Critical Approach to Childhood Consumption in the 21st Century* (pp. 53–60). Lund: Nordic Academic Press.

Curtis, P., James, A., & Ellis, K. (2010). Children's snacking, children's food: Food moralities and family life. *Children's Geographies, 8*(3), 291–302.

Dixon, J., & Banwell, C. (2004). Heading the table: Parenting and the junior consumer. *British Food Journal, 106*(3), 181–193.

Elliott, C. (2008). Marketing fun food: A profile and analysis of supermarket food messages targeted at children. *Canadian Public Policy, 34*(2), 259–274.

Elliott, C. (2009). Healthy food looks serious: How children interpret packaged food products. *Canadian Journal of Communication, 34*(3), 359–380.

Elliott, C. (2010). Eatertainment and the (re)classification of children's food. *Food, Culture and Society, 13*(4), 539–553.

Elliott, C. (2011). 'It's junk food and chicken nuggets': Children's perspectives on 'kids' food' and the question of food classification. *Journal of Consumer Behaviour, 10*(3), 133–140.

Federal Trade Commission (FTC) (2012). A review of food marketing to children and adolescents: Follow up. December Report. Available at: www.ftc.gov/sites/default/files/documents/reports/review-food-marketing-children-and-adolescents-follow-report/121221foodmarketingreport.pdf [Accessed 25 September 2014].

Food Standards Agency. (2012). Children in Scotland are still eating too much sugar. 5 October. Available at: www.food.gov.uk/scotland/news-updates/news/2012/5336/scot-eat [Accessed 18 December 2014].

Gamble, M., & Cotugna, N. (1999). A quarter century of TV food advertising targeted at children. *American Journal of Health Behaviour, 23*(3) 261–267.

Gevers, D. W. M., Kremers, S. P. J., de Vries, N. K., & van Assema, P. (2014). Clarifying concepts of food parenting practices. A Delphi study with an application to snacking behaviour. *Appetite, 79*(August), 51–57.

Gram, M. (2015). Buying food for the family: Negotiations in parent/child supermarket shopping: An Observational Study from Denmark and the United States. *Journal of Contemporary Ethnography, 44*(2), 169–195.

Grieshaber, S. (1997). Mealtime rituals: Power and resistance in the construction of mealtime rules. *British Journal of Sociology, 48*(4), 649–666.

Halkier, B., & Iben, J. (2011). Methodological challenges in using practice theory in consumption research. Examples from a study of handling nutritional contestations of food consumption. *Journal of Consumer Culture, 11*(1), 101–123.

Harman, V., & Cappellini, B. (2014). Unpacking fun food and children's leisure: mothers' perspectives on preparing lunchboxes. *Young Consumers, 15*(4), 312–322.

Harman, V., & Cappellini, B. (2015). Mothers on display: Lunchboxes, social class and moral accountability. *Sociology, 49*(4), 764–781.

Harris, J., Pomeranz, J., Lobstein, T., & Brownell, K. (2009). A crisis in the marketplace: How food marketing contributes to childhood obesity and what can be done. *Annual Review of Public Health, 30*(2), 211–225.

Hastings, G., Stead, M., McDermott, L., Forsyth, A., MacKintosh, A., Rayner, M., ... Angus, K. (2003). Review of Research on the Effects of Food Promotion to Children. Report commissioned by Food Standards Agency, September. Available at: www.foodstandards.gov.uk/multimedia/pdfs/promofoodchildrenexec.pdf [Accessed 11 May 2014].

International Obesity Task Force (2004). 'Childhood obesity out of control'. Extracts from Childhood Obesity Report, May, 2004. Available at: www.iotf.org/media/IOTFmay28.pdf [Accessed 8 October 2006].

Jackson, P. (Ed.) (2009). *Changing Families, Changing Food*. London: Palgrave Macmillan.

James, A. (1979). Confections, concoctions and conceptions. *Journal of the Anthropological Society of Oxford, 10*(2), 83–95.

Johansson, B. (2014). Lines of flight in children's foodscapes. Paper presented at 6th International Child and Teen Consumption Conference, University of Edinburgh Business School.

Johnson, G. H., & Anderson, G. H. (2010). Snacking definitions: Impact on interpretation of the literature and dietary recommendations. *Critical Reviews in Food Science and Nutrition, 50*(9), 848–871.

Kerrane, B., Hogg, M., & Bettany, S. M. (2012). Children's influence strategies in practice: Exploring the co-constructed nature of the child influence process in family consumption. *Journal of Marketing Management, 27*(7/8), 809–835.

Kline, S. (2011). *Globesity, Food Marketing and Family Lifestyles*. Basingstoke: Palgrave MacMillan.

Livingstone S., & Helsper, E. (2004). Advertising foods to children: Understanding promotion in the context of children's daily lives. Review of the literature prepared for the Research Department of Ofcom. Available at: www.ofcom.org.uk [Accessed 13 May 2015].

Marquis, M., Filion, Y. P., & Dagenais, F. (2005). Does eating while watching television influence children's food-related behaviours? *Canadian Journal of Dietetic Practice and Research, 66*(5), 12–19.

Marshall, D. (2005). Food as ritual, routine or convention. *Consumption, Markets and Culture, 8*(1), 69–85.

Marshall, D. (2010). What's in the cookie jar?: Young children's accounts of snacking. Paper presented at the ANR Colloque international consommations alimentaires, cultures enfantines et éducation Angoulême, 1–2 April 2010.

Marshall, D. (2014). Co-operation in the supermarket aisle: Young children's accounts of family food shopping. *International Journal of Retail & Distribution Management, 42*(11/12), 990–1003.

Marshall, D., & O'Donohoe, S. (2010). Children and food. In D. Marshall (Ed.), *Understanding Children as Consumers* (pp. 17–29). London: Sage.

Marshall, D., Kline, S., & O'Donohoe, S. (2006). Television promotion of children's snacks: Food for thought? In B. Tufte, & K. Ekström (Eds.), *Children Media and Consumption: On the Front Edge* (pp. 235–258). Lund: Nordicom.

Marshall, D., O'Donohoe, S., & Kline, S. (2007). Families, food, and pester power: Beyond the blame game? *Journal of Consumer Behaviour, 6*(4), 164–181.

Macdiarmid, J., Loe, J., Craig, L. C. A., Masson, L. F., Holmes, B., & McNeill, G. (2009). Meal and snacking patterns of school-aged children in Scotland. *European Journal of Clinical Nutrition, 63*(11), 1297–1304.

Mintel. (2013). The after school snack market shows untapped potential. Available at: www.mintel.com/blog/food-market-news/snack-market-trends-in-uk [Accessed 7 October 2015].

Moss, M. (2013). *Salt Sugar Fat: How the Food Giants Hooked Us.* London: Random House Publishing Group.

Murcott, A. (1982). On the social significance of the 'cooked dinner' in South Wales. *Social Science Information, 21*(4/5), 677–695.

Nørgaard, M. K., Brunso, K., Christensen, P. H., & Mikkelsen, M. R. (2007). Children's influence on and participation in the family decision process during food buying. *Young Consumers, 8*(3), 197–216.

O'Connell, R., & Brannen, J. (2014). Children's food, power and control: Negotiations in families with younger children in England. *Childhood, 21*(1), 87–102.

Ochs, E., & Shohet, M. (2006). The cultural structuring of mealtime socialization. *New Direction for Child and Adolescent Development, 111*(3), 35–49.

Ofcom (2006). Television advertising of food and drink products to children. Final statement. Available at: http://stakeholders.ofcom.org.uk/consultations/foodads_new/statement/ [Accessed 25 September 2014].

Ofcom (2013). UK Children's Media Literacy. Available at: http://stakeholders. ofcom.org.uk/binaries/research/media-literacy/october-2013/research07Oct2013. pdf [Accessed 25 September 2014].

Passy, C. (2014). What to pack your kids for lunch? New ways to spice up the humble lunch box. Marketwatch, 31 October, 2014. Available at: www.market-watch.com/story/what-to-pack-for-lunch-new-ways-to-spice-up-the-humble-lunch-box-2014-09-12 [Accessed 31 October 2014].

Pedersen, S., Grønhøj, A., & Thøgersen, J. (2015). Following family or friends: Social norms in adolescent healthy eating. *Appetite, 86*(1), 54–60.

Romani, S. (2005). Feeding post-modern families: Food preparation and consumption practices in new family structures. *European Advances in Consumer Research, 7*(1), 250–254.

Schatzki, T. R. (1997). Practices and actions: A Wittgensteinian critique of Bourdieu and Giddens. *Philosophy of the Social Sciences, 27*(3), 283–308.

Schor, J. B., & Ford, M. (2007). From tastes great to cool: Children's food marketing and the rise of the symbolic. *Journal of Law, Medicine and Ethics, 35*(1), 10–27.

Scully, P., Reid, O., Macken, A., Healy, M., Saunders, J., Leddin, D., … O'Gorman, C. S. (2014). Food and beverage cues in UK and Irish children-television programming. *Archives of Diseases in Childhood, 99*(11), 979–984.

Soni, P., & Vohra, J. (2014). Advertising foods to Indian children: What is the appeal? *Young Consumers, 15*(2), 178–192.

Valentine, G. (1999). Eating in home, consumption and identity. *The Sociological Review, 47*(3), 491–524.

Wansik, B., Payne, C. R., & Shimizu, M. (2010). 'Is this a meal or snack?': Situational cues that drive perceptions. *Appetite, 54*(5), 214–216.

Ward, S. (1974). Consumer socialization. *Journal of Consumer Research, 1*(September), 1–16.

Warde, A. (2005). Consumption and theories of practice. *Journal of Consumer Culture, 5*(2), 131–153.

Which? (2005). Marketing of foods to children. Report by the Food Commission for Which? Available at: www.which.co.uk/documents/pdf/marketing-of-foods-to-children-which-report-176877.pdf [Accessed 14 June 2014].

Yates, N., & Warde, A. (2015). The foods we eat now: Meal content in UK eating patterns, 1955–2012. *Appetite, 84*(1), 299–308.

YouGov (2013). Study reveals that a third of British children eat crisps every day. Available at: http://cdn.yougov.com/cumulus_uploads/document/4mi579uo6a/SnackingRelease.pdf [Accessed 12 June 2014].

Young, B. (2003). Does food advertising make children obese? *Young Consumers, 4*(3), 19–26.

Zeiher, H. (2001). Dependent, independent and interdependent relations: Children as members of the family household in West Berlin. In L. Alanen, & B. Mayall (Eds.), *Conceptualizing Child-Adult Relations* (pp. 108–129). London: Routledge.

Part IV
Disposal

14 The milk in the sink

Waste, date labelling and food disposal

Carl Yngfalk

Introduction: food waste, date labelling and disposal

One of the most recurrent issues emphasised in contemporary political concerns about sustainability in the marketplace is food waste (Swedish Environmental Protection Agency (SEPA), 2015; Stuart, 2009). In Sweden and the UK, discussions of sustainability have drawn attention to a relationship between date labelling (for example, use-by and best-before dates) and the unnecessary disposal of edible food in society (see SEPA, 2012; Waste and Resources Action Program (WRAP), 2008). Recent estimations suggest that consumers are disposing of between one-fifth and one-third of the food they purchase as waste (Smithers, 2013; SEPA, 2012).

Food date labelling is an important source of information for everyday consumption (e.g. acquisition, appreciation and disposal). The food market is characterised by pre-packaged food products hidden in paper and plastic, and contemporary consumers largely depend on date labelling in order to evaluate food quality and freshness. Labelling is thus also a powerful tool within the food industry and a key instrument within food policy, and it illustrates how food consumption is entwined with larger institutions that address public concerns such as food safety and public health. Accordingly, as a regulated industry practice within the European Union, date labelling appears on all pre-packaged products available in the marketplace. Whether it comprises 'best-before' dates (quality indicator), 'use-by' dates (risk indicator) or some similar terminology that denotes the freshness of pre-packaged food, date labelling facilitates consumption by way of suggesting when particular products should be consumed. Through date labelling individuals are encouraged by consumer policy to take more active and rationalised decisions in relation to the freshness of food. These decisions refer to whether one should eat, drink or dispose of a particular product beyond a particular date suggested by the best-before date and by using their senses (taste, smell, touch, and so on) to assess the relevance of the label (Swedish National Food Agency (NFA) 2015b). However, ongoing discussions suggest that consumers tend to be 'absorbed' by date labels and thus have trouble 'relying' on their bodily senses. This typically results in the unnecessary disposal of food due to the simple passing of a date (Smithers, 2013; WRAP, 2008).

That disposal is an important stage in the consumption process is clearly recognised in consumption studies (Evans, 2012; Cherrier, 2009; Gregson, Metcalfe, & Crewe, 2007). Previous research emphasises the role of disposal in the organisation of identity and social relations (see Cherrier, 2009; Price, Arnould, & Curasi, 2000). Following Munro (1995), Cappellini (2009) suggests that it is not merely in extraordinary consumption (for example, acquiring, appreciating, using) that we stage and reaffirm social relations, but also in everyday divestment practices such as consuming leftovers (see also Närvänen, Mesiranta, & Hukkanen, Chapter 15). Also previous research has further investigated the explicit relationship between date labelling and food waste. For instance, Milne (2013) argues that today's normative use of date labelling, that is, not disposing of food unnecessarily, has become part of the exercise of environmentally conscious consumer-citizenship (Milne, 2013; see also Mourad & Barnard, Chapter 16). However, extant research also stresses that date labels shape consumption by overriding sensory perception and may stigmatise expired products (Sen & Block, 2009; Wansink & Wright, 2006; Tsiros & Heilman, 2005). This suggests that date labelling expands the possibility that people will choose to dispose of products as waste rather than consuming them as it was intended.

The political interests served by food date labelling incorporate the autonomy and, to a certain extent, the very life and health of the consumer (Swedish Government, 2006). French philosopher Michel Foucault refers to this political exercise of power so characteristic of contemporary societies as 'bio-power' (Foucault, 1980). This chapter draws greater attention to this power and the potential that date labelling holds for the construction and shaping of consumption. More specifically, it addresses the associated determination of food disposal by investigating how it prompts consumers to reflect on their personal food consumption in relation to the body. This is achieved by drawing on a larger study and a qualitative discourse analysis of food date labelling in the Swedish market (Yngfalk, 2012). Accordingly, data have been gathered from readings of official government documents and materials collected from the Swedish NFA, and qualitative interviews with consumers using the date labels in the practice of the meal.

Making consumers: bio-power

For Foucault, bio-power entails a 'bio-politics' of the population directed at fundamental biological processes of people, 'propagation, births and mortality, the level of health, life expectancy and longevity' (Foucault, 1980: 139). In the context of everyday food consumption, bio-politics pervades the consuming body (Falk, 1997) through the aid of institutional instruments such as date labelling that are aimed at maximising consumer health via the minimising of risk related to the body in the marketplace.

Foucault argues that modern forms of bio-power are rooted in advanced neoliberalism (Foucault, 1997, 2000), which may carry different connotations in different contexts. In the European context, the rise of neoliberalism in society is broadly associated with the dismantlement of the welfare state, as well as the freedom and responsibility of individuals. A neoliberal understanding of consumer culture thus commonly translates into issues of consumer empowerment (Shankar, Cherrier, & Conniford, 2006), that is to say, it revolves around the understanding that consumers are supposedly empowered and free to make their own choices with regard to consumption. Accordingly, consumer choice is typically included as a key mechanism in the contemporary marketplace (Draper & Green, 2002) and one that entwines the consumer subject with the notion of people as citizens (see Trentmann, 2007). Bio-power does not therefore place the interests or self-knowledge of the consumer (that is, 'subjectivity') against the interests of experts or the state, but rather entails a consumer culture in which consumers increasingly experience life as an 'enterprise'. Put simply, consumers' actions and behaviours dictate their success or failure in life (Du Gay, 1996). In considering the self as an enterprise, food consumers may find that their bodily health, safety and well-being depend on their active choices and the 'proper' use of the information provided by, for example, food labelling. Accordingly, bio-power, as it comes to expression in food labelling, also relates to Foucault's notion of 'governmentality' (Foucault, 2000), that is, the rationality and mentality of government.

Governmentality refers to the ideas and principles that influence how one governs or, more specifically, how one aims 'to shape, guide or affect the conduct of some person or persons' (Gordon, 1991: 2). While the ultimate form of government entails a process of self-government and self-care in which consumers regulate themselves, Foucault views governmentality in a broader sense as both the government of the self and the government of the population. Date labelling conveys a governmentality that instructs people that they can, and moreover, should exercise individual choice in order to perform as responsible, that is, healthy and safe citizen-consumers. Accordingly bio-power, as it comes to expression in the date labelling policy, is ensured by governmentality. This is so because the latter does not merely discipline consumers by way of corrective technologies focused on the domination of others (Foucault, 1977), but also involves a care of the self through continual struggle (Foucault, 1990).

Food date labelling: the liberal arts of consumer governance

The intention of the date labelling policy is to protect consumers' interests in the marketplace, such as their right to make informed food consumption choices (NFA, 2015b). This section discusses this discourse of food date labelling and shows how it is accompanied by a bio-political governmentality that seeks to construct food consumption by promoting increased risk awareness and responsibility in consumption.

Increasing focus on information provision in the marketplace is a primary aspect of contemporary liberal regimens (Draper & Green, 2002), with the supposed empowerment and safety of consumers forming a central component of the date labelling policy (see Milne, 2013). Indeed, in Swedish consumer policy, information is generally considered a primary means by which to endorse the role of citizen-consumers and there exists a strong focus on building consumer trust in food labelling. The following outtakes drawn from, first, an official policy document and, second, the NFA's homepage, briefly illustrate this rationale:

> The goal of [Swedish] consumer policy is to give consumers the power and the possibility to make active and conscious choices. For this to work [...] information that is easy to grasp and consumer trust are central requirements.
>
> (Swedish Government, 2011)

> Food products should be labeled with the information that consumers need in order to make conscious and safe choices regarding the products.
>
> (NFA, 2015a)

As illustrated by these outtakes, while prompting consumers to make active and conscious choices, this consumer discourse entails a particular governmentality in which responsibilities are distributed in the marketplace through the freedom of choice (Rose, 2008). Here consumers are invested with rationalised forms of knowledge and encouraged to use the said labels to more actively orient themselves in relation to the risks they may encounter as food consumers.

In arguing that bio-power targets individuals within populations, Foucault further draws attention to how contemporary political regimens operate with regard to individuals and individual freedom (Foucault, 2000). While emphasising consumers' individual rights to choose freely in consumption, however, such governmentality also correlates such rights of people with a societal and collective duty to practice food consumption and dispose of products in prudent ways (Hodgson, 2002). In this sense, the governmentality of date labelling seeks to promote and develop consumer skills in the practice of a rationalised sense of food consumption. This rationalised consumption is discursively characterised by a capacity and willingness on behalf of individuals to correlate their conduct with a reflexive risk awareness (Thompson, 2005; Beck, 1992). The term 'best-before', for instance, originally emerged out of governmental concerns with the pre-existing term of 'use-by', which was seen as offering too little room for consumer choice and agency. Compared with 'use-by', the term 'best-before' implies that there is indeed an amount of risk attached to consuming particular products after particular dates. As such, date labels urge consumers to trust the information that they are presented with in order to account for the risks and threats that they are unable to tackle on their own as individual consumers. Although the initial purpose of the date labelling policy involved a strong emphasis on consumer protection on behalf of seemingly ignorant consumers (Milne, 2013), this contemporary political rationale works by inducing confidence in people to protect themselves and their bodies by bestowing agency upon the labels.

The focus on providing information to consumers that is embedded in the date labelling policy can thus be understood as necessitating a bio-political dimension that seeks to instil food safety and health discourses with the consumer by encouraging subjects to embrace an advanced view of bodily risk and risk management. Notably, such an understanding of, for instance, health risks is imposed upon consumers by way of an externally generated understanding of food 'freshness' or 'safety' that is controlled by the industry. As such, the bio-power of date labelling does not merely seek to discipline consumers, but also involves self-control and self-discipline. Importantly, it does so to the extent that it prompts individuals to internalise commercial norms of conduct that enable them to conduct themselves within the space of a regulated and, to a large extent, 'rationalised' sense of freedom (Rose, 2008: 22). In so doing, date labels endorse a struggle at the level of the self. This is demonstrated in the following section through an analysis of participating consumers' stories that tell of how they make use of date labels in everyday acts of food consumption.

Consumers struggling with date labels

For consumers, date labels function as a visual aid that assists them in the valuing of food freshness. They constitute a reference point that comes into expression in their choices and in their experiences of food consumption, that is to say, in their 'sensing of fresh food' through the utilisation of bodily or sensory perceptions.

Reading the date label or 'sensing food freshness'?

Date labels make food consumption and issues of food freshness 'more manageable' and in many ways 'less related' to the body, which participants typically see as generating more uncertain forms of knowledge. To take Ruth as an example, although the date label on a package of minced meat had been overrun by just one day, she considered examining the quality of the product to be out of the question and instead simply regarded the product as no longer edible because of the date alone. The minced meat was thus disposed of based on the information of the date label. While Ruth may indeed smell or taste any expired food in order to see if it is still fresh, she commonly disposes of such food directly and without doubt. In her own words:

> Minced meat often has a short date on it, so in this case it must be that it's best before the day after. And then I think, well, I will cook it tomorrow, so it's all right. But then maybe that doesn't happen because, well,

something else gets in the way, and one forgets about it [for a day or so]. So I throw it away.

(Ruth, 54)

For consumers like Ruth, date labels work as guidance for the uncertainty associated with the freshness of food, and thus the label becomes what Milne (2013) describes as an arbiter of waste. In this sense, a date label reduces the uncertainty associated with choices that are tied to the utilisation of the senses. For example, preferring 'fresher' food to 'less fresh' food, Ruth usually selects milk packages in the supermarket that have the 'longest' 'best-before dates'.

That's how it's done. I mean, if I go shopping for milk, then I look [at the label], do they all have 1 September or do some have 27 August? Then, of course, I put the older one back and only take 1 September with me, so that I have the same duration on all.

(Ruth, 54)

Similarly, Lisa, another participant, also feels that date labels aid her in avoiding the risk of becoming ill by consuming old food. For her, best-before labels play an important role in keeping the body safe and far from any harm that might influence her health in a negative manner. She explains:

[A]fter the date one should not drink it or eat it [. . .]. I mean, I really don't know, I guess I'm afraid of bacteria. That is, diseases or whatever. That's why I don't want to eat old food.

(Lisa, 24)

As illustrated here, by actively consuming food in accordance with best-before dates, consumers are able to avoid the risk of eating something that is no longer fresh that may potentially be of harm to them or taste bad. Accordingly, consumers use date labels to structure their eating and drinking in such a way that allows them to protect themselves and their bodies. Yet paradoxically, such conduct or self-care also entails the continuous removal of the body from consumption in the sense that eating is practised based on an externally generated understanding of freshness. For Lisa, for example, if products that have been kept in the refrigerator expire, deciding on whether they should still be consumed is not so much a matter of smelling or tasting the food because 'it still tends to smell or taste bad' (Lisa, 24).

Conversely, numerous participating consumers also express a desire not to waste 'expired products'. Although seemingly concerned with consulting the date labels on products, and then finding it hard to disregard the dates given as a guide to when food is meant to be consumed, consumers like Hans, 38, are concerned with the implications of food waste for society as a whole. As he explains:

One tries to be careful with what you've got in some way. The other thing is the public debate around the fact that it is not sustainable from the perspective of society to throw away things that one could use. Independent of what it is, I have a much better gut feeling if I throw away clothes, but clothes I seldom throw away, if they aren't completely worn out. And then I leave them to be recycled. But it is a really nice feeling, because then one has cleaned out clothes that one doesn't use, one thinks, 'Oh, it's so good', because one has created room for [new] things and so on. However, that nice feeling doesn't come with wasting food, it never feels good to throw away food.

(Hans, 38)

For Hans, the normative ideal suggests that it is not sustainable to waste things, especially not food. He makes a comparison with clothes as commercial items. Clothes, as he puts it, can be recycled but food cannot, which makes food harder to dispose of unnecessarily.

The participant consumers also express alternative views of the date labels in which they illustrate other ways of relating to food freshness. For consumers like John, 55, and his wife, nothing is disposed of as waste simply because of expired date labels. Instead they use their bodies – smelling, touching, tasting the food – in order to decide whether a product is edible or not:

No, no, we never do that [dispose of food because of the date label], but we always use our noses to assess if it's okay to eat or not. This goes for the food we have cooked, we save the rest, then one eats it as lunch the day after or the next. I mean, maybe not many do that. [...] Because we notice that a lot of friends, well, family or friends, they just dispose of everything.

(John, 55)

For John it is important not to dispose of food simply due to the information shown on the date label. He explains how he and his wife prefer to eat expired products rather than throwing such products away and they strive to smell and taste the food. Consumers like John and his wife thus come to develop self-technologies that allow them to care for the self by questioning the labels more actively in consumption.

Food disposal and the care of the self

The above illustrations indicate a struggle with date labels in which consumers, on the one hand, engage in a quest to make responsible choices concerning personal investment in the body and health (Yngfalk & Fyrberg Yngfalk, 2015) and, on the other hand, make an attempt to correlate such choices with, for instance, the environment and issues of sustainability (Milne, 2013). While the former involves both the pleasure of enjoying fresh food and ensuring one's personal safety in acts of consumption, the latter highlights other normative ideals to which such issues need to be related. Furthermore, consumers may attempt not to dispose of food on a whim but only to do so through more or less calculated practices that incorporate the aforementioned norms. As with the ancient Greek practices of the self, studied by Foucault (1990), the discourse enacted in the participants' practices shows a struggle with date labels that indicates the existence of bio-power. This bio-power is both voluntary and coercive and indicates processes through which people are called upon to exercise their rights, power and agency as citizen-consumers (see Foucault, 2000).

On the level of the self, date labels operate as a disciplinary institution within consumption through which people are reminded about and prompted to avert the risks and potential dangers embedded in deviant conduct (Foucault, 1977). If food is not consumed in a responsible manner, that is to say, in a way that avoids the potential risks and dangers, then no one is to blame but oneself. In order to cope with such responsibility, the consumers assessed herein express a care of the self that involves monitoring, calculation and organisation with regard to the ways in which food is consumed and dis-posed of at home, as well as in relation to how it is selected during the shop-ping process. Consumers buy products based on date labels, organise their cooking practices in line with date labels, dispose of products in reference to date labels and so on. Accordingly, the products stored in the participants' refrigerators formed part of a calculated scheme for consumption. For the participants herein this scheme could be interrupted by unexpected events, such as an unplanned visit to a restaurant that leads to products in the refri-gerator passing their best-before dates. Such an event would disrupt order in the refrigerator by overriding previous calculations and food planning (Munro, 1995). Here date labels could then be used once again to restore order and regain control by facilitating the disposal of products with 'bad dates' without further concern for the environment or personal doubt. Illus-trating reflexive risk awareness, such conduct reproduces underlying cultural anxieties that are relieved through consumption (disposal) as a risk-reducing practice (Thompson, 2005: 246). As such, for consumers like Ruth and Lisa food disposal aided by date labelling is a way of practising care of the self/body. Notably, such self-care involves a process that minimises the seemingly irrational and lay conduct of the body and practices such as smelling, tasting, feeling, and so on.

Accordingly, date labelling offers consumers an opportunity to assume control over their bodies and health, otherwise potentially consuming harmful food products from which they are distanced in terms of production and packaging. Either by disposing of the food as waste when the date label expires, like Ruth and Lisa, or by eating such food instead, like John and his wife, consumers are prone to practice consumption in relation to the labels and in accordance with what they perceive as being 'in control'.

Conclusion: food waste as a consequence of bio-political consumption

The consumption practices actualised within the governmentality discourse of date labelling can be seen as an expression of individuals conducting themselves in responsible ways in relation to their bodies. Through labelling, consumers are educated to have a choice in food consumption and these choices should, preferably, be conducted based on formalised forms of expert intelligence (for example, date labels) rather than informal, alternative embodied forms of knowledge (for example, taste, smell, touch and feeling). Accordingly, in largely constraining the ability of consumers to sense food consumption by imposing upon them an externally generated form of 'expert knowledge', date labelling seeks to construct and control consumption in terms of risk. Through such control, failing to make the right choice and conduct oneself in a 'rational manner' is a failure not merely towards the self but also towards society. As a consequence of this form of responsibility the waste mountain grows: date labels increase the demand for food at an aggregate level in society, which is largely characterised by excess production.

To conclude, the present chapter has argued that the political rationality of date labelling conveys a bio-politics and governmentality of consumption that promotes excess food disposal, and thus waste, through increased risk awareness and responsibility in consumption. Whereas the bio-politics of traditional societies used to relate the human body to social life by maximising natural processes (Foucault, 1980: 139), namely the use of the senses (smell, touch, taste and so on), the governmentality actualised by date labelling promotes a consumer culture that seeks to minimise corporeality through the advancement of 'rational conduct' and control in the market.

References

Beck, U. (1992). *Risk Society: Towards a New Modernity*. London: Sage.

Cappellini, B. (2009). The sacrifice of re-use: The travels of leftovers and family relations. *Journal of Consumer Behaviour, 8*(6), 365–375.

Cherrier, H. (2009). Disposal and simple living: Exploring the circulation of goods and the development of sacred consumption. *Journal of Consumer Behaviour, 8*(6), 327–339.

Draper, A., & Green, J. (2002). Food safety and consumers: Constructions of choice and risk. *Social Policy and Administration, 36*(6), 610–625.

Du Gay, P. (1996). *Consumption and Identity at Work*. London: Sage.

Evans, D. (2012). Binning, gifting and recovery: The conduits of disposal in household food consumption. *Environment and Planning D: Society and Space, 30*(6), 1123–1137.

Falk, P. (1997). *The Consuming Body*. London: Sage.

Foucault, M. (1977). *Discipline and Punish*. London: Penguin.

Foucault, M. (1980). *The History of Sexuality, Vol. 1: The Will to Knowledge*. London: Penguin.

Foucault, M. (1990). *The History of Sexuality, Vol. 3: The Care of the Self*. London: Penguin.

Foucault, M. (1997). The Birth of Biopolitics. In P. Rabinow (Ed.), *Essential Works of Foucault, 1954–1984, Vol. 1: Ethics* (pp. 77–89). New York: The New Press.

Foucault, M. (2000). Governmentality. In J. D. Faubion (Ed.), *Essential Works of Foucault, 1954–1984, Vol. 3: Power* (pp. 120–135). New York: The New Press.

Gordon, C. (1991). Governmental rationality: An introduction. In G. Burchell, C. Gordon, & P. Miller (Eds.), *The Foucault Effect: Studies in Governmentality* (pp. 1–51). Chicago: The University of Chicago Press.

Gregson, N., Metcalfe, A., & Crewe, L. (2007). Identity, mobility, and the throw-away society. *Environment and Planning D: Society and Space, 25*(4), 682–700.

Hodgson, D. (2002). Know your customer: Marketing, governmentality and the new consumer of financial services. *Management Decision, 40*(4), 318–328.

Milne, R. (2013). Arbiters of waste: Date labels, the consumer and knowing good, safe food. *The Sociological Review, 60*(S2), 84–101.

Munro, R. (1995). Disposal of the meal. In D. Marshall, (Ed.), *Food Choice and the Consumer* (pp. 313–325). London: Blackie Academic and Professional.

NFA. Swedish National Food Agency. (2015a). Food labelling. Available at: www.livsmedelsverket.se/en/sok/Search/?q=labelling%2C+production%2C+handling+and+control [Accessed 22 December 2015].

NFA. Swedish National Food Agency. (2015b). Shelf life dates. Available at: http://www.livsmedelsverket.se/en/sok/?q=shelf+life+date [Accessed 22 December 2015].

Price, L. L., Arnould, E. J., & Curasi, C. F. (2000). Older consumers' disposition of special possessions. *Journal of Consumer Research, 27*(2), 179–201.

Rose, N. (2008). *Powers of Freedom: Reframing Political Thought.* Cambridge: Cambridge University Press.

Sen, S., & Block, L. G. (2009). Why my mother never threw anything out: The effect of product freshness on consumption. *Journal of Consumer Research, 36*(3), 47–55.

Shankar, A., Cherrier, H., & Canniford, R. (2006). Consumer empowerment: A Foucauldian interpretation. *European Journal of Marketing, 40*(9/10), 1013–1030.

Smithers, R. (2013). Food waste: national campaign aims to stop the rot by 2020. The Guardian. 11 November. Available at: www.theguardian.com/environment/2013/nov/11/food-waste-ban-landfill-campaign [Accessed 20 November 2014].

Stuart, T. (2009). *Waste: Uncovering the Global Food Scandal.* London: Penguin.

Swedish Environmental Protection Agency. (2012). Food Waste in Sweden 2012 (sv. Matavfallsmängder i Sverige 2012). Stockholm: Swedish Environmental Protection Agency.

Swedish Environmental Protection Agency. (2015). Food Waste (sv. Matsvinn), (16 January 2015). Available at: www.naturvardsverket.se/Miljoarbete-i-samhallet/Miljoarbete-i-Sverige/Uppdelat-efter-omrade/Avfall/Avfallsforebyggande-program/Matsvinn/ [Accessed 20 May 2015].

Swedish Government. (2006). Food Act (2006: 804). In *Ministry of Agriculture* (Ed.), Government Offices of Sweden.

Swedish Government. (2011). Consumer Policy at the EU Level. Government Offices of Sweden.

Thompson, C. J. (2005). Consumer risk perceptions in a community of reflexive doubt. *Journal of Consumer Research, 32*(2), 235–248.

Trentmann, F. (2007). Citizenship and consumption. *Journal of Consumer Culture, 7*(2), 147–158.

Tsiros, M., & Heilman C. M. (2005). The effect of expiration dates and perceived risk on purchasing behavior in grocery store perishable categories. *Journal of Marketing, 69*(2), 114–129.

Wansink, B., & Wright, A. O. (2006). 'Best if used by…' How freshness dating influences food acceptance. *Journal of Food Science, 71*(4), 354.

Waste and Resources Action Programme (WRAP). (2008). *The Food We Waste.* Banbury: WRAP, 237.

Yngfalk, C. (2012). *The Constitution of Consumption: Food Labeling and the Politics of Consumerism.* School of Business. Stockholm: Stockholm University.

Yngfalk, C., & Fyrberg Yngfalk, A. (2015). Creating the cautious consumer: Marketing managerialism and bio-power in health consumption. *Journal of Macromarketing.* DOI 10.1177/0276146715571459.

15 The quest for an empty fridge

Examining consumers' mindful food disposition

*Elina Närvänen, Nina Mesiranta and
Annilotta Hukkanen*

Introduction

Throwing food away is an alarming environmental concern in Western consumer societies (Imeche.org, 2013). Accumulating household food waste has an enormous impact on sustainability even though it takes place in everyday life and is therefore not often consciously reflected upon (Stefan, van Herpen, Tudoran, & Lähteenmäki, 2013; Røpke, 2009). However, routine practices in food purchasing and provisioning play a key role in moving towards sustainability and having a greener lifestyle. This chapter focuses on how consumers collectively reduce their food waste by modifying their current food disposition practices and developing new ones.

The full consumption cycle has recently gained increasing research interest, given the under-researched stage of disposition (Black & Cherrier, 2012; Albinsson, Wolf, & Kopf, 2010; Albinsson & Perera, 2009; Parsons & Maclaran, 2009). Food disposition has also been studied aside from recycling, donating or exchanging durable goods. However, as a phenomenon, the disposition of food is rather complex because of the nature of food as a consumable, perishable good. Therefore, food waste emerges in the intersection of several different influences. These influences include the way the food industry produces, stores, packages, delivers and promotes food; the way food is purchased and stored at home; personal values and habits; social and cultural norms; knowledge and skills; and facilities and resources available for consumers (Quested, Parry, Easteal, & Swannell, 2011). Although research has been conducted on household food disposition practices (Evans 2012a, 2012b; Cappellini, 2009), consumers' active pursuit of and practices in reducing food waste still require further research.

This chapter looks at one interesting case of consumers taking charge of reducing their household food waste. The data come from a netnography of Finnish food bloggers' campaign called 'From Waste to Delicacy'. We apply a practice theoretical framework (Warde, 2005, 2014; Reckwitz, 2002) to analyse how food disposition practices are interlinked to the ways in which consumers purchase, store and cook food as well as how they consciously reflect upon their practices and share them with others in their quest for a more sustainable lifestyle.

Disposing food in households

Aside from being recently highlighted as a potential and interesting research topic, food waste has also become a widely discussed theme in the areas of policy, regulation, environment and cultural politics (Evans, Campbell, & Murcott, 2012). Reducing food waste has become essential from both environmental and economic perspectives, especially after the global financial crisis. Policies at the European Union (EU) level to reduce biodegradable waste have been introduced (European Commission, 2011). For instance, in the United Kingdom, the Waste and Resources Action Programme[1] has had a wide influence on increasing awareness of the issue. This programme and other non-profit organisations have created an agenda for reducing food waste. They have published staggering statistics of household food waste, which is estimated to be up to one-third of the food purchased. The European Commission has estimated that about 90 million tonnes of food waste is currently produced in the EU area. At the same time, in 2011 every tenth EU citizen 'reported that they could not afford a meal with meat, chicken or fish or a vegetarian equivalent every second day' (European Federation of Food Banks, 2013).

Studying waste, particularly food waste, is a relatively new research area. Traditionally, waste is conceptualised as 'rejected and worthless stuff that needs to be distanced from the societies that produce it' (Evans et al., 2012: 6–7). Other definitions of waste are that it is a static category and that it accumulates at the end of a linear process in which food is produced, consumed and disposed. Recently, many scholars have been paying more attention to waste as a dynamic and contextually bound complex issue. Evans (2011, 2012a, 2012b) has studied household food disposition and food waste ethnographically. He criticises public debates and policy interventions that try to blame food waste on individual consumers by emphasising the need for attitude and behavioural change. He and other researchers claim that changing behaviour is actually about changing everyday social practices and the material and social conditions in which these practices take place (Evans, 2011; Hargreaves, 2011; Røpke, 2009). Evans' findings (2011) reveal the various ways in which consumers attempt to balance the norms of eating healthily and properly with the need to avoid waste. He considers consumers to be concerned about wasting food, and thus avoiding food waste is not merely a question of wrong attitude or not having enough knowledge (see also Abeliotis, Lasaridi, & Chroni, 2013). Rather, it is more about the social organisation of food practices in terms of purchasing, storing, preparing and consuming food (see Yngfalk, Chapter 14). Cappellini's (2009) findings on the role of leftover food in British families illustrate that food can reinforce and sustain family bonds as being a member of the family is required before leftovers can be eaten. Moreover, Cappellini (2009) draws on Miller's (1998) concept of thrift practices and concludes that transforming leftovers back into acceptable meal status during weekdays enables families to invest more time, energy and money into special meals during the weekend.

Mobilising consumers through blogging

As discussed above, food waste as a phenomenon is usually addressed through public policy initiatives that emphasise attitude change and increased consumer awareness. However, research shows that the challenge cannot be overcome only by lecturing consumers. Rather, consumers should be informed and have good intentions to reduce their food waste. However, they are impeded by their practices and the socio-material context, such as social norms and cultural values that the consumers have, or the material ingredients and devices that they can use for cooking. In our study, we focus on the activities of reducing food waste initiated by consumers themselves.

Cultural practices related to ecological consumption, such as food waste reduction, can be studied in-depth in online communities where people constantly negotiate them (Rokka & Moisander, 2009). Online communities have become arenas for collective innovation, not only for user-led product development but also for reflecting and discussing consumption practices and lifestyles (Närvänen, Kartastenpää, & Kuusela, 2013; Kozinets, Hemetsberger, & Schau, 2008).

Recently, blogs have gained increasing attention in consumer research as a specific type of online community. Blogs revolve around the blogger, whose lifestyle, consumption interests and practices are at the centre of discussion. Nevertheless, the blogosphere forms a larger community that connects bloggers with similar interests, such as fashion (Kulmala, Mesiranta, & Tuominen, 2013; McQuarrie, Miller, & Phillips, 2013; Scaraboto & Fischer, 2013) and interior design (Arsel & Bean, 2013). Blogs give an opportunity to seek an audience for bloggers' acts of consumption (McQuarrie et al., 2013) and a way to manifest opinions, share experiences, and represent taste and know-how (Scaraboto & Fischer, 2013). Therefore, for researchers, blogs offer an insightful and fertile context in which to observe consumer practices as they are explicitly reflected and verbalised (see Truninger, Chapter 7). Moreover, blogging and blog campaigns have become a way to enact consumer-citizenship and identity projects. An example is the collective quest by plus-size bloggers to influence mainstream fashion retailers to have greater product variety (Scaraboto & Fischer, 2013).

Method

The netnography of a blog campaign in Finland was used to generate data for the study. We observed 33 food blogs participating in the campaign that aims to reduce food waste. In accordance with the principles of netnography, we examined the social and cultural features of interaction in the blogs (Kozinets, 2002, 2009). According to Hookway (2008), social researchers can observe blogs to gain insight of the dynamics of everyday life from a first-person viewpoint. In addition, blogs offer publicly available, naturally occurring data. We analysed the data from a practice theoretical perspective, highlighting the intertwined practical, material and symbolic aspects of bloggers' activities (Shove, Pantzar, & Watson, 2012; Røpke, 2009; Reckwitz, 2002).

A food blogger started the campaign in May 2012 after becoming concerned about food waste. She challenged other bloggers to join her. Although initially the campaign was planned to last for a month, after two years it is still more or less ongoing. In her starting manifesto, the blogger wrote:

> In general, every one of us carries food to the garbage bin with both hands. Together with about thirty other food bloggers, we decided that something must be done.... We want to inspire rather than lecture you all to magically transform waste into delicacy and at the same time reduce our own food waste.
>
> (From Waste to Delicacy Blog Manifesto, Salt and Honey blog).

We collected and downloaded all blog entries between May 2012 and January 2013. We selected altogether 293 entries that included the From Waste to Delicacy tag. Also audience comments to those blog entries were included as data. We asked permission from each blogger to conduct the study. Aside from downloading the entries, we closely observed the blogs by reading them throughout the study period. We did not focus on the individual consumers but on the representations of collectively shared practices as they emerged from the online interaction. Hence our study was not about the actual behaviour of consumers but rather how they talked about their daily practices. As Hookway (2008: 97) points out: 'even if bloggers do not tell the "truth", these "fabrications" still tell us something about the manner in which specific social and cultural ideas […] are constructed'.

The textual data from the blog entries and comments are considered cultural text that gives access to cultural forms and understanding, according to which people make sense of the world and perform their practices (Rokka & Moisander, 2009).

The data analysis was conducted following the standard procedure for qualitative research outlined by Spiggle (1994), including the processes of categorising data, abstracting the categories to a higher level, comparing the categories to each other, dimensionalising them through interaction with the theoretical framework and continuing the analysis until we felt the data had told its story. In this chapter, we analysed the bloggers' practices as a holistic process, from planning and acquiring food (i.e. visiting the grocery store) to cooking and storing it at home, as well as the meanings related to reducing food waste. For the analysis, we used the framework of acquisition, appropriation and appreciation (see also Warde, 2005, 2014). By acquisition we mean how consumers plan for and do shopping for groceries. Appropriation refers to 'the incorporation, adaptation and using up of items to serve practical purposes' (Warde, 2014: 283–284). Appreciation deals with the social and cultural meanings related to practices.

Findings

Acquisition

Reducing food waste can be done at home even before we go to the grocery store. According to a study, planning and shopping practices predict food waste, and reducing waste is possible by changing these practices (Stefan et al., 2013). Bloggers are more aware of the need to plan in advance than they were prior to the campaign. This move requires more physical and mental effort, for example, in terms of making an inventory of the contents of the fridge, writing a shopping list or eating before going shopping to avoid feeling hungry while in the grocery store.

> Before going to the store, I promise to look in my fridge in case there's something I can use. I'll make a shopping list and plan in advance in order to avoid impulse buying. I'll not go to the store feeling hungry.
>
> (Terhi's Kitchen)

> I promise to reflect on this issue next month. I'll plan my grocery shopping more carefully. I'll check my fridge more rigorously before the next shopping trip, and I'll not fall so easily for impulse purchases.
>
> (Soul Kitchen)

While in the store, bloggers admit to changing their shopping habits. For example, they look for items with approaching expiry dates that are discounted. They understand this practice as economical and ecological consumption on a larger scale. Changing their practices may mean doing something completely opposite to what they are used to.

> Inspired by the 'From Waste to Delicacy' theme, I decided to be a superwoman. Aside from saving my own kitchen, I also save the nearby food stores from threatening waste.... Whereas before I usually try to find the most recent products from the back row and put them into my shopping cart, this time I get only the products marked with a 'NB! Expiry Date Approaching' sticker.
>
> (Gobbler)

However, the bloggers also face difficulties in changing their shopping practices. Food disposition in general also causes anxiety and contradiction between the ideal and the real. While in the store, the bloggers admit to buying food on impulse despite knowing that it will likely go to waste. They want to follow the norm of eating healthily and buying fruits and vegetables, but they act differently at home.

> I just happen to have this bad habit of buying apples and mandarins that nobody even eats in my household as well as boxes of salad that usually become leftovers. I also tend to buy vegetables using my gut feeling. Because of lack of planning, these vegetables always end up in the compost.
>
> (Princess Kitchen)

The practices of retailers and the food industry also play an important role in influencing bloggers to act against their better judgement. Volume discounts encourage them to buy more than they plan and need. Moreover, the food industry produces too-large packages for small households. For example, in Finland, bread is mostly sold in large quantities in supermarkets rather than in small bakeries. During the campaign, many bloggers decided to forego grocery shopping as much as possible to avoid the temptations in the store. This reflects the view of living in a society of abundance where shopping for more is a habit rather than a necessity (Albinsson et al., 2010).

> I'm going to skip grocery shopping today. I'm sure there's a lot of food stuff in my kitchen cupboards and in the freezer. I'll save money and the world.
>
> (Ankerias Vipunen)

Appropriation

At home, appropriating food in different storage containers and adopting different cooking practices are part of food waste reduction. The bloggers discuss and reflect on preventive practices and those that focus on re-using leftovers or food waste. They share tips on how to best preserve food and organise the storage of food at home. One audience member of a blog gives a detailed preventive suggestion on how to store food in the freezer with the help of a freezer map.

> As I am a visual person, I've made a so-called freezer map. It is a sheet of paper that charts the sections of my freezer. I use small (4.5 cm × 1.5 cm) Post-it notes to mark what I have in each section and how many portions. This system enables me to get the frozen stuff moving faster. Without the map, they will no doubt be forgotten in the darkness of the freezer.
>
> (Comment in In the soup)

In general, the bloggers consider having home-cooked food as a way to reduce their food waste. For example, one blogger optimises the amount of bread in her household by baking it herself. The following quote is in accordance with the norm of home-cooked meals being more 'proper' food (Evans, 2012a).

> After I started baking bread at home, bread waste has been almost non-existent in our household.
>
> (Flour in the Mouth)

The most salient feature of the campaign is the sharing of recipes, especially those that create new dishes out of leftovers. These recipes include typical Finnish dishes, such as pies, casseroles and soups. Some bloggers introduce recipes from foreign cultures as well. The bloggers also discuss specific ingredients with various uses and kitchen appliances that can be used to process food required in recipes. Some of the recipes even change the category of a dish, for example, from a salad to a smoothie. Similar trends can be seen in recent popular TV cooking shows such as 'Chopped' or 'Masterchef' using leftovers to innovate new dishes.

> In the Far East, fried rice is an ordinary everyday dish for which you use not only yesterday's rice but also anything that is available. It is therefore a good way to get rid of leftovers in the vegetable drawer, fridge or freezer.
>
> (Cooks and Pots)

> When reducing food waste, baking flatbread is practical because you can use yesterday's boiled potatoes or mashed potatoes and just adjust the amount of water.... When you have baked the flatbread, using the toaster to heat it can help you to reduce waste. The flatbread is of course at its best on the day it is baked, but it still tastes good for several days when you toast it.
>
> (Salt and Honey)

Food bloggers also report being proud of themselves when they are able to save food from going to waste. Therefore, as a result of their reflection on their practices, they are able to use food items on the verge of becoming food waste. They use the information they gained on good (still edible) versus bad (spoilt) waste as well as trust their senses more than the expiry dates on the food packages (see Meah, 2014).

> Yesterday, I used half a litre of cream even though it had expired over a week ago. I've learnt something at least.
>
> (Ankerias Vipunen)

> Food bloggers' 'From Waste to Delicacy' campaign slowly changes your own thinking. Instead of throwing dry buns in the garbage bin as usual, I started to consider creating a second life for them.
>
> (In the Soup)

In the latter quote, the blogger reflects upon a practice in which food that is considered almost a useless excess (Evans, 2012b) is brought back to the category of food that can still be used. The consumer negotiates the boundary between putting something in the bin and thus into the waste stream and keeping it in use and inventing a 'second life' for it. This practice is similar to recycling other durable consumer items (Albinsson & Perera, 2009), such as giving an old sweater a new life as a sofa cushion. In our findings, creating new uses for food waste is not restricted to cooking. The bloggers also share innovative new practices to take advantage of food waste before throwing it in the garbage bin.

> I even use orange peels for easy-to-make detergent. And did you know that banana peels are great for polishing shoes?
>
> (Oranges and Honey)

Appreciation

As part of the campaign, bloggers engage in changing the meanings associated with leftovers and food waste. These meanings are not considered negative but as having the potential for innovation. Bloggers are also able to develop their cooking skills. Similar to Fernandez, Brittain and Bennet's (2011) study on dumpster-diving, consumers engage in turning trash into something valuable. One of the related new skills that the bloggers develop is avoiding the use of recipes and improvising instead.

> I absolutely love leftovers and the challenge of conjuring up something new to eat instead of just warming it up and eating it as such.
>
> (On the Foodie's Plate)

> Creating exact recipes from 'From Waste to Delicacy' dishes is quite hard because the amount of food you have is rarely equal to any exact recipe.
>
> (Cooks and Pots)

Therefore, our findings seem to contrast with some of the earlier findings, especially those on families who do not necessarily want to innovate and try out new things because of fixed routines or the pressure of feeding the family in a proper way (Evans, 2012a). In general, the bloggers represent themselves as good cooks instead of lazy ones with poor taste. They see the campaign as a challenge that makes them inventive and explore new ideas. Cooking with leftovers begins with looking at the ingredients in a new light rather than as part of a recipe. One way to appreciate ingredients in a novel way is to highlight their ecological, moral and sustainable characteristics. From this perspective, throwing food away becomes a great moral anxiety.

> Cooking to reduce food waste turned out to be a task that encouraged invention. After typing 'Zucchini recipe' in Google, the world's largest

cookbook, I searched for recipes more than once before I had used up a giant zucchini.

(Salt and Honey)

The 'From Waste to Delicacy' challenge encourages one to engage in everyday creativity. I catch myself examining each ingredient I hold in my hand from a totally new perspective.

(Kitchen Chameleon)

In this quest, it helps to be ecological and thrifty as well as respectful of other people's work in producing food from raw materials or from a butchered animal.

(That's an Onion)

Cultural traditions and heritage are evident in the bloggers' reflective accounts. For instance, one blogger describes the Finnish tradition of serving party leftovers for a second group of guests. Gifting leftover food has been found problematic and is therefore not a common practice in other studies (Evans, 2011, 2012b). The reason is that food easily spoils and is therefore risky. Nevertheless, cultural differences can be found in the appropriateness of this practice. Another blogger looks for reasons behind her practices in her family background. She belongs to a generation whose parents were forced to minimise food waste during wartime. Similarly to the East German informants in Albinsson et al. (2010), the thrifty values and consumption patterns of the past have an influence on current practices.

'Rääppiäiset' – what a lovely old Finnish word! It means the after-party, i.e. the party that is held after the official guests have left but there is still plenty of food left. Just recently, we celebrated our kid's birthday with relatives.... Even though the day had been long, and the birthday girl was already tired, we sent out SMS messages right away to our friends. Come and save us from food waste!

(Tommy's Kitchen)

I prepare food from scratch by myself, and I don't use any ready-made meals or convenience food. Utilizing leftovers has always been close to my heart. I don't like it when food goes to waste. I've been thinking if the reason for that is that I'm the firstborn of two people born during the war.

(On the Foodie's Plate)

Through blogging activities, consumers want to overcome the guilt of wasting food. Avoiding food wastage is considered a personal quest or a heroic deed that requires many sacrifices. These sacrifices include eating too much to avoid throwing food items in the garbage or making the effort to plan meals more carefully. Succeeding in the quest for an empty fridge, that is, zero food waste, is a gratifying experience. Similar to families who consider consuming leftovers to be associated with thrifty practices and sacrifice so that the family could devote more resources to special occasions (Cappellini, 2009), the bloggers attempt to achieve higher personal and collective goals. Moreover, whereas in the family context, as these practices are considered intimate and restricted to members of the family only, the bloggers decide to reveal and discuss their practices openly. Sharing their personal development publicly and inspiring others in their blogs are important in this journey.

> I'm putting on the saint's crown here because the result is so much better than what I could ever dream of . . . but it does not come without pain.
>
> (Salt and Honey)

Conclusion

Whereas previous research emphasises the reasons why food waste occurs and the routines and socio-material contexts in which it happens, our study focused more on how consumers actively attempt to change their practices and reduce food waste (see Mourad & Barnard, Chapter 16). Our study examined how consumers collectively reduce their food waste by modifying their current food disposition practices and developing new ones. Our analysis of a food blog campaign in Finland, initiated by the consumers themselves, showed that food waste reduction is dynamic and complex. It is not only related to disposition but also to acquisition, appropriation and appreciation of food. The process is not linear but different stages are interlinked. Also, through blogging, reducing food waste becomes a collective project of innovation.

Our findings indicate that food waste reduction requires consumers to more comprehensively change their consumption patterns. Food waste reduction seems to be equal to preventing and reducing food waste. Prevention starts from planning and storing practices, and reduction means using leftovers or innovating new dishes. The bloggers are also willing to make a significant effort to change their practices. Based on our findings, blogging campaigns and blogging about mindful consumption may be more successful than campaigns initiated by public organisations. By consciously reflecting and sharing their private practices with each other through blogs, consumers also inspire and mobilise a larger audience. Therefore, informing consumers about the amount of food waste in kilos per household is not enough as it is only the tip of the iceberg. Encouraging consumers to take action themselves is one of the ways to attain more sustainable food consumption.

As a consequence of the campaign, bloggers reflect and become more aware of their food consumption practices (see Askegaard, Kristensen, & Ulver, Chapter 2), the reasons why they waste food and the current and new ways to reduce it. Blogging about their practices also helps them to document the changes in their everyday activities publicly. It offers a rich opportunity for us researchers to analyse the habitual and routine household patterns that are usually private and unreflected. Therefore, blogs are specific social sites where consumers can reflect, discuss and attempt to change their practices related to food waste.

Note

1 See www.wrap.org.uk/ [Accessed 7 October 2015].

References

Abeliotis, K., Lasaridi, K., & Chroni, C. (2014). Attitudes and behaviour of Greek households regarding food waste prevention. *Waste Management & Research, 32*(3), 237–240.

Albinsson, P. A., & Perera, B. Y. (2009). From trash to treasure and beyond: The meaning of voluntary disposition. *Journal of Consumer Behaviour, 8*(6), 340–353.

Albinsson, P. A., Wolf, M., & Kopf, D. A. (2010). Anti-consumption in East Germany: Consumer resistance to hyperconsumption. *Journal of Consumer Behaviour, 9*(6), 412–425.

Arsel, Z., & Bean, J. (2013). Taste regimes and market-mediated practice. *Journal of Consumer Research, 39*(5), 899–917.

Black, I., & Cherrier, H. (2012). Recycling: Yes, but caring for my loved ones first: Exploring identity conflicts amongst 'green' working mothers. In R. Ahluwalia, T. L. Chartrand, & R. K. Ratner (Eds.), *Advances in Consumer Research, Vol. 39 (pp. 34–35)*. Duluth, MN: Association for Consumer Research.

Cappellini, B. (2009). The sacrifice of re-use: The travels of leftovers and family relations. *Journal of Consumer Behaviour, 8*(6), 365–375.

European Commission. (2011). Roadmap to a resource efficient Europe: COM/ 2011/0571 final. Available at: http://eur-lex.europa.eu/legal-content/EN/TXT/ ?uri=CELEX:52011DC0571 [Accessed 22 March 2013].

European Federation of Food Banks. (2013). Aid to the most deprived: European Parliament and Council agree to €3.5 billion for 2014–2020. Available at: www. eurofoodbank.eu/portail/index.php?option=com_content&view=category&layout =blog&id=26&Itemid=45&lang=en [Accessed 22 March 2013].

Evans, D. (2011). Blaming the consumer – once again: The social and material contexts of everyday food waste practices in some UK households. *Critical Public Health, 21*(4), 429–440.

Evans, D. (2012a). Beyond the throwaway society: Ordinary domestic practice and a sociological approach to household food waste. *Sociology, 46*(1), 41–56.

Evans, D. (2012b). Binning, gifting and recovery: The conduits of disposal in household food consumption. *Environment and Planning D: Society and Space, 30*(6), 1123–1137.

Evans, D., Campbell, H., & Murcott, A. (2012). A brief pre-history of food waste and the social sciences. *The Sociological Review, 60*(S2), 5–26.

Fernandez, K. V., Brittain, A. J., & Bennett, S. D. (2011). 'Doing the duck': Negotiating the resistant-consumer identity. *European Journal of Marketing, 45*(11/12), 1779–1788.

Hargreaves, T. (2011). Practice-ing behaviour change: Applying social practice theory to pro-environmental behaviour change. *Journal of Consumer Culture, 11*(1), 79–99.

Hookway, N. (2008). Entering the blogosphere: Some strategies for using blogs in social research. *Qualitative Research, 8*(1), 91–113.

Imeche.org. (2013). Global food: Waste not, want not. Institution of Mechanical Engineers. Available at: www.imeche.org/knowledge/themes/environment/global-food [Accessed 22 May 2014].

Kozinets, R. V. (2002). The field behind the screen: Using netnography for marketing research in online communities. *Journal of Marketing Research, 39*(1), 61–72.

Kozinets, R. V. (2009). *Netnography: Doing Ethnographic Research Online.* London: Sage.

Kozinets, R. V., Hemetsberger, A., & Schau, H. J. (2008). The wisdom of consumer crowds: Collective innovation in the age of networked marketing. *Journal of Macromarketing, 28*(4), 339–354.

Kulmala, M., Mesiranta, N., & Tuominen, P. (2013). Organic and amplified eWOM in consumer fashion blogs. *Journal of Fashion Marketing and Management, 17*(1), 20–37.

McQuarrie, E. F., Miller, J., & Phillips, B. J. (2013). The megaphone effect: Taste and audience in fashion blogging. *Journal of Consumer Research, 40*(1), 136–158.

Meah, A. (2014). Still blaming the consumer? Geographies of responsibility in domestic food safety practices. *Critical Public Health, 24*(1), 88–103.

Miller, D. (1998). *A Theory of Shopping.* Ithaca, NY: Cornell University Press.

Närvänen, E., Kartastenpää, E., & Kuusela, H. (2013). Online lifestyle consumption community dynamics: A practice-based analysis. *Journal of Consumer Behaviour, 12*(5), 358–369.

Parsons, E., & Maclaran, P. (2009). 'Unpacking disposal': Introduction to the special issue. *Journal of Consumer Behaviour, 8*(6), 301–304.

Quested, T. E., Parry, A. D., Easteal, S., & Swannell, R. (2011). Food and drink waste from households in the UK. *Nutrition Bulletin, 36*(4), 460–467.

Reckwitz, A. (2002). Toward a theory of social practices: A development in culturalist theorizing. *European Journal of Social Theory, 5*(2), 243–263.

Rokka, J., & Moisander, J. (2009). Environmental dialogue in online communities: Negotiating ecological citizenship among global travellers. *International Journal of Consumer Studies, 33*(2), 199–205.

Røpke, I. (2009). Theories of practice: New inspiration for ecological economic studies on consumption. *Ecological Economics, 68*(10), 2490–2497.

Scaraboto, D., & Fischer, E. (2013). Frustrated fatshionistas: An institutional theory perspective on consumer quests for greater choice in mainstream markets. *Journal of Consumer Research, 39*(6), 1234–1257.

Shove, E., Pantzar, M., & Watson, M. (2012). *The Dynamics of Social Practice: Everyday Life and How It Changes.* London: Sage.

Spiggle, S. (1994). Analysis and interpretation of qualitative data in consumer research. *Journal of Consumer Research, 21*(3), 491–503.

Stefan, V., van Herpen, E., Tudoran, A. A., & Lähteenmäki, L. (2013). Avoiding food waste by Romanian consumers: The importance of planning and shopping routines. *Food Quality and Preference, 28*(1), 375–381.

Warde, A. (2005). Consumption and theories of practice. *Journal of Consumer Culture, 5*(2), 131–153.

Warde, A. (2014). After taste: Culture, consumption and theories of practice. *Journal of Consumer Culture, 14*(3), 279–303.

16 'Don't waste the waste'

Dumpster dinners among garbage gourmands

Marie Mourad and Alex Barnard

Introduction: dumpster dinners

On a Wednesday night in May 2012, Janet, a 45-year-old high school Spanish teacher, and Jonathan, a 25-year-old self-described anarchist and full-time activist, are washing and cutting courgettes in the kitchen of a cosy apartment in Queens, New York. As they work, they chat amicably about how best to prepare the vegetable stir fry and debate over whether the meal should be vegan. Around them, ten other people are helping with the preparation. This scene is reminiscent of the classic American potluck, where each participant brings a dish to share or ingredients to prepare with the others, except for one key difference: the night before, all of the food being prepared had been at the bottom of 50-litre dark plastic trash bags, placed on the pavement and destined for the landfill. This meal started where other meals usually end: disposal.

Janet and Jonathan are part of a group of 'freegans' in New York City. Freegans are people who adopt the practice of eating from the garbage as part of a 'total boycott' of an economic system they see as wasteful, exploitative, and unsustainable.[1] They call this Wednesday night's event a 'freegan feast': a meal where all the ingredients – except for some spices and cooking oil – have been 'dumpster-dived' outside of commercial establishments. Although dumpster-diving for food, clothing, or other household items has a long history as a survival strategy for the poor and marginalised, an increasing number of groups and individuals around the Western world use *voluntary waste recovery* as a form of political action (see Nguyen, Chen, & Mukherjee, 2014; Barnard, 2011; Gross, 2009; Edwards & Mercer, 2007).

Across the Atlantic in the summer of 2013, Adrien and Marine, a haphazardly dressed and eccentric-looking young couple sharing an apartment in the 18th arrondissement of Paris, have also organised a free meal in their community garden. Marine is a part-time French tutor, while Adrien works – ironically enough – for a gastronomic guidebook. He puts his knowledge of French culinary culture to good use, preparing a barbecue that brings together a diverse group from the neighbourhood around food that has been almost entirely rescued from the trash. The pair have been dumpster-diving for four years and, as they stated on an advertisement posted in March 2013 for a room in their shared apartment, 'Nine-tenths of our food comes from rescue!'[2] They represent a growing trend of dumpster-divers who recover waste for reasons that vary from sustainability to amusement or thrift, particularly in response to the economic downturn in 2008 (Guillard & Roux, 2014; Brosius, Fernandez, & Cherrier, 2013; Carolsfeld & Erikson, 2013; Fernandez, Brittain, & Bennett, 2011; see also Cappellini, Marilli, & Parsons, Chapter 4).

Drawing on practice theories, which underline the importance of the material dimensions of everyday life (Røpke, 2009; Shove, Trentmann, & Wilk, 2009; Warde, 2005), we show how certain objects – such as discarded food – can reshape human action in surprising ways. By analysing dumpster-dived meals as a 'compound practice' (Warde, 2013), breaking it down into the 'sub-practices' or acquiring, preparing, eating, and disposing of discarded food, we reveal the contradictions between the political and ethical meanings and the 'doings' (Magaudda, 2011) of this practice (see Canniford & Bradshaw, Chapter 17).

As we find, 'dumpster dinners', free from the usual economic pressures of purchasing food, are still shaped by different cultural and social rules about how foods should be separated or combined, peeled or not-peeled, discarded or preserved. These expectations and habits at times block dumpster-divers from realising their purported commitments to reduce waste. These tensions are invisible in existing studies of dumpster-diving as a form of ethical consumption which focuses primarily, or solely, on the *acquisition* of wasted goods and not their subsequent trajectory (Guillard & Roux, 2014; Carolsfeld & Erikson, 2013; Edwards & Mercer, 2007; see also Närvänen, Mesiranta, & Hukkanen, Chapter 15). At a time when various public policies and activist movements aim to encourage ethical or sustainable consumption, analyses such as this are vital for showing how such changes must focus on complete *systems* of practices – whether from acquisition to disposal or disposal to consumption – and the way they interact with and constrain one another.

We base our analysis on ethnographic observations of the activist network freegan.info in New York City from 2007 to 2012 and of Disco Soupe – a movement founded in 2012 that organises public cooking events that use discarded ingredients in order to 'raise awareness' on food waste in a musical and 'festive' atmosphere[3] – in Paris from 2013 to 2014. In addition to our participation in these groups, we conducted semi-structured interviews with 29 dumpster-divers in the US and nine in France. These data are complemented by ongoing, embodied participation in dumpster-diving by both authors between 2009 and 2014.

Acquisition: pavement shopping

On a warm night in June 2012, around 9 p.m., Jonathan rises from the couch he scavenged from a kerbside for his squatted apartment and announces to the first author that he 'feel[s] like a bacon sandwich'. In a city with thousands of restaurants and delis, this is not a particularly difficult wish to fulfil – except that Jonathan has not bought food in over nine months. Nonetheless, he confidently rides his bike to a gourmet store in the SoHo neighbourhood that he knows as a good 'spot'. When he arrives, he begins feeling the outsides of the mound of plastic bags, trying to discern which contain edible food and which contain genuine garbage. Suddenly he exclaims, 'Whoa! There is sushi!' Like grocery store shoppers who leave the house with a specific list, yet are lured by sales and advertisements and fill their carts with unintended purchases, Jonathan begins piling up his finds on the pavement: bagged lettuce, fruit salads, pastries, and, at last, a bacon sandwich (with the $10 price sticker still attached).

In some surprising ways, dumpster-diving – even when undertaken by anti-consumption activists – looks a lot like shopping. Regulars know where to go to find one type of food or another: in NYC, donuts at Dunkin Donuts or packaged food at Trader Joe's; in Paris, pastries and bread at Paul Bakery, organic vegetables at Naturalia, or cheese and yogurts at Monoprix. Many dumpster-divers develop a weekly routine, built around the rhythm of stores putting out waste and municipal collection services coming to pick it up. One New York diver even said in an interview that she would check inside neighbourhood grocery stores to see what foods were near their expiration date that day and plan her night's route accordingly.

Of course, 'shopping' in dumpsters does not quite have all the conveniences of consumption in modern capitalism. Although they can choose the places and times, divers can't really choose the products themselves. Dumpster-divers often describe what they do as a modern day version of hunter-gathering – or, 'urban foraging', as some NYC freegans call it – but in truth, it's a bit more like fishing. In opening a garbage bag, freegans are casting a line into the vast waste stream of the metropolis, often with a half-joking, pseudo-religious plea to the 'dumpster gods'[4] to deliver a hoped-for item. Dumpster-divers spend a lot of time waiting for garbage to appear and frequently boast about their findings; freegan meetings in New York, for example, often begin with a ritualistic sharing of finds from the much celebrated Pom and Odwalla Dumpsters, the erstwhile final resting places for high-end pomegranate juice and energy bars, respectively.

Dumpster-diving practices mirror fishing in one other way: sometimes catches have to be let go. While freegans are fond of describing the food they find as 'perfectly good' – thus critiquing the seemingly arbitrary decisions that lead some items to be discarded while others are eaten – even they admit that not all food that ends up in the garbage is edible. This capacity to differentiate the good from the bad is a source of distinction for dumpster-divers, a sign that they have not fallen prey to the widely-derided 'de-skilling' of Western consumers (see Meah & Watson, 2011). As another freegan lectured a group of students who had come for a 'trash tour' – a publicly announced dumpster dive open to newcomers – in February 2009: 'We have false ideas about what constitutes fresh food. A lot of food tastes better when it looks worse. But those are not the tactile and aesthetic qualities people look for when they purchase produce.'

By rejecting the importance of perfect looking food and instead relying on senses of touch, taste, or smell, dumpster-divers believe they have developed practices that are more sustainable than mainstream consumers' reliance on supermarket sell-by dates and aesthetic standards (the latter leading to the rejection of up to 30 per cent of fruits and vegetables harvested in the Western world) (see Institution of Mechanical Engineers, 2013). Yet expectations about what constitutes so-called 'good' food are not easy to change. Freegan trash tours, particularly those attended by large numbers of newcomers, often devolve into a scramble for the least-blemished and most shapely items. Even movements like Disco Soupe, which explicitly attempt to change consumer practices through encouraging the consumption of 'ugly produce',5 struggle with the desire to present food that is visually appealing and concerns about how those very same aesthetics may generate waste.

This omnipresent tension between the dumpster-diver-as-consumer and dumpster-diver-as-activist presents itself in other ways. Janet explains during an interview in 2009 that she sees dumpster-diving as an 'educational' activity and, as a consequence, avidly shares her favourite spots with newcomers and with the media. On the night he found the bonanza of sushi, Jonathan attempted to pass some of it off on a passer-by he knew, assuring her, 'You're not gonna be sick, I already ate a lot of sushi here, it's always good!' Yet at other sites, Jonathan often went so far as to actively hide evidence that he had dived from others – fearful that if his favourite spots, as he put it, 'dried up', he would have to return to work and drop some of his activist commitments.

The temporary gatherings that form around dumpsters, then, can take markedly different forms. On one evening in the 10th district of Paris in 2014, Adrien and Marine meet in front of a high-end organic grocery store. With a small group of people that include a dreadlocked vegan and a hunched pensioner, they wait patiently until the store manager brings out a 1.5m-high green plastic dumpster. They paw through layers of cardboard and plastic to get what is in the bottom: potatoes, peppers, broccoli, spinach and fruits – all organic, all usually fetching a premium price. This day they are lucky, also finding quinoa-flour bread and yogurts. The assembled divers assess each others' preferences – 'Do you like chard?' – and the elderly woman repeatedly attempts to push more food onto the young couple before taking any herself. It is a moment characterised by solidarity, sharing, and community, one which many divers see as a sharp contrast to a world in which more people shop, cook, and eat alone. As one diver notes in an interview,

> It has become a trend, dumpster diving. We go and find people already there, putting their foodstuff out and trying different things, laughing and having a beer.... Half the time I'll find some friends at my favorite dumpster when I go there.

Yet, on this night in Paris, before they part, the dreadlocked vegan recounts a story of a recent fight over garbage she witnessed at another store. In New York, the stories are the same: as Janet describes it during a follow-up interview in 2012: 'I had a pretty crazy experience, a dive where someone grabbed a bag [of trash] and was growling over it like an animal.' As more and more people have become aware of the free abundance that discarded food represents – especially in an era of stagnant wages and unemployment – dumpster-diving begins to look less like a way of getting back to our forager roots in an urban environment and more like a frenzied, everything-must-go closeout sale. While dumpster-divers may see themselves as distinctive 'ethical consumers' (see Dubuisson-Quellier, 2013), they are nonetheless limited by the deeply ingrained practices of a standardised market-based food system.

Preparation: the food-rescue recipe

Although Jonathan asserts, during a conversation with the first author in the summer of 2012, that he 'always' eventually finds what he needs among the seemingly infinite waste of New York City, it can take him three hours walking in Manhattan to find his favourite pizza. By contrast, *preparing* a dumpstered meal can be almost effortless. As Western consumers work longer hours and spend less time cooking (Warde, Cheng, Olsen, & Southerton, 2007), supermarkets have devoted an increasing amount of shelf space to pre-packed, pre-prepared foods. Although food packaging is often touted as a potential *solution* to consumer-level food waste (Conseil National de l'Emballage, 2011), the contents of supermarket dumpsters suggest that processed or cooked offerings – like baby carrots, rotisserie chickens, or salad bars – are wasted at higher rates than their unprocessed counterparts. The materiality of food, after all, is 'unforgiving' (Evans, 2011: 11), as cut skins or removing peels drastically diminishes food's shelf life. For his part, Jonathan composes most of his diet from these offerings: pizza, ready-made salads, sandwiches and, on special occasions, sushi.

Most freegans, however, see procurement as only one of the ways they break with more mainstream food practice. Maximus, a freegan in Boston who briefly attempted to start a free restaurant with rescued ingredients in April 2013, notes in an interview that the diver's difference in mentality extends to the kitchen:

> Most people walk into the kitchen and think, 'What do I want?' which quickly transforms into, 'What product should I buy?' We think differently. When we walk into the kitchen, we ask, 'What do we have? What can we make with it?' We use whatever resources we have available.

Dumpster-divers often reverse the usual assumption of the right way to cook: they know the means – the individual ingredients – before the final dish. Cooking in this way requires creativity, improvisation, and a knowledge of the material qualities of food. As Jason, one New York diver, sums it up during the preparation for a freegan feast in his Brooklyn apartment: 'If it looks like green onions, I cook it like green onions, whatever it actually is.' In France, Adrien and Marine laugh as they describe how dumpster-diving means that they eat 'improbable' food all the time even as they still follow the classic French multi-course scheme for dinner: entrée, main dish and side, cheese and bread, and dessert.

At other times, though, the culinary traditions that dumpster-divers think they are resuscitating and their actions to reduce waste mix uneasily. On a cold morning in January 2014, the authors participate in a Disco Soupe event. An older man with a long white beard who had been passing by joins in the preparation, which until then had been carried out mostly by young, highly-educated Disco Soupe activists. He immediately begins to enforce a strict separation of ingredients between the two soups, following traditional French culinary rules. He then announces that certain ingredients are not of high enough quality for either. When he begins cutting vegetables, he admonishes the participants, 'You have to peel the carrots! Otherwise it's disgusting!' Disco Soupe itself does not take a position on the weighty question of 'to peel or not to peel?': some activists see peeling as wasteful while others are concerned about pesticides on the outside of food. In the end, taste and tradition have to be balanced against environmental concern. In this case, two North African women with experience preparing food for 300-person weddings join in the debate and announce that peeling is obligatory, because 'that's the way you have to do it'.

In fact, while Disco Soupe participants believe that the very practice of cooking with discarded ingredients 'sensitises' people about food waste and changing representations of what should and should not be eaten, the group is reluctant to consider one major source of waste: hygiene concerns. As Watson and Meah (2012) elaborate, in an era of lengthening supply chains, increasing disconnection from agriculture, and well-publicised food safety scares, 'best-before' or 'use-by' dates have proliferated – with major consequences for the production of waste[6] (see Yngfalk, Chapter 14). While helping in the washing of vegetables during the Disco Soupe event, Aurélien, a 28-year-old journalist and core member of the Parisian team, tells Amelle, a 35-year-old teacher: 'You should add vinegar to the water.' Without waiting for a response, he starts re-rinsing – with vinegar – vegetables that she has already cleaned. Amelle looks surprised: 'Are you going to re-rinse everything? Do you rinse your own dumpster-dived food with vinegar at home?' to which he answers, 'No, but at least I know where that is from!' Besides the obvious irony in the response – Aurélien has little idea where the food he routinely dives comes from (other than that it comes from a dumpster) – the anecdote highlights how working with surplus or excess food may actually *increase* hygiene requirements. As such, the sub-practice of *preparing* dumpster-dived food could conflict with the principles behind the overall practice itself:

wasting as little food as possible, in part through questioning the hygiene and convenience standards usually associated with processed and mass-marketed food.

Eating: 'garbage, not trash'

Once the meal is ready, it is no longer 'waste': as a member of freegan.info proudly stated to one reporter during a TV interview in 2008, 'We may eat garbage, but we don't eat trash.' Many of the dumpster-divers we interviewed avowed that they actually ate better food when dumpster-diving than they ever would if they were buying it. Adrien and Marine describe a diet full of choice cuts of meat, fancy cheese, and *foie gras* – all delicacies that, given their income, they could scarcely afford to actually buy. At one dumpster frequented by the authors in Paris, several regulars repeatedly turn down offers of any food that isn't organic. For some, the abundance of dumpster-diving converts otherwise shoestring purchasers into garbage *gourmands*: 'I've become very picky', Jonathan observes, something that was not the case when he was buying food on a student's budget.

Beyond just allowing them to eat certain *types* of food, the social relationships forged around freegan meals can help freegans cope with other problems their lifestyle poses. Jonathan describes how his decision not to purchase food – and the anti-capitalist ideology behind it – leaves him feeling isolated, given that so many social interactions, like having coffee with a friend, involve buying something:

> I always stand around in a room full of people and think, 'Oh my God, no one is an anti-capitalist here.' I feel so alone, I feel so out of place.... It's so lonely. It's depressing as hell to live here [in New York].

In her own interview, Janet mentions a similar feeling, noting:

> You can sit in a room of five or ten people, and they're talking about bargains and sales and 'Where'd you buy that?' and what the latest technology is, and you can really feel like you don't want to participate at all, or that you have to guard it [your freeganism].

Freegan feasts, on the other hand, create a space of conviviality where worldviews and ideologies that would be otherwise derided as extreme can be shared openly. In August 2008, the menu at one feast in a Brooklyn apartment included broccoli rabe, vegetable stew, bread with hummus, stir fry, and, for dessert, a fruit smoothie. Someone commented how rare it was to be at an event where, as a vegan, she could eat every single dish served. This comment served as a spark for several freegans to open up and share beliefs that would put them on the fringes of the mainstream animal rights or environmental movements. Jason brought up that he thought the example of early hunter-gatherers indicated the possibility that some forms of meat eating could be ethical, a proposition that proved quite contentious. Sasha countered,

> I feel one-hundred times happier when I'm not eating animals because I know my biology is not set up for being an animal eater.... I don't want to kill any animals, and I don't really want to eat them. That's just how I am. I feel like it's a better life to be more at peace with nature.

As with other sub-practices, though, these 'garbage dinners' expose tensions between the 'meanings' and the 'doings' of dumpster-diving. Although the menu at the freegan feast mentioned above included a healthy range of fruits and vegetables, it was almost entirely lacking in protein. While the authors' own experience is that virtually every product on offer inside a store – including seeming non-perishables like canned goods or honey – eventually winds up in the dumpsters outside it,[7] healthier items and vegetarian sources of protein are rare.

The difficulty that even picky dumpster-divers face in putting together healthy meals from the garbage raises questions about some of the strategies commonly proposed to reduce food waste. Reports often sum up the total calories that are discarded and then proceed to infer how many people could be fed by that food: by one calculation, current avoidable global food waste is enough to feed 1.9 billion people 2,100 kcal per capita per day (Kummu, de Moel, Porkka, Siebert, Varis, & Ward, 2012). The implication is clear: that any excess food should be donated and used to feed the hungry. Yet a recent study from the US Department of Agriculture found nearly half of the calories in discarded food come from added fats and added sweeteners (Buzby, Hodan, & Jeffrey, 2014). In recognition of this reality, Janet once even cautioned new attendees at a trash tour about the risks of an all-dumpster-dived pastry diet, ruefully observing that she had gained weight since she started rescuing food. Sometimes what gets thrown out – even technically *edible* food – really *is* trash.

The nature of how and what food is *procured* by dumpster-divers often shapes the way food is *eaten* in contradictory ways, showing the tensions within the 'compound' practice of dumpster-divers. Adrien and Marine state that while they might prefer to be vegetarian – as Marine exclaimed during a dinner in 2014, 'I'm tired of all this meat!' – they feel a duty to eat the meat they find because of its high ecological footprint and economic value. But precisely because many divers see taking discarded food as having no impact on the environment, they can consume these (former) commodities with less reflection about whether their sub-practices of preparing or eating the meals would make sense in a less-wasteful world where they *wouldn't* dumpster dive. In New York, the freegan.info group had put some thought and effort into how they would feed themselves in a post-capitalist world – engaging in community gardening projects and 'wild food foraging' tours in city parks

– but, as one freegan remarked: 'I'd rather not eat dandelions. Dumpsters have tastier food.' While dumpster-divers may have found a way to live more ethically as individuals *within* the existing food system, they struggled to envision the practices of a food system that would be more ethical at a structural level.

Disposal: 'don't waste the waste'

Our description of dumpster-divers' practices of procuring, preparing, and eating meals has already shown how 'back-end' practices of our food system – that is, disposal – can have implications for the 'front-end' (see Cappellini, 2009). As suggested by other recent studies on waste (Crang, Hughes, Gregson, Norris, & Ahamed, 2013; Reno, 2009), the act of disposal is not an end point, but can actually begin a complex trajectory that ends in re-valuation and reuse. Having already saved their food 'from the jaws of the trash compactor' – as one freegan puts it during a speech delivered during a trash tour – many freegans are reticent to dispose of it *again*, and will go to great lengths to avoid doing so. For her part, Janet evokes a sense of moral 'obligation to rescue stuff', adding,

> I can quit my job, and quit sleeping, and spend all of my time fixing what people have done wrong with the things they throw out and not recycling – all the bagels and donuts and salads – all of it is going wrong and it's terribly frustrating to ignore.

Janet often arrives at freegan events laden with bags of bizarre items and attempts to convince others to take them.

On one evening in 2012, while the first author is spending time at Jonathan's apartment, Lucy, one of the temporary roommates and a regular dumpster-diver, opens the 'dumpster box' – a cardboard box full of bread and pastries – and declares, 'This bread is getting stale.' Jonathan replies dismissively, 'Just throw it out, we'll get more tonight.' Lucy hesitates, and Jonathan adds, 'You're just *re*-wasting it!' Unconvinced, Lucy defiantly takes a bite with a loud 'crunch' and retorts, 'Don't waste the waste!'

For Jonathan, like other groups of anti-waste activists, *re*-wasting is an unavoidable and necessary part of his practices. The fact that the food is already rescued makes it first, more likely, and second, more legitimate, to let it to go to waste. At one architecture and music festival in 2014 where Disco Soupe cooked for hundreds of people, kilos of strawberries had to be thrown away because there was not enough time to sort the bad from the good ones and not enough broilers to cook jam.

Clearly, because dumpster-dived food is free and has been destined for the landfill anyway, some divers feel comfortable throwing it out. One resident of a freegan cooperative house in New York confesses in a conversation during a dumpster dive in 2009: 'Because we're diving, there's way too much food [and] people aren't worried about leaving it out or throwing it away.' Adrien and Marine's fridge almost always seemed to contain things in various states of decay: it is often easier to take more than they need while diving and then throw the excess out later. In fact, the authors themselves even discovered that they produced *more* waste than they did when they were not dumpster-diving – partly because of the temptation of taking too much, and partly because of a much greater proportion of packaged food. While at the core of dumpster-divers' – and freegans' in particular – critique of capitalism is the notion that, in capitalist societies, useful things that cannot be sold are considered valueless, freegans themselves struggle to develop practices of care and stewardship for free things. Seeing this, however, required following dumpster-divers beyond the dumpster and into the spaces where they carried out the rest of their culinary practices.

Changing the world one dumpster at a time?

The practice of rescuing discarded objects to achieve ethical or political goals within the current food system entails often contradictory sub-practices related to acquiring, preparing, eating and potentially discarding food. The fact that dumpster-divers engage in the practice of recovering items that have been labelled as 'waste' often leads them to adopt other sub-practices that they would never consider, such as eating meat or throwing out excess food. This contradiction leads us to broader questions about the rise of ethical and sustainable consumption. Scholars have charted the dramatic rise in purchases of 'organic' food or 'fair trade' coffee (Dubuisson-Quellier, 2013). We wonder, however, whether purchasing these commodities may actually help actors overlook *other* elements of their practices that are contradictory or, even by their own standards, *un*ethical.

And what, in the end, do all the efforts that freegans and other dumpster-divers put into acquiring, preparing, eating, and (re)disposing of wasted food add up to? For Jonathan, eating dumpster-dived food is one among many strategies – alongside voluntary unemployment, squatting, bicycling and hitchhiking – which helps him keep away from capitalism. Janet sees dumpster-diving as a way to focus media and popular attention on mass consumerism, which in her eyes is 'destroying the planet'. In contrast, Adrien sees dumpster-diving less as a political statement, as he states in an interview with the first author in February 2014:

> You know the food is there.... It seems logical to me.... There is food, you can eat it, you eat it. It's common sense. I am not really into the 'fighting against food waste' thing.

In fact, Adrien is conscious of, and even agrees with, the frequent criticism of dumpster-divers that they are parasites on the very system they claim to be resisting:

You don't fight against the system. On the contrary, you live off the system's leftovers.... You have no impact. If you really want to change something, you buy directly from producers at a price paying both the labour and the product.

In the end, though, he affirms, 'Even if I had money, I'd still do it [dumpster dive]. It's fun, it's an adventure.' Irrespective of its diverse motives and goals, voluntary dumpster-diving has had an influence – if not necessarily the one divers intended. In reviewing the factors that have spurred increasing public and private interest in food waste, Evans, Campbell and Murcott (2012) cite the spectacle of well-educated, middle-class individuals surviving off of discards as having sparked outrage at the scale of food waste. But perhaps a more important question is what – if anything – dumpster-divers can tell us about *addressing* food waste. With reports from the EU and United Nations declaring much of the 40 per cent of world food production that goes to waste is discarded by consumers, attention has shifted to consumer practices – not 'capitalism' – as a target for reform (Gustavsson, Cederberg, Sonesson, van Otterdijk, & Meybeck, 2011; European Commission, 2010). Both social movements like Disco Soupe and public campaigns emphasise change through individual practices of procuring, preparing and eating food. As the United Nation's recently-launched 'Think.Eat.Save' website assures us, 'with relative ease and a few simple changes to our habits, we can significantly shift this paradigm' of waste.[8]

Yet are changes to culinary practices as simple as activists and policymakers seem to assume? We find that even dumpster-divers – individuals often willing to renounce their privileged backgrounds and live on the margins of society, while facing the stigma attached to contact with waste – struggle to adopt truly sustainable practices. True, their meals may be 'no impact' in the sense that they have not financially contributed to the ecological or human costs of the food system. Some sub-practices that go along with dumpster-diving, such as eating non-organic, non-seasonal, highly processed food and throwing away a large quantity of packaging, look surprisingly 'normal' in their level of ecological consideration (or lack thereof). Ultimately, by focusing on individual practices, campaigns around food waste may be missing the extent to which these practices are constrained by the existing organisation of food production, distribution and consumption.

Notes

1 See freegan.info [Accessed 8 January 2015].
2 All quotes from French informants are translated by the first author.
3 See Discosoupe.org [Accessed 8 January 2015].
4 Expression used by Marine during various dumpster-dives in Paris in 2013.
5 Based on Discosoupe.org [Accessed 8 January 2015].
6 Surveys find that only 15 per cent of consumers correctly understand date labels, and one study observed that consumers cited labels in explaining 30 per cent of instances of wasting food (Lyndhurst, 2011).

7 This claim is based on 60 observations in Paris between December 2013 and May 2014, during which the authors tracked the types, locations, and times of the products recovered.
8 www.thinkeatsave.org/index.php/about [Accessed 14 February 2014].

References

Barnard, A. V. (2011). 'Waving the banana' at Capitalism: Political theater and social movement strategy among New York's 'freegan' dumpster divers. *Ethnography, 12*(4), 419–444.

Brosius, N., Fernandez, K. V., & Cherrier, H. (2013). Reacquiring consumer waste: Treasure in our trash? *Journal of Public Policy and Marketing, 32*(2), 286–301.

Buzby, J., Hodan, W., & Jeffrey, H. (2014). *The Estimated Amount, Value, and Calories of Postharvest Food Losses at the Retail and Consumer Levels in the United States.* Washington, DC: US Department of Agriculture.

Cappellini, B. (2009). The sacrifice of re-use: The travels of leftovers and family relations. *Journal of Consumer Behaviour, 8*(6), 365–375.

Carolsfeld, A. L., & Erikson, S. L. (2013). Beyond desperation: Motivations for dumpster™ diving for food in Vancouver. *Food and Foodways, 21*(4), 245–266.

Conseil National de l'Emballage. (2011). *Prévention du gaspillage et des pertes: Le rôle clé de l'emballage.* Paris, France. Available at: http://www.conseil-emballage.org/la-prevention-du-gaspillage-et-des-pertes-des-produits-de-grande-consommation-le-role-cle-de-lemballage/ [Accessed 8 January 2015].

Crang, M., Hughes, A., Gregson, N., Norris, L., & Ahamed, F. (2013). Rethinking governance and value in commodity chains through global recycling networks. *Transactions of the Institute of British Geographers, 38*(1), 12–24.

Dubuisson-Quellier, S. 2013. *Ethical Consumption.* Halifax, Canada: Fernwood Books.

Edwards, F., & Mercer, D. (2007). Gleaning from gluttony: An Australian youth subculture confronts the ethics of waste. *Australian Geographer, 38*(3), 279–296.

European Commission. (2010). *Preparatory Study on Food Waste Across EU 27.* Paris, France: Bio Intelligence Service Available at: http://ec.europa.eu/environment/eussd/pdf/bio_foodwaste_report.pdf [Accessed 26 January 2014].

Evans, D. (2011). Beyond the throwaway society: Ordinary domestic practice and a sociological approach to household food waste. *Sociology, 46*(1), 41–56.

Evans, D., Campbell, H., & Murcott, A. (2012). A brief pre-history of food waste and the social sciences. *The Sociological Review, 60*(S2), 5–26.

Fernandez, K. V., Brittain, A. J., & Bennett, S. D. (2011). 'Doing the duck': Negotiating the resistant-consumer identity. *European Journal of Marketing, 45*(11/12), 1779–1788.

Gross, J. (2009). Capitalism and its discontents: Back-to-the-lander and freegan foodways in rural Oregon. *Food and Foodways, 17*(2), 57–79.

Guillard, V., & Roux, D. (2014). Macromarketing issues on the sidewalk: How 'gleaners' and 'disposers' (re)create a sustainable economy. *Journal of Macromarketing, 34*(3), 291–312.

Gustavsson, J., Cederberg, C., Sonesson, U., van Otterdijk, R., & Meybeck, A. (2011). *Global Food Losses and Food Waste.* Rome, Italy: UN Food and Agricultural Organization. Available at: www.fao.org/fileadmin/user_upload/ags/publications/GFL_web.pdf [Accessed 1 December 2011].

Institution of Mechanical Engineers. (2013). *Global Food: Waste Not Want Not.* London, UK. Available at: www.imeche.org/knowledge/themes/environment/global-food [Accessed 1 January 2014].

Kummu, M., de Moel, H., Porka, M., Siebert, S., Varis O., & Ward, P. J. (2012). Lost food, wasted resources: Global food supply chain losses and their impacts on freshwater, cropland, and fertiliser use. *Science of The Total Environment, 438*(November), 477–489.

Lyndhurst, B. (2011). *Consumer Insight: Date Labels and Storage Guidance.* Banbury, UK: Waste and Resources Action Program.

Magaudda, P. (2011). When materiality 'bites back': Digital music consumption practices in the age of dematerialization. *Journal of Consumer Culture, 11*(1), 15–36.

Meah, A., & Watson, M. (2011). Saints and slackers: Challenging discourses about the decline of domestic cooking. *Sociological Research Online, 16*(2), 6. Available at: www.socresonline.org.uk/16/2/6.html [Accessed 13 May 2014].

Nguyen, H. P., Chen, S., & Mukherjee, S. (2014). Reverse stigma in the freegan community. *Journal of Business Research, 67*(9), 1877–1884.

Reno, J. (2009). Your trash is someone's treasure. *Journal of Material Culture, 14*(1), 29–46.

Røpke, I. (2009). Theories of practice: New inspiration for ecological economic studies on consumption. *Ecological Economics, 68*(10), 2490–2497.

Shove, E., Trentmann, F., & Wilk, R. R. (2009). *Time, Consumption and Everyday Life Practice, Materiality and Culture.* Oxford, UK: Berg.

Warde, A. (2005). Consumption and theories of practice. *Journal of Consumer Culture, 5*(2), 131–153.

Warde, A. (2013). What sort of a practice is eating? In *Sustainable Practices: Social Theory and Climate Change* (pp. 17–30). London, UK: Routledge.

Warde, A., Cheng, S.-L., Olsen, W., & Southerton, D. (2007). Changes in the practice of eating: A comparative analysis of time-use. *Acta Sociologica, 50*(4), 363–385.

Watson, M., & Meah, A. (2012). Food, waste and safety: Negotiating conflicting social anxieties into the practices of domestic provisioning. *The Sociological Review, 60*, 102–120.

17 Shit happens

The fears that constitute waste

Robin Canniford and Alan Bradshaw

The outcome of the meal

Faeces, from the Latin *faex* – residue or dregs – is a material with a rich history of social, spiritual and material consequences (Laporte, 2000) that has nevertheless received scant attention in the social sciences. A notable exception is the work of Norbert Elias (2000 [1939]) who shows that practices of eating have been subject to increasingly stringent codes of social and personal conduct, particularly in respect of bodily functions and fluids. In particular, during the fifteenth century, eating, spitting, urination and defecation appear to have been practices that prompted censure: 'Before you sit down, make sure your seat has not been fouled', warns one text (Elias, 2000: 110). That such advice was required indicates an important detail: that it was conceivable for practices of eating and excretion to intersect during the meal!

To be sure, the medieval table was a place of mixings: Elias notes that people might chomp on a bone before returning it to the communal bowl (precursor to *double-dipping* one's crudité in the tzatziki). Alternatively they might relieve themselves on their hosts' curtains, a feature common enough at the Brunswick Court to have warranted this advice during the advent of modernity: 'Let no one, whoever he may be, before, at, or after meals, early or late, foul the staircases, corridors or closets with urine or other filth, but go to suitable, prescribed places for such relief' (Elias, 2000: 112). Elias explains that over the course of centuries, these performances of manners are internalised and embodied as a 'superego' or 'habitus' that layers increasing levels of restraint and foresight over practices of ingestion, digestion and egestion.

Importantly, as these connected processes became regulated in this way, they also became temporally and spatially ordered and separated. For example, through the passage of modernity the meal comes to be served in increasing numbers of courses, which become more homogeneous – a fish course, a meat course – and separated into planned sequences (see Flandrin, 2007). Moreover, unlike the mid-meal relief that medieval subjects might have enjoyed, *modern digestion* is temporally separated from the meal. In high-modernity this may have first entailed time in the smoking room, where the quacks and pongs of gentlemanly farts are disguised by guffaws and cigar smoke. Finally, expulsion is carried out alone in tiled cubicles where the object of disgust plonks beneath water, lest its stench might linger.

Changing temporal and spatial orderings of meals, and the progressive separation of what occurs afterwards are of sociological consequence. Elias (2000) explains how these separations arise from a need to exhibit taste and etiquette as a means of social advancement in court societies in which previous methods of advancement – notably direct physical violence – had been centralised under state authority (cf. Foucault, 1991). Moreover, Elias explains that imperatives to exhibit distinctions in matters of eating and subsequent bodily ejections became more cramping as modernity wore on, since emerging middle-classes aped manners that ordered these higher social circles. This upward pressure justified a kind of etiquette arms race – a race *from* the bottom – in which distinction was maintained through increasingly elaborate manners and fears surrounding excrement and associated emissions (Elias, 2000). Contravention of these orders resulted in experiences of shame and embarrassment, further limiting contact with excremental matters (Bradshaw & Canniford, 2010; LaCom, 2007; Elias, 2000).

Matter out of place?

Elias shows that excrement is ripe with material and symbolic impact, and that the construction of certain materials and practices as 'dirty' establishes social orders (see Mourad & Barnard, Chapter 16). It follows that by maintaining or contravening these boundaries, subjects show themselves to be clean or dirty respectively. In this sense, *dirt is matter out of place*, both in the sense of dirty materials and dirty people. Mary Douglas' trope regards material to take on a negative symbolism within certain material orders and practices, where it is not fitting, especially where this betrays an established order of one kind or another (Douglas, 2002 [1966]). Beyond Elias' contexts of court societies and early Western modernity, Douglas illustrates that order and disorder have revolved around bodily issues in a variety of cultures and historical periods. If bodily waste is not flushed away quickly, personal identities and social orders are threatened.

So vital is the treatment of waste at both personal and societal levels, that it has become a communal and national issue of concern and pride (Laporte, 2000). On the personal level, lack of bowel control is challenging to self-identity (Atkinson, 2012) – the guarded boundaries of the body are disrupted when wastes flow uninhibited. On the societal level, Al-Mohammad (2007) describes how the (re)emergence of excrement is both a symptom and driver of disorder as a State breaks down. When it comes to waste and dregs, sewers materialise the internalisation of shame that citizens embody in their desires to avoid waste. More specifically, the sewer is a mode of disposal designed to limit any sensory engagement with waste (Laporte, 2000). As we have become affectively conditioned to abhor the smell and sight of excrement, we become dependent on these material structures, a situation in which 'the civilized citizen's physical, moral and spiritual cleanliness, internalized as manners for the avoidance of shame and embarrassment, is underpinned by … cubicles, toilets, drains' (Bradshaw & Canniford, 2010: 105).

Figuring dirt as matter out of place is an important way to consider the relations between excrement and social order at psychic, social and material levels of analysis. The corollary of this figure however, is that this matter *is* acceptable – read *not dirt anymore* – if it's in the 'right' place. We do not dispute that what is dirty is symbolically contextualised within specific social milieus. However, we do consider that what is considered dirty often changes through time and space, since certain materials and practices become dirty through long periods, and because these processes are tied to class and gender politics. The mixing of spittle in the communal bowl is a good example of this: acceptable once, unthinkable now. To figure dirt through a simple duality of clean/dirty therefore can belie the complexity of 'dirty' substances, which are always flowing and changing, crossing material and symbolic boundaries (see Närvänen, Mesiranta, & Hukkanen, Chapter 15). More specifically, understanding dirt as simply clean *or* dirty belies the flowing nature of excrement for two reasons:

First, we note that excrement is meals that have *become* dirty. Shit is embodied through spatial practices of mealtimes and processes of ingestion, digestion and egestion that are seldom mapped outside of medical contexts. Though shit often assumes an overall negative reference point among bodily secretions, a benchmark of dirtiness and index-point of disgust, it has to become this way: *out of place* is as much of a journey as a location, something requiring *work*. Second, though there is little research that explains the variability in the temporality of figuring dirt through time, it is clear that there are contextual reversals of this work and social order established as boundaries of dirtiness; a 'lowering of all that is high, spiritual, ideal, abstract … to the sphere of earth and body' (Bakhtin, 2009: 19–20). Related to this, there are (backstage) contexts of disordure in which excrement as dirt can *take flight*, transforming into spiritual, aesthetic and pleasurable experiences (Griffiths, 2013; Bataille, 2009; Weisberg, 1993), or into materials of torture, exile and alienation (Al-Mohammad, 2007; LaCom, 2007; Kristeva, 1982). Both contextual modes subvert linear orders of civilising processes and associated classed spaces. For these reasons, we wish to examine the movements and topologies of dirt, to discover more about what lies between the common duality of clean and dirty.

Historical topologies of dirt

Although there is rarely an 'in place' for shit, where the matter is not dirty, we suggest that meanings of clean and dirty need always to be examined as historical movements within the conjoined space-times of both bodies and societies. Bakhtin (2009) is instructive here in his emphasis on the upward–downward topological movements of dirt. Specifically, he posits the topographical and metaphysical correspondence between the head down to the belly and buttocks.[1] In this system, meals become dirtier as they move onwards and downwards. How might such an association of higher and lower bear out in practice?

Consider the meal mentioned in Part III, ordered in courses and separated by flavours. The epitome of polite society dining is the multiple course meal, perhaps a red cabbage gazpacho; a snail porridge with ham and fennel; followed by a jelly of quail, with liver parfaits, oak moss and truffle toasts; and then lamb with green peppers and caviar oil; etc. Fashionable tasting menus such as these[2] are passed on serving spoons, to the personal plates of polite diners. To eat off another's plate in this scene is rude; to take from another's mouth would see the offending diner ejected from the restaurant. And though animals regurgitate food for their young, and may extract nutrients from scat, comparable practices would have a diner committed to an institution. In short, food starts clean and then begins a journey of becoming dirty. The further from the serving plate, the dirtier food becomes, and the more degrading the experience of any encounter with this *travelling matter*.

Politically, this spatial ordering bears out in manners of distinction. The upper classes enjoy drawn-out ingestive practices, and thus more elaborate journeys from cleanliness to dirtiness. It is of no coincidence that stew is associated with the lower classes, with peasants. Stew is a mixed feast, left in a pressure cooker for hours to soften tough meat. The meal comes practically pre-chewed and partially digested before serving, and therefore, nearer on the journey to shit than those tasting plates served in neat, orderly portions. Stew is not commonly served in restaurants because it is considered a *dirtier* thing. Baby food is another example that can turn stomachs, because this mush comes already half-digested, and is likewise closer to shit.

Instead of a binary of excrement being clean *or* dirty, therefore, we wish to examine the journeys between these poles, and the practices and places through which inbetween matter is more or less kept at bay, amounting to work by which the *image* of the duality is reconstructed. Previously we have argued that practices such as these amount to a conspiracy of silence around the issue of bodily waste (Bradshaw & Canniford, 2010). So long as bodily functions are kept secret via psychic, embodied and material orders, then clean/dirty dichotomy is reconstituted and the social orders that rely on this constitution are defended. Instead of figuring shit through the figure of clean *or* dirty therefore, we intend to interrogate what lies behind, between and beyond the framing of excrement. Elias's explanations largely stem from fears of shame and embarrassment (Scheff, 2004), which arise from potential failures to maintain manners of bodily functions and consequent infractures of social class orders. Next therefore, we examine two epistemes of fear that orbit excrement, via a duality of inside and outside. Through this analysis we explain divergent outcomes of dirt generally, and excrement in particular.

Celia shits: the fear of the inside

Psychoanalysis points towards early relationships with excreta as framing experiences in later life, forming part of the tissue of who we are, and crucially, who we understand ourselves *not* to be. Freud (2001 [1908]) explained that toilet training brings children into a society of boundaries between bodies and spaces, tying the bowel and the world together. Here, the shame layered on the functions of the gut over centuries (Elias, 2000 [1939]) is cast upon each nascent individual, demanding silence concerning matters of bodily products. Faeces, however, confronts the trained subject with a problem, because it *will* flow. Indeed, Kubie (1937) writing contemporaneously to Elias, suggests that we fear all that is inside the body, because this is a space of shame and filthiness that always threatens to reveal itself to others.

According to Spillius, Milton, Garvey, Couve and Steiner (2011: 40) this fear of what emerges from our bodies is 'a mental and emotional image of an external object that has been taken inside the self'. In our case, the 'external object' is our waste, and the emotional image is the negative affective associations – shame and embarrassment – that are internalised to ensure self-restraint, as Elias (2000) notes. If we bring Melanie Klein's ideas of object relations to bear here, we might say that excrement, having acquired unconscious significance as an external object, then features in phantasies of expelling the *bad object*: a psychological defence manoeuvre associated with avoiding the negative emotional associations of the external object by disassociating from that object (Spillius et al., 2011; Klein, 1952). Considering the internalisation of architectures and manners that bind the potty-trained body to a nexus of classed material resources and social affectations, it seems justifiable that we would seek to *flush and forget* the issue, as it were.

Nevertheless, digestion is a Sisyphean affair, and excrement continues to haunt the subject (Laplanche & Pontalis, 1973), the bad object constantly returning. This perspective helps us to understand why shit structures both psychological and social identity, not only as a negative reference point, but as a means of externalising *the other*, and materialising fear around the other. In particular, Kristeva (1982) explores the ambiguous tension that exists between objects that are *inside* and *outside* the body. Crucially the act of expelling an object from the body is also the act of producing the body as a person, or as a discrete subject, while the expelled object takes on an 'abject' form. '"I" do not assimilate it, "I" expel it.... I expel *myself*, I spit *myself* out' (Kristeva, 1982: 3). In other words the excrement is not an alien form, but rather is produced as external, and then as abject, through the act of expulsion, which simultaneously produces the discreet subject.

Jonathan Swift explores the result of such abjection in *The Lady's Dressing Room* (1732), in which a naïve lover, Strephon, stalks the personal chambers of Celia, the woman he adores, rifling through and snuffling at her most intimate objects. Instead of the erotic exercise he desires, however, he is appalled by what he discovers: the remnants of greasy armpits in a dirty smock, 'Sweat, dandruff, powder, lead and hair' in her brush. Her towels are 'Begummed, bemattered, and beslimed with dirt and sweat'; her handkerchiefs are 'varnished o'er with snuff and snot'. The denouement occurs when he searches her most intimate of closets, whereupon his nostrils are assaulted:

> And up exhales a greasy stench,
> For which you curse the careless wench;
> So things, which must not be expressed,
> When plumped into the reeking chest,
> Send up an excremental smell
> To taint the parts from whence they fell.
> ...
> Thus finishing his grand survey,
> Disgusted Strephon stole away
> Repeating in his amorous fits,
> Oh! Celia, Celia, Celia shits!

Swift's verse can be read in a variety of ways; first, as expression of misogyny in a traumatic and humiliating undoing of women's privy abjections. To be sure, human waste as bad object made visible can be an instrument of torture and mortification (see Al-Mohammad, 2007; Goffman, 1961). An alternative reading, however, would have Swift's satirical target Strephon as an idiot whose illusions stem from a gendered and classed habitus. A more generous reading could suggest that Swift's poem de-fetishises the female body as an object of desire that has succeeded in abjecting its excess. Might the real obscenity be binding a lover into a material-semiotic nexus that refuses to acknowledge the reality of the other? The work can thus be read as forcing us to abandon our contrivances about shit-free bodies which coerce us all into conspiracies of silence and disavowals of our universal experiences. *Or* perhaps, and let *us* not be naïve, Strephon is yielding to unconscious scatological desire (Freud, 1995), 'the disturbing implication that in fantasy we find the subject relating to its shit' (Dean, 2003: 265). Dean postulates that such 'horrifying results' might be an end point of struggling 'against the affect-laden social norms regulating sexuality', and therefore might be thought of as not just the negative effort to resist norms, but also as, 'intense almost superhuman loving' (2003: 268). Amorous fits, indeed.

Toilet humours: the fear of the outside

So far we have explained the significance of social orders of distinction and abjection as conditioning digestion and egestion as indicative of social and personal orders. These affective boundaries are conserved by a fear of shame, repugnance over what emerges from within us. Recently, however, historian Shighisa Kuriyama (2008) has investigated alternative explanations concerning fears of excrement. He argues that preceding the fear of what emerges from inside is a fear of what is outside of the body, especially with respect to food and drink. This is a largely forgotten system of knowledge that requires delving back into early modernity to relate a story of a largely forgotten discourse, namely *humours*.

Between the fifth and fourth centuries BC and the eighteenth century, humours were often understood as harmful. Bile and phlegm in particular were thought to arise from certain environmental circumstances – such as excessive heat or cold – triggering all manner of ailments. Although the presence of humours in various parts of the body was aetiologically complex, in essence they were considered poisonous, wreaking fluid havoc in the bodies of unfortunate patients, who waited – phlegmatically or biliously – for a physician's attention. Treatment consisted of purging the menacing fluids by cupping, blistering, leeching, bleeding, draining, or administering emetics or enemas (see Dixon, 1993). Importantly, the indication of these humoural imbalances was excreta: 'cloudy foam in urine, black streaks in feces, fetid stink in vomit' (Kuriyama, 2008: 427). Around the body's output orbited fear over signs of the inner body's workings. 'Until not so very long ago, the anxieties surrounding excrement haunted minds in a way that is now hard to comprehend fully' (Kuriyama, 2008: 429).

This is not the same fear as that examined above however. To be sure, rather than excrement as relegated to discrete space-times separate from the other practices of daily life such that it is unthinkable to look upon, touch or smell excrement, evacuation was a serious and open matter, demanding sensory focus and the engagement of knowledge. Early modern kings, for instance, were attended during their ablutions. Henries VII and VIII, received their *privy* council within chambers where the regal elimination was bared to the inner court, chief among whom was the *Groom of the Stool*. Indeed, over centuries, regal turds were examined as an indicator of the Monarch's health (in *The Madness of King George*, for instance, a court doctor exclaims, 'I've always found the stool more eloquent than the pulse'). Excrement as explained at the beginning of this chapter is what is left, the dregs of the eaten food. Hence, 'food was fraught with danger. If it contained the nutriments needed to replace the natural deterioration of the body, it also contained superfluities, which could harm or destroy the body' (Kuriyama, 2008: 430). Of course, the water closet and the underground sewer would have been anathema to this system of knowledge.

Where have these overriding desires to purge the body of such poisons gone? Kuriyama explains how longstanding forms of knowledge concerning humours fades from memory and cultural practice as though through an epistemological accident, or more specifically to a certain pretentiousness on the part of medicine. This was a desire to align theories of humours with natural philosophy. Put simply, the theory of the four humours was shoehorned into the theory of the four elements. The effect of this was in some ways to lead physicians to look upwards, away from the bedpan, and towards the stars; from inner to outer space.

However, as these magical suppositions around the body were gradually cast-out by anatomical investigations and resulting medical *gazes* (Foucault, 1973), the theoretical symmetries and preoccupations with imaginary flux of fluids were flushed away also. In this sense, evacuation has perhaps become less symbolically significant than it once was. Hence, this particular way of fearing excrement has fallen from public life, leaving behind its psychoanalytic bedfellow, that fear of disorder and abjection emerging from the body. Let us not be hasty however. In the next section we digest contemporary popular culture's entanglements with ingestion and digestion, using these two kinds of fear that we have explained. What emerges from our tract suggests that the fear of the inside is at work in society, but that the fear of the outside is experiencing a scatological renaissance.

Jamie's stool dinners

Jamie Oliver's crusades against fatty foodstuffs exemplify the fear of the inside in practice. Despite the wealth of evidence that these foods offer poor nutrition, the techniques that celebrity protesters like Oliver use to champion healthy eating are often based less upon nutritional evidence and more on darker arts. In his *School Dinners* campaign, Oliver has not been averse to such alchemy: his mushing up of the fundamentals of a school dinner – turkey twizzlers, and fizzy pop – into a sludgy mess on a tarpaulin to prove how *crappy* school food is (*Jamie's School Dinners*, 2005) serves as a good example. In a sense, this technique exemplifies the theory set out above: rendering food in a mushy manner is tantamount to serving up shit. Oliver puts the public off twizzlers by leveraging their aversion to mushed-up food that stems from their fear of excrement.

Nevertheless, this affective technique is mired in class politics and abjection. As journalist Charlie Brooker (2006) has commented, red cabbage gazpacho, snail porridge, oak moss and truffle toasts, etc. would also turn to shit if mashed up on a tarpaulin laid out on the floor. In rendering food *shitty* like this, Oliver exploits the fear of shit, but this is also layered with the fact that his crusade occurs in working-class communities, already metaphorically dirtied by 'lower' status. What we draw from this example is that the dieticians' and food technologists' evidence-based techniques of dietary management are not necessarily applied in entirely rational ways. Rather, these disciplinary techniques are hybridised with manipulations of our affective conditioning, designed to take certain foods and associated diners of these foods on a journey related to the internalisation of objects and restraints.

It is interesting that the renewal of the fear of the outside also figures in these meaning-making practices. This renewal is illustrated in Gwyneth Paltrow's popular blog *Goop*,[3] which recently explored fringe-scientist Masuru Emoto's (2004) claims that water is sensitive to your 'vibes'. With scientific evidence of the kind normally available only to prime ministers and presidents who need to justify poor decisions in a hurry, Paltrow's readership are illuminated as to water's tendency to freeze differently, depending on the words it encounters. Say nasty things to freezing water, and ice crystals look bad; but say nice things and the crystals blossom prettily. Since we are composed of some 70 per cent water, the conclusion is that we should all say nice things to one another; else the water in us might do ugly things too, and then where would we be?

> Water in a river remains pure because it is moving. When water becomes trapped, it dies. Therefore, water must constantly be circulated. The water – or blood – in the bodies of the sick is usually stagnant. When blood stops flowing, the body starts to decay.... But why does blood become stagnant? We can see this condition as the stagnation of the emotions.
>
> (Emoto, 2004: xvi)

Here, once again is a fear of what is outside the body as disrupting natural balances. In a passage reminiscent of the treatment of bodily humours, Emoto argues that it is important that we purify our waters, else our bodies and souls become 'stagnant'.

Conclusion: the politics of inside and outside

At the beginning of this chapter, we noted that the practices and materialities of excrement remain hidden behind a veil of secrecy, absenting excreta from accounts of meals and eating. Specifically, we have argued that contrary to simple notions of cleanliness and dirtiness, waste cannot and should not be conceived of in a simple fashion. Rather, through an interrogation of what lies either *inside* or *outside* the body, we have explained that the nature of these fears has neither been consistent through history, nor in contemporary discourses on meals. Currently, two ways of figuring excrement through fear coexist, and these we suggest, tell us a lot about how we treat waste, and what prevents us from engaging with waste as a subject.

'All well and good', you might say, 'but what are we to do with our shit if not flush it away?' Is there a political substance that can amount to more than just another self-satisfying act of critical pooh-poohing? To answer this question, our final move is to unite the perspectives on the fear of inside and outside, and assert that the body is an extended ring in which inside and outside are connected. Thus, it is the differentials constructed between the two that are of political importance.

Considering ideas of the abject, or the acceptance of excrement into the world of humours, we can see that boundaries of inside and outside are upheld for 'purposes of social regulation and control' (Butler, 1990). Butler argues that in moments of producing the discreet subject via abjection, we see how other forms of fear come into fruition. The boundary between the inner and outer is confounded by those excremental passages in which the inner effectively becomes outer, and this excreting function becomes, as it were, the model by which other forms of identity-differentiation are accomplished. In effect, this is the mode by which '*Others* become shit' (1990: 182).

Butler argues, if the inner world is to remain distinct from the outer world, the surface of the body must become impermeable and there must be a sealing of bodily boundaries. Accordingly, when excrement pours, it always arrives as an explosion of 'precisely that excremental filth that it fears' (1990: 182). Of course, as our opening maxim in this chapter affirms, sealing is impossible; hence it at this juncture that the metaphoric world of shit becomes clearer. Although each body is an extended ring, inside and outside as one, in practice, false borders are bolstered by the disturbing separation of inside and outside via fears of excrement. This conflation of fear of 'the other', as inside and outside can be seen in the pathological and psychotic roots of racism, for instance, Enoch Powell's Rivers of Blood speech, in 1968. Recounting the (probably fictitious) story of a Birmingham constituent, Powell stated:

> She is becoming afraid to go out.... She finds excreta pushed through her letterbox. When she goes to the shops, she is followed by children, charming, wide-grinning piccaninnies.

Rustin (1991) interprets Powell's speech as an instance of the primitive mental associations of internal objects that lie at the heart of racism. Similar to Butler's reading of Kristeva in which 'Others become shit', Rustin writes: 'disgusting and degraded aspects of the self are here being dealt with by being either ascribed to, or literally dumped on, the unwanted group' (1991: 67). Importantly for us, Rustin sees anxieties concerning food as defining forms of racism, citing the example of a family being harassed in London during the 1980s when the 'next door neighbor banged on the door to inform them that "Your curry is making the whole street stink"'.

Rustin explains that 'disgusts ... evoked by food habits reveal deep preoccupations with, and probably confusions about, bodily functions and their inner meanings' (1991: 67). Let us return to the connection made earlier with stews; curry in this context is *the stew of the other* and therefore, reveals an intersectional system (Collins, 2000) of otherness. The shit here is associated with lower classes, women, and immigrants. Indeed the association of shit and women as a root of mysogny is further explored by Rose's (2014) analysis of the hatred encountered by Rosa Luxemberg – for instance, August Bebel spoke of Luxemberg's 'wretched female squirts of poison', while Viktor Adler insisted 'we will not allow her to spit in our soup'. Rose interprets such misogyny, which frames women as vile liquid, as stemming from 'their (women's) ability to force to the surface of the everyday parts of the inner life – its visceral reality, its stubborn unruliness – which in the normal course of our exchanges we like to think we have subdued'.

Following such psychoanalytic insight, we see concerns about our experience of the other as abounding with phantasies of permeations and incorporations of bodies and the identification of the other as embodying what we fear in ourselves, the other as shit.

What then are we to do with our excremental status quo, in which identifications are made on the basis of casting away excess from a corporeal ideal, and simultaneously producing the other as shit? Zizek points out how the urgency of this political status of excrement is embodied in the injustice experienced by the Indian Untouchables, a group 'doubly marked by the excremental logic: they not only deal with impure excrements, (but) their own formal status within the social body is that of excrement' (2010: 23). The solution, for Zizek, is to universalise this excremental status to the whole of humanity. We say therefore, that if the mouth constitutes society through the meal (see Falk, 1994) then so does the anus and therefore, perhaps it is time to finally accept, as per the earlier discussion of Dean, that the universal object petit *a* has been none other than the proverbial poo all along (oh don't look so surprised). Distasteful, offensive? Perhaps, but in explaining that issues of 'good and bad taste' in this arena are bound to class, race and gender politics, it is a scholarly community's responsibility to figure the boundaries of inside and outside, the emotions that attend these boundaries, and the social effects that result. We must then accept collective responsibility because as B. R. Ambedkar stated, there can be 'no castes without outcasts'.

Notes

1 Forms of 'dirt' that extend from the body can be placed in a hierarchy of emotional avoidance (say, tears, to spittle, nasal mucous, to genital expulsions and secretions, all the way down to shit) that often conform to a physical topology of high to low. Nevertheless, we acknowledge the affective constructions of excrement are likely to vary among subjects, professions, and in different environments.
2 Courtesy here of the *Fat Duck* restaurant.
3 www.goop.com/journal/go/286/goop-mag-16 [Accessed 24 May 2014].

References

Al-Mohammad, H. (2007). Ordure and disorder: The case of Basra and the anthropology of excrement. *Anthropology of the Middle East, 2*(2), 1–23.

Atkinson, M. (2012). Norbert Elias and the body. In B. Turner (Ed.), *The Routledge Handbook of Body Studies* (pp. 45–63). London: Routledge.

Bakhtin, M. (2009). *Rabelais and His World*. IN: Indiana University Press.

Bataille, G. (2009). *Divine Filth: Lost Writings*. IL: Solar.

Bradshaw, A., & Canniford, R. (2010). Excremental theory development. *Journal of Consumer Behaviour, 9*(2), 102–112.

Brooker, C. (2006). Supposing … you are not what you eat. *The Guardian.* 6 October. Available at: www.theguardian.com/commentisfree/2006/oct/06/food. health [Accessed 23 September 2014].

Butler, J. (1990). *Gender Trouble*. London: Routledge.

Collins, P. H. (2000). *Black Feminist Thought: Knowledge, Consciousness, and the Politics of Empowerment*. London: Routledge.

Dean, T. (2003). *Beyond Sexuality*. IL: Chicago University Press.

Dixon, L. S. (1993). Some penetrating insights: The imagery of enemas in art. *Art Journal, 52*(3), 28–35.

Douglas, M. (2002 [1966]). *Purity and Danger: An Analysis of Concepts of Pollution and Taboo*. London: Routledge.

Elias, N. (2000 [1939]). *The Civilizing Process, Vols. 1 and 2*. Oxford: Blackwell.

Emoto, M. (2004). *The Hidden Messages in Water*. Oregon: Beyond Words.

Falk, P. (1994). *The Consuming Body*. London: Sage.

Flandrin, J. (2007). *Arranging the Meal: A History of Table Service in France*. Berkeley: University of California Press.

Foucault, M. (1973). *The Birth of the Clinic: The Archeology of Medical Perception*. London: Vintage.

Foucault, M. (1991). *Discipline and Punish*. London: Penguin.

Freud, S. (1995). *The Freud Reader*. P. Gay (Ed.). London: Vintage.

Freud, S. (2001 [1908]). *The Complete Psychological Works of Sigmund Freud*. London: Vintage Classics.

Goffman, E. (1961). *Asylums: Essays on the Social Situation of Mental Patients and Other Inmates*. London: Penguin.

Griffiths, M. (2013). Eproctophilia in a young adult male. *Archives of Sexual Behaviour, 42*(3), 1383–1386.

Jamie's School Dinners (2005). Available at: http://www.channel4.com/programmes/jamies-school-dinners [Accessed 7 October 2015].

Klein, M. (1952). The origins of transference. *International Journal of Psychoanalytic, 33*(1), 433–438.

Kristeva, J. (1982). *The Powers of Horror: An Essay on Abjection*. NY: Colombia University Press.

Kubie, L. (1937). The fantasy of dirt. *Psychoanalytic Quarterly, 6*(4), 388–425.

Kuriyama, S. (2008). The forgotten fear of excrement. *Journal of Medieval and Early Modern Studies, 38*(3), 413–442.

LaCom, C. (2007). Filthy bodies, porous boundaries: The politics of shit in disability studies. *Disability Studies Quarterly, 27*(1), 1–2.

Laplanche, J., & Pontalis, J. (1973). *The Language of Psychoanalysis*. London: Karnac.

Laporte, D. (2000 [1978]). *History of Shit*. London: MIT Press.

Rose, J. (2014). *Women in Dark Times*. London: Bloomsbury.

Rustin, M. (1991). *The Good Society and the Inner World*. London: Verso.

Scheff, T. (2004). Elias, Freud and Goffman: Shame as the master emotion. In K. Quilley, & G. Loyal (Eds.), *The Sociology of Norbert Elias* (pp. 67–82). Cambridge: Cambridge University Press.

Spillius, E. B., Milton, J., Garvey, J., Couve, J., & Steiner, D. (2011). *The New Dictionary of Kleinian Thought*. London: Routledge.

Swift, J. (1732). *The Lady's Dressing Room*. Available at: http://www.poetryfoundation.org/poem/180934 [Accessed 7 October 2015].

Weisberg, G. (1993). Scatological Art. *Art Journal, 52*(3), 18–19.

Zizek, S. (2010). *Living in the End Times*. London: Verso.

18 Concluding remarks

Benedetta Cappellini, David Marshall and
Elizabeth Parsons

As Mary Douglas (1975) eloquently reminds us in her seminal essay on deciphering a meal, putting things in order is a matter of imposing classifications, boundaries and structures reflecting a cosmology of norms and conventions that goes beyond the dining table. In trying to impose some order to such a messy reality, we have followed previous studies on consumption and food consumption (Warde, 2005; Marshall, 1995; Goody, 1982), applying a cyclical framework starting with acquisition and ending with disposal. This framework provides a useful template for ordering this collection of chapters on the practice of the meal, unpacking the complexities of the process of acquiring, appropriating, appreciating and disposing of the food. However, the reality of the meal does not follow a fixed menu but reveals a series of interlinked, juxtaposed and sometimes contrasting practices. Appropriation is interlinked with disposal and the boundaries between appreciation and appropriation are often blurred. Places can be the site of more than one practice. For example, the supermarket bin can be a place wherein food is abandoned but also a place of acquisition and appreciation. Time is also a crucial factor as some aspects of the meal change over time, while other elements remain almost untouched. Objects have trajectories that cross borders and can be reclassified and returned to the dining table after having being disposed of. The meal is also linked and often in opposition with sports, studying, professional and leisure practices.

If the practice of the meal is a messy network of networks of objects, bodies, times and spaces do we still need to talk about it as a single unit of analysis? We think we do. What emerges from this collection is an integrative bundle (Schatzki, 1996) of interconnecting practices, without a clear beginning or end, that impact on each other, restraining or promoting the emergence of a practice-as-entity (see Bellotti & Mora, 2014). Similarly, our collection has shown how the practice of the meal as a single entity emerges from an assemblage of dispersed practices in time and space, involving brands, objects, media, bodies, relations, routines and ideals of family life. These are organised around norms and conventions about social class, gender and mothering, governance of the body and ethics. We learn how the practice of the meal as an entity emerges from a complex process of negotiation, reflection, accountability and discipline that reveals the powerful and seductive ideal of family life around a dining table.

The market and brands are an unavoidable feature of our meals, whether it be in seeking authenticity in our food and distinguishing between 'good' and 'bad' brands, or adapting and shifting our meals to accommodate cultural anomalies in the availability of certain foods as we appropriate and accommodate what the market has to offer. Brands do not simply reflect the status quo, but also reshape it; they provide appealing narratives that offer solutions to the contemporary challenges of food provisioning, offering identity, authenticity and convenience that are acceptable to some and rejected by others. The marketisation of the meal is inevitable but consumers are finding ways to counter the commercial hegemony and challenge the status quo while remaining true to their ideas about food provisioning and meal practice.

Supermarket aisles and bins are not the only significant places wherein consumers reflect on their meals. The kitchen is indeed a crucial space wherein consumers do not simply prepare their meal but also reflect on the way they have changed their cooking. The presence of new kitchen technologies has modified the way consumers plan, prepare, cook, serve and remember their dishes. This redistribution of competences and skills between consumers and devices makes certain culinary projects and tasks achievable and indeed facilitates the storing and sharing of recipes and cooking techniques in online spaces. It reflects the continued intrusion of the market in our meal planning and the expansion beyond the kitchen and the immediate family to include external online communities that offer advice on anything from recipes to ways of dealing with food waste and austerity. In fighting austerity women have 'rediscovered' some abandoned practices, reactivating some of their skills and knowledge previously abandoned or delegated to the marketplace. Perhaps one of the most striking changes that emerges from this reflection on meal practices is the extent to which we have delegated everyday food practices to the marketplace as we look for ingredients (and their expiry dates), ideas and recipes in store and online. This in itself is not new; there have always been recipe books and family favourites but the ability to retrieve a recipe and then source ingredients from retailers highlights the degree to which our eating is reliant on the market. A main challenge remains our ability to keep up with these changes and understand what is actually on offer. In reactivating some of their bodily skills of selecting food from their fridges and cupboards, consumers interpret, reflect on and contest the government and the market discourses of food safety.

If meal is an assemblage of practices dispersed across places, some actors seem to be more involved than others in such practices. This book reaffirms the role of mothers as being morally accountable for the everyday meal (from planning, preparation and serving) but suggests a widening of that responsibility to include other family members. If some parents are prepared to compromise the convivial element of their meal, eating dinners without their children, others reshape their entire daily activities in order to share their meals with the whole family. Meals are shifting into new spaces. Other eating occasions, including lunch and snacks seem to be less anchored to the idea of conviviality and family bonding. Self-discipline remains a central theme of the practice of the meal and mothers are constantly evaluating themselves in relation to the ideals of good mothering and good family life; these women operate a strict self-discipline regime seeking to achieve an often unachievable target. Disciplining the self is also a central theme across the four parts as consumers discipline themselves and the others around them while they select 'good' brands, re-classify 'good' and 'bad' food, choose a snack and rework leftovers. The body is also a central aspect of this disciplining process. Abstinence and excess are common aspects of the everyday meal, showing how the body is often tamed around the dining table, during snacking occasions and in the bathroom. Being the last point of a degrading hierarchical order of the life of the meal, the body represents the irreversible end point of a unidirectional process in which the decomposition of food inside the body represents a collective fear.

To conclude, we hope that with this collection we have shown how the practice of the meal emerges as an entity colliding disrupted and dispersed practices, objects, brands and ideals. From Australia to China, from Sweden to the US, this collection has shown how the everyday meal is indeed in good health and it does not risk extinction. In this collection authors have unpacked networks of places, times, objects, brands, technologies, bodies, celebrities, media and government discourses surrounding the thinking, planning, preparing, serving, sharing and disposing of a meal. Modified in times and spaces the meal remains a practice holding people together, revamping our passions and fears, generating political activism and ethical dilemmas, provoking the reinvigoration of ideals about the world we dream of, and the way we would like to feed our children and care for the unknown others and the environment we live in. Being a bundle of contradictory feelings, anxieties and emotions, it is not surprising to see how deciphering a meal is a topic fascinating artists, musicians, poets and scholars of all times, generating an endless list of contributions. We hope that this collection will be added to the list.

References

Bellotti, E., & Mora E. (2014). Network of practices in critical consumption. *Journal of Consumer Culture*. Available at: http://joc.sagepub.com/content/early/2014/05/25/1469540514536191.abstract [Accessed 22 December 2015].

Douglas, M. (1975). Deciphering a meal. *Daedalus, 101*(1), 61–81.

Goody, J. (1982). *Cooking, Cuisine and Class: A Study in Comparative Sociology*. Cambridge: Cambridge University Press.

Marshall, D. (Ed.) (1995). *Food Choice and the Consumer*. London: Chapman and Hall.

Schatzki, T. R. (1996). *Social Practices: A Wittgensteinian Approach to Human Activity and the Social*. Cambridge: Cambridge University Press.

Warde, A. (2005). Consumption and theories of practice. *Journal of Consumer Culture, 5*(2), 131–153.

Index

 Taylor & Francis eBooks

Helping you to choose the right eBooks for your Library

Add Routledge titles to your library's digital collection today. Taylor and Francis ebooks contains over 50,000 titles in the Humanities, Social Sciences, Behavioural Sciences, Built Environment and Law.

Choose from a range of subject packages or create your own!

Benefits for you

- » Free MARC records
- » COUNTER-compliant usage statistics
- » Flexible purchase and pricing options
- » All titles DRM-free.

 Free Trials Available
We offer free trials to qualifying academic, corporate and government customers.

Benefits for your user

- » Off-site, anytime access via Athens or referring URL
- » Print or copy pages or chapters
- » Full content search
- » Bookmark, highlight and annotate text
- » Access to thousands of pages of quality research at the click of a button.

eCollections – Choose from over 30 subject eCollections, including:

Archaeology	Language Learning
Architecture	Law
Asian Studies	Literature
Business & Management	Media & Communication
Classical Studies	Middle East Studies
Construction	Music
Creative & Media Arts	Philosophy
Criminology & Criminal Justice	Planning
Economics	Politics
Education	Psychology & Mental Health
Energy	Religion
Engineering	Security
English Language & Linguistics	Social Work
Environment & Sustainability	Sociology
Geography	Sport
Health Studies	Theatre & Performance
History	Tourism, Hospitality & Events

For more information, pricing enquiries or to order a free trial, please contact your local sales team:
www.tandfebooks.com/page/sales

For Product Safety Concerns and Information please contact our EU
representative GPSR@taylorandfrancis.com
Taylor & Francis Verlag GmbH, Kaufingerstraße 24, 80331 München, Germany